Hacking Gmail™

Hacking Gmail™

Ben Hammersley

WILEY

Wiley Publishing, Inc.

Hacking Gmail™

Published by
Wiley Publishing, Inc.
10475 Crosspoint Boulevard
Indianapolis, IN 46256
www.wiley.com

Copyright © 2006 by Wiley Publishing, Inc., Indianapolis, Indiana

Published simultaneously in Canada

ISBN-13: 978-0-7645-9611-7
ISBN-10: 0-7645-9611-X

Manufactured in the United States of America

10 9 8 7 6 5 4 3 2 1

1B/RU/RS/QV/IN

For general information on our other products and services or to obtain technical support, please contact our Customer Care Department within the U.S. at (800) 762-2974, outside the U.S. at (317) 572-3993 or fax (317) 572-4002.

Wiley also publishes its books in a variety of electronic formats. Some content that appears in print may not be available in electronic books.

Library of Congress Cataloging-in-Publication Data

Hammersley, Ben.
  Hacking Gmail / Ben Hammersley.
     p. cm.
  Includes index.
  ISBN-13: 978-0-7645-9611-7 (paper/website)
  ISBN-10: 0-7645-9611-X (paper/website)
  1. Gmail (Electronic resource) 2. Electronic mail systems. 3. Internet programming. I. Title.
  TK5105.74.G55H36 2006
  004.692—dc22
                              2005029719

Meanwhile, back in Florence, Anna, Lucy, Mischa, and Pico ignored the swearing and kept me fed. Love, as ever, to them.

About the Author

Armed only with a PowerBook and some fine pipe tobacco, **Ben Hammersley** is a journalist, writer, explorer, and an errant developer and explainer of semantic web technology. He's also liable to spread his dirty, dirty words over at *The Guardian*.

As an Englishman of the clichéd sort, Ben's angle brackets always balance, and his tweed is always pressed. He's not worn trousers for six months now. Ask him about it sometime.

Credits

Executive Editor
Chris Webb

Development Editor
Brian Herrmann

Technical Editor
Justin Blanton

Production Editor
Kenyon Brown

Copy Editor
Nancy Rapoport

Editorial Manager
Mary Beth Wakefield

Production Manager
Tim Tate

Vice President and Executive Group Publisher
Richard Swadley

Vice President and Executive Publisher
Joseph B. Wikert

Project Coordinator
Michael Kruzil

Graphics and Production Specialists
Carrie A. Foster
Lynsey Osborn
Melanee Prendergast

Quality Control Technicians
Leeann Harney, Jessica Kramer,
Charles Spencer, Brian H. Walls

Proofreading and Indexing
TECHBOOKS Production Services

Cover Design
Anthony Bunyan

Contents at a Glance

Acknowledgments xvii
Introduction xix

Part I: Starting to Use Gmail 1
Chapter 1: Desktop Integration 3
Chapter 2: Integrating Your Existing Mail 11
Chapter 3: Gmail Power Tips 15

Part II: Getting Inside Gmail 27
Chapter 4: Skinning Gmail 29
Chapter 5: How Gmail Works 53
Chapter 6: Gmail and Greasemonkey 91
Chapter 7: Gmail Libraries 117
Chapter 8: Checking for Mail 137
Chapter 9: Reading Mail 151
Chapter 10: Sending Mail 161

Part III: Conquering Gmail 167
Chapter 11: Dealing with Labels 169
Chapter 12: Addressing Addresses 177
Chapter 13: Building an API from the HTML-Only Version of Gmail 183
Chapter 14: Exporting Your Mail 197
Chapter 15: Using Gmail to 203
Chapter 16: Using GmailFS 213

Appendix: Long Code Listings 223

Index 275

Contents

Acknowledgments xvii

Introduction xix

Part I: Starting to Use Gmail   1

Chapter 1: Desktop Integration 3

New Mail Notification 3
    Windows 3
    Mac OS X 5
    Linux, etc. 5
Redirecting mailto: 6
    Windows 7
    Multiplatform/Mozilla 7
    OS X 8
    GmailerXP 8
And Now 9

Chapter 2: Integrating Your Existing Mail 11

Importing Your Mail into Gmail 11
    Gmail Loader 11
Setting Up Pop Access Inside Gmail 12
Setting Up Pop Within an Application 13
IMAP for Gmail 14
And Now 14

Chapter 3: Gmail Power Tips 15

Keyboard Shortcuts 15
Plus Addressing and Filtering 20
    Other Addressing Tips 21
Quickly Mark a Group of E-Mails 23
Send Executables as Attachments 23
Advanced Searching 24
And Now 26

Part II: Getting Inside Gmail   27

Chapter 4: Skinning Gmail 29

Deconstructing Gmail 29
    The Top Section 33
    The Navigation Menu 35
    The Activity Area 38
    The Bottom Section 42
Applying a New Style 44
Creating Gmail Lite 44
Walking Through the Style Sheet 45
Removing Google's Advertising 51
And Now 51

Chapter 5: How Gmail Works 53

What the Devil Is Going On? 53
    Preloading the Interface 54
Introducing XMLHttpRequest 55
    Using XMLHttpRequest Yourself 55
    Finding XMLHttpRequest within the Gmail code 61
Sniffing the Network Traffic 62
    Firing Up Tcpflow 62
Prodding Gmail to Hear It Squeak 67
    Preparing to Watch the Gmail Boot Sequence 67
    Cleaning Up the Log 68
Stepping Through the Gmail Boot Sequence 68
    Logging In 69
    The First Cookie 71
    Loading the Inbox 74
    Reading an Individual Mail 81
And Now 89

Chapter 6: Gmail and Greasemonkey 91

What Is Greasemonkey? 91
The Userscripts 92
    Displaying Bloglines Within Gmail 92
    How It Works 100
    Add a Delete Button 101
    GmailSecure 108
    MailtoComposeInGmail 110
Other Userscripts 114
    Mark Read Button 114
    Multiple Signatures 115
    Hide Invites 115
    Random Signatures 115
And Now 115

Chapter 7: Gmail Libraries 117

PHP — Gmailer 118
   Getting and Installing the Library. 118
   How to Use It 119
Perl — Mail::Webmail::Gmail 127
   Getting and Installing the Library. 127
   Using the Library 128
Python — Libgmail 131
   Getting and Installing the Library. 131
   How to Use It 132
   Reading the First Message in the Inbox. 134
Setting Yourselves Up for the Remaining Chapters 135
And Now 136

Chapter 8: Checking for Mail. 137

The Basics in Perl 137
The Basics in PHP 139
The Basics in Python. 140
Building on the Basics 142
   New Mail Count in RSS 142
   New Mail Count to AOL Instant Messenger. 144
And Now 149

Chapter 9: Reading Mail 151

Reading Mail with Perl. 151
   The Basics 151
   Accessing All the Data of a Message 152
   Listing the Mail and Displaying a Chosen Message 153
   Dealing with Attachments. 155
   Making an RSS Feed of Your Inbox. 155
And Now 159

Chapter 10: Sending Mail. 161

Sending Mail with Gmail SMTP 161
   Sending Mail with Perl 162
And Now 166

Part III: Conquering Gmail   167

Chapter 11: Dealing with Labels 169

Listing the Existing Labels. 169
Setting New Labels. 173
   Creating a New Label 175
Removing Labels 175
And Now 176

Chapter 12: Addressing Addresses **177**

The Contacts List 177
Importing Contacts. 178
Showing Your Current Contacts 180
Exporting Contacts. 181
And Now 182

Chapter 13: Building an API from the HTML-Only Version of Gmail . . . **183**

A First Look at the HTML Version 183
Introducing Basic Scraping. 186
HTML::TokeParser 186
Parsing the Inbox 188
Retrieving the Individual Page. 192
Dealing with Threads 195
Dealing with Other Folders 195
And Now 196

Chapter 14: Exporting Your Mail **197**

Exporting as a Massive Text File 197
Converting to Mbox 199
Appending to IMAP 200
And Now 201

Chapter 15: Using Gmail to **203**

Using Gmail as a To-Do List 203
Using Filters 203
Using gmtodo 205
Using Gmail to Find Information in RSS Feeds. 205
Using Gmail to Find Torrent Files 206
Using Gmail as a Notepad 207
Using Gmail as a Spam Filter 209
An Even Simpler Way of Doing It 210
Using Gmail as Storage for a Photo Gallery 210
And Now 211

Chapter 16: Using GmailFS **213**

The Underlying Idea 213
Installing GmailFS 213
The Correct Python 213
Installing FUSE 215
Installing Libgmail. 215
Installing GmailFS 215
Using GmailFS 216
Mounting GmailFS from the Command Line 216
Mounting GmailFS from fstab 217
Passing Commands to the File System 217

How GmailFS Works 218

What Makes Up a File? 218

Representing All of This in E-Mail 220

The Actual Data in Action 220

And Now 221

Appendix: Long Code Listings **223**

Index **275**

Acknowledgments

Books of this nature are tremendously difficult to write. Without support from Google (we didn't ask, admittedly) and with Gmail being in perpetual Beta throughout the writing process, we often found ourselves with chapters being made obsolete overnight. Deadlines passed, were rescheduled, passed again. Editors wept salt tears. Publishers, that sainted breed, were patient and handsome and generally lovely. Chris Webb and Brian Herrmann, both of the Wiley clan, stood by the project so faithfully that their names will be forever legend. Men of the Far North will sing songs to their honor. Justin Blanton, the technical editor, managed to combine a Law Degree with the task: there's not enough beer in the world to pay him back. Thanks to all of them, and everyone else at Wiley.

Introduction

Welcome to *Hacking Gmail*. Thanks for buying this book. If you haven't bought it, you should. It's very good, and once you buy it you can stop loitering around the bookstore stacks. Go on: Buy it, sit down, have a coffee. See? Comfier isn't it? Ah. Hacking Gmail. It's a manly hobby, and this book will tell you how. Sorry? What's Gmail, you ask? Well, let me tell you . . .

What's Gmail?

March 31, 2004. A watershed in human history. Google's web-based e-mail service, still now at the time of this writing in Beta, and available only to people invited by other existing users, was launched. Offering a gigabyte of storage, an incredibly advanced JavaScript interface, and a series of user interface innovations, Gmail was an instant hit among those who could get access to the system. Today, more than a year later, Gmail is proving to be one of the flagship applications on the web—a truly rich application within the browser, combined with the server-based power of the world's leading search engine.

Hacking Gmail?

Of course, all that power just begs to be abused. Power corrupts, as they say, and hackers are nothing but a corrupt bunch: Almost as soon as Gmail was launched, hackers were looking at ways to use those capabilities for other purposes. They investigated the incredibly rich interface, and saw how much of the processing is done on the user's own machine; they burrowed into the communication between the browser and the server; and they developed a series of interfaces for scripting languages to allow you to control Gmail from your own programs.

This book shows what they did, how to do it yourself, and what to do after you've mastered the techniques. Meanwhile, you'll also learn all about Ajax, the terribly fashionable JavaScript technique that Gmail brought into the mainstream. Two topics for the price of one!

What's in This Book?

There are three parts to this book, each lovingly crafted to bring you, young Jedi, to the peak of Gmailing excellence. They are:

Part I: Starting to Use Gmail

Where you learn to use Gmail like a professional. A professional Gmail user, no less. A really skilled professional Gmail user. With a degree in Gmail. A Gmail ninja. A Gmail ninja with a black belt in Gmail from the secret Gmail training school on Mount Gmail. You might actually be part Gmail. Perhaps you've named your first born child after Gmail. You live in the Google Headquarters. You are Larry Page. You get the idea.

Part II: Getting Inside Gmail

Where you find out how Gmail works, and how you can use modern scripting languages to control it.

Part III: Conquering Gmail

Where you put these new skills to the test, wrangling Gmail into fiendishly clever uses, totally unlike those Google intended.

Whom Is This Book For?

You. Of course it is. If you picked up a book called *Hacking Gmail*, you're very likely to want it. If you're a programmer looking to use Gmail in wacky ways, this book is for you. If you're a power user looking to hack together scripts to do dangerously efficient things with your mail, this book is for you. If you're the parent, best friend, or lover of someone who answers to that description, this book is for them, and you should buy two copies. Really. It's great. And the shiny cover looks cool, no? I tell you, metallic covers are all the thing.

Hacking Carefully

It must be said here in plain English, and elsewhere by a battalion of scary lawyer folk, that I take no responsibility whatsoever for anything anyone does after reading this book. If you lose data; get folded, spindled, or mutilated; or have your Gmail account suspended, it is not my fault. The fine folks at Google, it has to be said, have played no part in the writing of this book, and most likely do not approve of the contents within. They may have me killed. Either way, I take no responsibility for anything. You're on your own, kiddo. As am I.

Companion Website

For links and updates, please visit this book's companion website at `www.wiley.com/go/extremetech`.

Hacking Gmail™

Starting to Use Gmail

First things first, then. Before you get into the deeper workings of Gmail, you need to get yourself up to scratch with the more public side of the application. Being able to hack Gmail is one thing, but it's very helpful to have a full understanding of how the system is meant to work before taking it apart and doing silly things with it.

In this part, therefore, you look at how to integrate Gmail with your desktop (Chapter 1). Then in Chapter 2 you look at merging your existing mail into the application, and finally in Chapter 3 you look at some of the cunning ways people use Gmail to its utmost.

in this part

Chapter 1
Desktop Integration

Chapter 2
Integrating Your
Existing Mail

Chapter 3
Gmail Power Tips

Desktop Integration

The first part of this book really highlights its entire theme: that the Gmail service, although ostensibly a website, can be dragged over to touch the desktop in ways that make new and exciting applications possible.

The first five chapters deal with this on a very basic level, allowing you to use Gmail to its limits before delving into the nitty gritty of code and some rather extreme uses of the system.

This chapter deals with the situations that arise when you continue to use Gmail within the browser but want to use it as your day-to-day e-mail system. There are two areas to cover: new mail notification and `mailto:` link redirection.

in this chapter

☑ New mail notification

☑ Available applications

☑ Redirecting mailto:

New Mail Notification

Gmail's great features have inspired many early adopters to move their entire e-mail regime over to the service. But unlike other e-mail clients, Gmail requires you to have your web browser open to see if you have any new mail. Even with tabbed browsing, this is annoying. The alternative is to use a new-mail notifier application. This section details some of the best notifiers, grouped by platform. This is not a definitive list even at the time of this writing. By the time you read this, there will be even more options. But this is a good start.

Windows

Perhaps not the operating system of choice for the readers of this book, but certainly one with a lot of users, Windows is gifted with a wide range of Gmail integration products.

Google Gmail Notifier

The first and most obvious application comes from Google itself. Their Gmail Notifier sits in the system tray, and displays an unread mail count, and the subject line, sender, and a synopsis of newly arriving mail, all shown in Figure 1-1. At the time of writing, it, like Gmail itself, is in beta. Get the Gmail Notifier from `http://toolbar.google.com/gmail-helper/`.

FIGURE 1-1: Google's own Gmail Notifier in action

Mozilla Extension Gmail Notifier

Technically, this will work on any platform that can run Mozilla-based browsers, but I'll put Doron Rosenberg's Gmail Notifier browser extension here (see Figure 1-2). Although it doesn't provide the same level of interface as a taskbar-based application, for people who spend a lot of time in their web browser, the Mozilla extension is very convenient.

You can find the extension at `http://nexgenmedia.net/extensions/`.

FIGURE 1-2: Mozilla
Gmail Notifier in the
Firefox status bar

Mac OS X

OS X users have a choice of two applications, both very similar to each other, and doing pretty much the same thing: placing the mail notification in the menu bar at the top of the screen.

GmailStatus

Carsten Guenther's GmailStatus (`http://homepage.mac.com/carsten.guenther/GmailStatus/`) is a good example. It displays new mail counts for the Inbox, and each individual label you might have set up, adds a hotkey to launch Gmail in your browser, supports Growl notifications (see `http://growl.info/` for more on that), and gives a hotkey to write a new message in Gmail (see Figure 1-3).

FIGURE 1-3: GmailStatus in action, with Growl notification

gCount

Nathan Spindel's gCount (`www.ocf.berkeley.edu/~natan/gcount/`), shown in Figure 1-4, is very similar indeed to GmailStatus in terms of functionality, with perhaps two interesting additions. First, you can have a new mail count in the dock, and second, it takes your Gmail username and password from the keychain. This is a nice touch.

Linux, etc.

People using Linux, or any other Unix-style operating system with the option to compile things, have a whole series of potential Gmail applications to choose from. Linux users will also find the scripting done in the later stages of this book to be very simple to implement.

FIGURE **1-4:** gCount, showing the preference menu

Mail Notification

Jean-Yves Lefort's Mail Notification system for Linux desktops supports Gmail as well as most of the other common e-mail systems. You can get it from www. nongnu.org/mailnotify/ where it is released under the GPL. According to Lefort, it works with system trays implementing the freedesktop.org System Tray Specification, such as the Gnome Panel Notification Area, the Xfce Notification Area, and the KDE System Tray.

Wmgmail

Remarkably useful for the clarity of its Python-based code, Pasi Savolainen's Wmgmail is intended for use with WindowMaker or fluxbox window managers on the operating system of your choice. (If that sentence means nothing to you, this is not for you, in other words.)

It's a standard new mail notification app, with new mail preview added in, but it also has one very nice feature that is perfect for the hacker: You can set it to run another program whenever new mail arrives.

You can find Wmgmail at http://osx.freshmeat.net/projects/wmgmail/.

Redirecting mailto:

Now that you have your desktop telling you when you have new mail within your Gmail account, the only remaining integration is to ensure that clicking on a mailto: link on a web page opens Gmail instead of your operating system's default e-mail client.

Windows

Again, as with new mail notification, Windows users have the pick of the crop. The Google-authored Gmail Notifier, as mentioned previously, gives you the option to redirect `mailto:` links when you install it.

If you really want to, you can manually edit the Windows Registry to enact the same effect. The website `www.rabidsquirrel.net/G-Mailto/` gives a rundown of just how to do this.

Multiplatform/Mozilla

Other than the Mozilla extension, at the time of this writing there is no `mailto:` link diversion for the Linux desktop. But happily, by far the best way of repurposing `mailto:` links is to do it in the browser, and specifically in a Mozilla-based browser, which runs on all of the platforms used in this book: Windows, OS X, and Linux. The platforms can use Jed Brown's WebMailCompose extension (see Figure 1-5), installable from `http://jedbrown.net/mozilla/extensions/ #WebMailCompose`.

FIGURE 1-5: WebMailCompose in action in Firefox 1.0 on OS X

This extension also allows `mailto:` links to point to many other web-based e-mail systems, should you tire of all of this coolness.

OS X

GmailStatus, mentioned earlier, also has the effect of changing `mailto:` links to launch Gmail instead of `Mail.app`. But if you don't want to use GmailStatus, a good example for OS X users is Gmailto, found at `http://gu.st/code/Gmailto/`. Gmailto is simple to use: Just download and run it, and then go to `Mail.app`'s preference panel to change the default reader application to Gmailto (displayed in Figure 1-6) instead of `Mail.app`. Why the preference panel is inside the application you no longer wish to use is beyond the reckoning of mortal men.

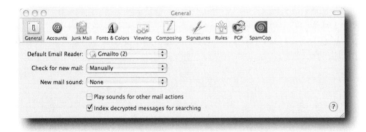

FIGURE 1-6: Selecting Gmailto in Mail.app's preferences

GmailerXP

Well worth its own section, if only because it's really weird, the Windows software GmailerXP — `http://gmailerxp.sourceforge.net` — does all of the above but adds in a desktop version of all of the other Gmail features as well: labels, stars, setting filters and contacts, and so on (see Figure 1-7). I'm not sure when you would use it, but it is a brilliant example of a Gmail hack.

The second half of this book looks at how applications such as GmailerXP work and how to make your own.

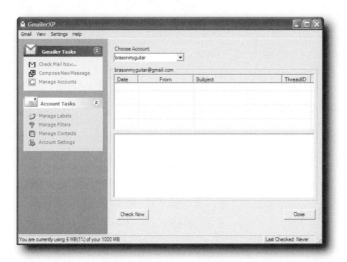

FIGURE 1-7: GmailerXP in action

And Now . . .

By now you should be happily using Gmail, with new mail showing up on your desktop and `mailto:` links on the web causing Gmail to open, not the default mail reader you got with the operating system. In the next chapter, you look at using the POP interface to pull your Gmail mail down into that very reader.

Integrating Your Existing Mail

☑ Importing your mail

☑ Using Pop3 with Gmail

☑ Imap for Gmail?

Gmail is probably not your first e-mail account, but its features may well make it your best. Certainly it's likely to be the one with the biggest amount of storage available and such an exemplary search system.

Importing Your Mail into Gmail

The most important thing for me, when starting to use Gmail properly, was getting all of my existing mail into the Gmail system. Alas, Gmail doesn't have an import facility, so in this chapter you have to make use of someone else's hack to get your existing mail into the system. There are a few applications available to do this, but none are as good as the one concentrated on in the following section: Gmail Loader.

Gmail Loader

Mark Lyon's Gmail Loader (shown in Figure 2-1), which you can find at www.marklyon.org/gmail/default.htm, does the trick very nicely indeed. It's available in versions for Windows, OS X, and Linux, and in a source-code version. To quote the author, "The GMail Loader is a graphical, cross-platform, Python-based utility that supports two mBox formats (Netscape, Mozilla, Thunderbird, Most Other Clients), MailDir (Qmail, others), MMDF (Mutt), MH (NMH), and Babyl (Emacs RMAIL). Eventually, I plan to add support for direct sending of IMAP accounts, and am working on a library that can read and export Microsoft Outlook PST files." (This was in December 2004. That addition may well have happened by now.)

FIGURE 2-1: Gmail Loader on Windows

Mark Lyon's own instructions (www.marklyon.org/gmail/instruction.htm) are perfectly good, so you don't need to walk through them here. There are some general problems to point out, however, which are a result of the shortcomings of the way the system has to work. Because there is no direct method to import mail into the system, Gmail Loader (and its clones) rely on just forwarding the mail from your existing account. This means that all date information is based on the time the mail was received by Gmail, not on the time you originally received it elsewhere. There's no real way around this, although it can be worked around if you want to find mail from, say, one particular month: Just use the search box to look for it, or create a filter.

Setting Up Pop Access Inside Gmail

Log in to Gmail and click on the settings link at the top-right of the screen. Once there, click on Forwarding and Pop. You should see a screen similar to Figure 2-2.

Figure 2-2: The Pop mail settings inside Gmail

Setting Up Pop Within an Application

Full instructions on setting up the Pop mail access within individual e-mail applications are available directly from Gmail at `http://gmail.google.com/support/bin/answer.py?answer=12103`

For expert users, the settings, shown in Table 2-1, are very simple indeed.

Table 2-1   Pop Settings in Gmail

The Setting	What You Set It To
Incoming Mail (POP3) Server requires SSL Use SSL: Yes Port: 995	pop.gmail.com
Outgoing Mail (SMTP) Server requires TLS Use Authentication: Yes Use STARTTLS: Yes (some clients call this SSL) Port: 465 or 587	smtp.gmail.com (use authentication)
Account Name	Your Gmail username (including @gmail.com)
E-mail Address	Your full Gmail e-mail address (username@gmail.com)
Password	Your Gmail password

IMAP for Gmail

Gmail's features, the labeling and stars specifically, do not have counterparts in the standard e-mail world. There's no facility within any e-mail format to apply labels, for example, to your mail. It's not surprising, therefore, that there is no existing mail application that could understand or use them. Mail exported from Gmail does not take its label with it.

Nor once the mail has been exported can the exported copy have any effect on the original. Moving an exported mail into a different locally stored folder doesn't change anything on Gmail itself.

Both of these facts are, in my view, great disadvantages to the idea of offline working with Gmail. The first is a difficult problem, but the second can be solved by replacing the Pop interface with one based on another standard: IMAP.

Gmail does not support IMAP at the time of this writing. No matter: The second half of this book looks at building a Gmail-to-IMAP proxy server.

And Now . . .

In this chapter, you have moved your existing mail over to Gmail, integrated Gmail into your desktop, and looked at settings that will allow you to access Gmail from other applications and devices. Altogether, this means that Gmail can now be used as your primary e-mail application.

In the next chapter, you look at ways to improve how you use Gmail itself: power tips and the tricks of the advanced user. Once you know those, you can move on to reverse engineering Gmail and use it to power your own applications.

Gmail Power Tips

chapter

3

in this chapter

☑ Keyboard shortcuts

☑ Plus addressing

☑ Filters

☑ Advanced searching

Now you've integrated Gmail into your desktop and moved all of your mail over into it, but before you start to rip the application apart, you should look at the ways to use Gmail to its limits. This chapter does just that. This book is not just about using Gmail itself but rather hacking the application to do other things. Nevertheless, you'll need the techniques you are about to discover in later chapters. They are also all very useful in their own right.

Keyboard Shortcuts

The keyboard shortcuts available within Gmail are, without any doubt, the quickest route to speedy productivity within the application. The time investment in learning the keyboard shortcuts of all of your computer's applications always pays off, as you are able to navigate your system much more quickly than before. Instead of reaching off the keyboard, grasping the mouse, moving it to the right place and clicking, keyboard shortcuts allow you to press just one button. You don't lift your hands off the keyboard, and when you're really good at typing, you don't even need to look at the screen.

Activating the keyboard shortcuts is simple. Go to the Settings page and turn them on there, as shown in Figure 3-1.

FIGURE 3-1: The keyboard shortcuts checkbox

Save the settings, and you will find that the bottom of your Inbox screen has changed to show some of the keyboard shortcut commands, as shown in Figure 3-2.

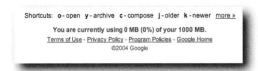

FIGURE 3-2: The bottom of the Inbox with keyboard shortcuts turned on

To see what keyboard shortcuts are about, press the c key now. Immediately, the page changes to the Compose Message window, with your cursor in the To: addressing area. Type an e-mail address, and then press Tab. Your cursor moves to the Subject line. Type something, and hit Tab again, and you're in the message box. So far so good. Now a snag. Hit Tab again, and then Enter, and in Internet Explorer your message is sent. In any other browser — Firefox, say — the final tab puts your cursor up into the search box. Hitting Enter brings up a warning box (shown in Figure 3-3) asking if you are willing to lose the newly typed, and unsaved, message.

FIGURE 3-3: You're about to lose your work. Eek!

You most likely don't want to do that.

Tip If you're not using Internet Explorer—and for the sake of this book, at least, I recommend you do not, and employ Firefox (as I am in this chapter's screenshots) or Mozilla instead—this is a drawback to the keyboard shortcuts. Grasp your mouse, and click the Send button instead.

The keyboard shortcuts come into their own when dealing with spam. Figure 3-4 shows my Inbox full of the stuff.

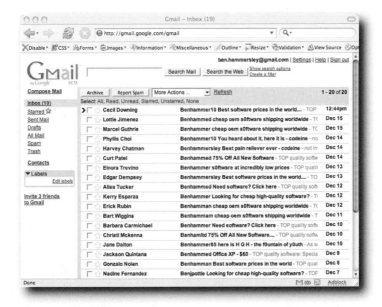

FIGURE 3-4: An Inbox full of spam

(I have to be honest here—Gmail's spam filters caught all of this before it hit my Inbox. I just moved it out there for the sake of this demonstration.)

If you wake to find an Inbox full of such nastiness, it's easy to get rid of. Press o to open a message, and when it has opened, press the exclamation point (!) to mark it as spam. By using my left hand to press the Shift+1 to make the exclamation point, and my right hand to press o, I find I can get quite a satisfying rhythm going and my Inbox clear in little to no time. Making "Pow!" noises is also recommended.

You can, of course, use the mouse to select the ones you want and then hit an exclamation point.

The keyboard shortcuts are many and various, and are all good to know about. But they're also very simple. By now you should have the hang of their power. Here then, before moving on, in Table 3-1 is a complete rundown of the keyboard shortcuts available at the time of this writing.

Table 3-1   Gmail's Keyboard Shortcuts

Key	Definition	Action
c	Compose	Allows you to compose a new message. Shift+c allows you to compose a message in a new window.
/	Search	Puts your cursor in the search box.
k	Move to newer conversation	Opens or moves your cursor to a more recent conversation. You can hit Enter to expand a conversation.
j	Move to older conversation	Opens or moves your cursor to the next oldest conversation. You can hit Enter to expand a conversation.
n	Next message	Moves your cursor to the next message. You can hit Enter to expand or collapse a message. (Applicable only in Conversation View.)
p	Previous message	Moves your cursor to the previous message. You can hit Enter to expand or collapse a message. (Applicable only in Conversation View.)
Enter	Open	Opens your conversation. Also expands or collapses a message if you are in Conversation View.
u	Return to conversation list	Refreshes your page and returns you to the Inbox, or list of conversations.
y	Archive (Remove from current view)	Automatically removes the message or conversation from your current view. From Inbox, y means Archive. From Starred, y means Unstar. From Spam, y means Unmark as spam and move to Inbox. From Trash, y means move to Inbox. From any label, y means Remove the label. Pressing y has no effect if you're in Sent or All Mail.

Key	Definition	Action
x	Select conversation	Automatically checks and selects a conversation so you can archive, apply a label, or choose an action from the drop-down menu to apply to that conversation.
s	Star a message or conversation	Adds a star to or removes a star from a message or conversation. Stars allow you to give a message or conversation a special status.
!	Report spam	Marks a message as spam and removes it from your conversation list.
r	Reply	Reply to the message sender. Shift+r allows you to reply to a message in a new window. (Applicable only in Conversation View.)
a	Reply all	Reply to all message recipients. Shift+a allows you to reply to all message recipients in a new window. (Applicable only in Conversation View.)
f	Forward	Forward a message. Shift+f allows you to forward a message in a new window. (Applicable only in Conversation View.)
esc	Escape from input field	Removes the cursor from your current input field.

Now that you're familiar with Gmail's keyboard shortcuts, Table 3-2 outlines the combo-key shortcuts.

Table 3-2   Combo-Keys Shortcuts

Shortcut Key	Definition	Action
Tab then Enter	Send message	After composing your message, use this combination to automatically send it. (Supported in Internet Explorer only.)
y then o	Archive and next	Archive your conversation and move to the next one.
g then a	Go to All Mail	Takes you to All Mail, the storage place for all the mail you've ever sent or received, but haven't deleted.
g then s	Go to Starred	Takes you to all of the conversations that you've starred.
g then c	Go to Contacts	Takes you to your Contacts list.
g then d	Go to Drafts	Takes you to all the drafts that you've saved.
g then i	Go to Inbox	Takes you back to the Inbox.

Moving on from the keyboard shortcuts, the next section shows you how you can avoid them altogether by using filters.

Plus Addressing and Filtering

One little-known feature of the more old school e-mail systems is the one called *plus addressing*. It can be exceptionally useful both in Gmail and in your other e-mail systems, and I use it extensively for things such as mailing lists and weblog commenting.

In a nutshell, Gmail ignores anything in the first half of an e-mail address after a plus sign. So ben.hammersley+chapter_three_comments@gmail.com is treated in exactly the same way as ben.hammersley@gmail.com. It is not, as you might expect, a different address. You can put anything after the plus sign except for a space or an at (@) sign, and it always gets delivered to your real Inbox. Figure 3-5 should prove that it works.

FIGURE 3-5: Plus addressing in action

Plus addressing is remarkably useful, as it enables you to set up filters for your incoming mail. In order to do set up filters, click the "Create a filter" link to the right of the search bar. You will be presented with a screen containing something very much like Figure 3-6.

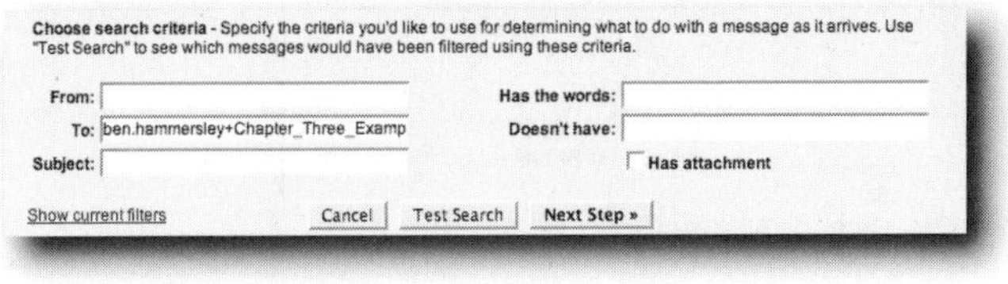

FIGURE **3-6: The first stage in setting up a filter**

Copy, as shown, the address into the To: box, and click the Next Step button. Of course, this is how you create filters for any other part of the message as well. I'll leave it to the reader's intelligence to see how this works. Figure 3-7 shows the next stage.

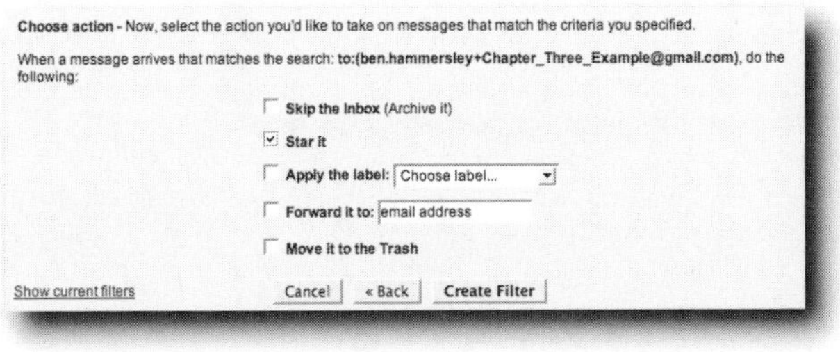

FIGURE **3-7: Selecting the action you want Gmail to take when a message arrives**

A filter can move, star, directly archive, label, forward, trash, or a combination of the five, any message that triggers it. Select the actions you want, and click the Create Filter button. Figure 3-8 shows the final result.

Because plus addressing effectively gives you an unlimited number of e-mail addresses to the same Gmail inbox, it allows you to assign one to each mailing list, website, and so on that you subscribe to. You can also use it to track which e-mail addresses have been sold to spammers, and send those to Trash automatically.

Other Addressing Tips

Gmail has a few other features to its addressing. First, the dot in the middle of most people's Gmail addresses is entirely optional. As Figure 3-9 shows, benhammersley@gmail.com is exactly the same as ben.hammersley@gmail.com.

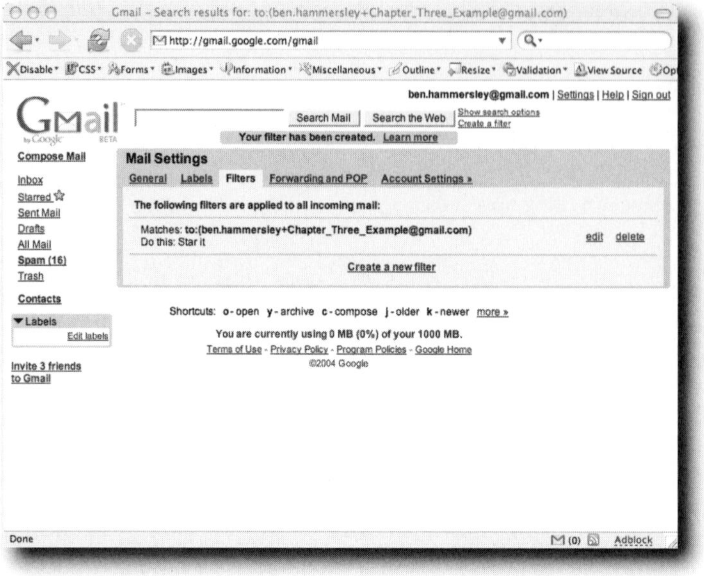

FIGURE 3-8: A filter, set up

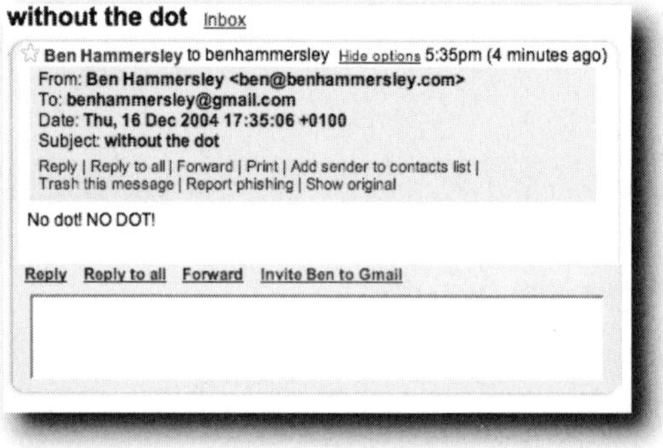

FIGURE 3-9: Receiving mail from anti-dot fanatic

Indeed, as Figure 3-10 shows, the dot is basically ignored. Put it anywhere you like or leave it out entirely: yet another way to produce filterable e-mail addresses inside Gmail.

From: **Ben Hammersley**
      <ben@benhammersley.com>
To: b.enhammersley@gmail.com
Date: Thu, 16 Dec 2004 17:45:40 +0100
Subject: **dot test**

FIGURE 3-10: The blessing of the
wandering dot

Note

One final thing about addressing: If you are sending a mail to someone else's Gmail account, you needn't add the @gmail.com section of the address. Just type the first half and it is delivered perfectly well.

Quickly Mark a Group of E-Mails

Like most desktop applications, Gmail actually allows you to *mark* a group of items without having to select each one individually (by mark, I mean to put a check in the checkbox next to an e-mail when you are presented with a list of e-mails). With Gmail, if you'd like to select a group of consecutive messages without marking each one separately, you simply need to check the first one in the list, and then hold down the Shift key and check the last one you want to include in the group of marked messages — the two e-mails you checked and all of the e-mails between them will now be marked. You can use the same method to unmark e-mails and to star or unstar them. Note, however, that this might not work in all browsers.

Send Executables as Attachments

When you receive an e-mail from an address that doesn't end in @gmail.com, Gmail looks at attachments for file extensions known to be executable (such as .dll, .exe, .vbs, and so forth), so if someone sends you one of these file types, their message will bounce back. This goes for files within ZIP archives as well — Gmail looks inside these for executable extensions and the e-mail bounces back to the sender if it contains any. Gmail doesn't look inside other archive formats, such as RAR or ACE, so you might want to use one of these formats instead of going through the hassle of the following workaround.

To get around this annoyance, you can use the same trick that has been used for years. Simply tell the sender to rename the extension of the file to something Gmail will allow (such as .jpg), and when you receive the file, rename it back to the type it really is (for example, change file.jpg to file.exe).

It seems that Gmail *will* allow you to send and receive executable attachments between Gmail accounts and from Gmail to outside accounts.

Advanced Searching

Gmail is run by Google, so it's obvious that its built-in search engine is going to be extremely powerful indeed. Everyone is used to the ordinary search technique of putting keywords into the box and pressing Enter, but not everyone is aware of the additional operators you can use. Table 3-3 gives a rundown.

Table 3-3   Gmail's Search Operators

Operator	Definition	Example(s)
from:	Used to specify the sender.	Example: from:amy Meaning: Messages from Amy.
to:	Used to specify a recipient.	Example: to:david Meaning: All messages that were sent to David (by you or someone else).
subject:	Search for words in the subject line.	Example: subject:dinner Meaning: Messages that have the word "dinner" in the subject.
OR	Search for messages matching term A or term B. OR must be in all caps.	Example: from:amy OR from:david Meaning: Messages from Amy or from David.
- (hyphen)	Used to exclude messages from your search.	Example: dinner-movie Meaning: Messages that contain the word "dinner" but do not contain the word "movie".
label:	Search for messages by label. There isn't a search operator for unlabeled messages.	Example: from:amy label:friends Meaning: Messages from Amy that have the label "friends". Example: from:david label:my-family Meaning: Messages from David that have the label My Family.
has:attachment	Search for messages with an attachment.	Example: from:david has:attachment Meaning: Messages from David that have an attachment.

Operator	Definition	Example(s)
filename:	Search for an attachment by name or type.	Example: filename:physicshomework.txt Meaning: Messages with an attachment named physicshomework.txt. Example: label:work filename:pdf Meaning: Messages labeled work that also have a PDF file as an attachment.
" " (quotes)	Used to search for an exact phrase. Capitalization isn't taken into consideration.	Example: "i'm feeling lucky" Meaning: Messages containing the phrase "i'm feeling lucky" or "I'm feeling lucky". Example: subject:"dinner and a movie" Meaning: Messages containing the phrase "dinner and a movie" in the subject.
( )	Used to group words. Used to specify terms that shouldn't be excluded.	Example: from:amy(dinner OR movie) Meaning: Messages from Amy that contain either the word "dinner" or the word "movie". Example: subject:(dinner movie) Meaning: Messages in which the subject contains both the word "dinner" and the word "movie".
in:anywhere	Search for messages anywhere in your account. Messages in Spam and Trash are excluded from searches by default.	Example: in:anywhere subject:movie Meaning: Messages in All Mail, Spam, and Trash that contain the word "movie".
in:inbox in:trash in:spam	Search for messages in Inbox, Trash, or Spam.	Example: in:trash from:amy Meaning: Messages from Amy that are in the trash.
is:starred is:unread is:read	Search for messages that are starred, unread, or read.	Example: is:read is:starred from:David Meaning: Messages from David that have been read and are marked with a star.
cc: bcc:	Used to specify recipients in the cc: or bcc: fields. Search on bcc: cannot retrieve messages on which you were blind carbon copied.	Example: cc:david Meaning: Messages that were cc-ed to David.
after: before:	Search for messages after or before a certain date. Date must be in yyyy/mm/dd format.	Example: after:2004/04/17 before:2004/04/18 Meaning: Messages sent on April 17, 2004. More precisely: Messages sent on or after April 17, 2004, but before April 18, 2004.

The operators detailed in Table 3-3 are all self-explanatory and can be combined. For example, consider the following search parameters:

```
in:inbox from:BenHammersley "fancy a pint?"
```

This search would result in any message from my Gmail account, in your Inbox, suggesting a visit to the pub. In order to bring any unread mail sent before New Year's Eve 2004, with an attachment, and the subject line New Year's Eve Invitation, you would conduct the following search:

```
is:unread before:2004/12/31has:attachment  subject:"New Years Eve
Invitation"
```

Very simple indeed.

For more information on advanced searching with Google, a good place to start is *Google For Dummies*.

And Now . . .

You've reached the end of Chapter 3. You should feel confident using Gmail itself, in getting your mail into and out of the system, and in using the system with some sort of flair. From the next chapter onward, you're going to delve into Gmail's inner workings. Things get much more technical from now on. Let's go.

Getting Inside Gmail

So, by now you should be up to speed with actually using Gmail. It's time to get a bit dirtier. Time to get under the hood, so to speak, and fiddle with the application. In this part, you look at how Gmail works and how to make it work for you.

First, you look at skinning Gmail in Chapter 4. Making Gmail look different might seem to be a strange thing to do, but it's both fun and educational. The knowledge you pick up there, and in Chapter 5 where you investigate the JavaScript-ybased workings of the application, will enable you to fully understand how Gmail works. In Chapter 6, you learn how Greasemonkey and Firefox can be used to radically improve your Gmail experience and to build your own Greasemonkey scripts.

In Chapter 7, you encounter the various programming language libraries available for use with Gmail, and you start to use them: writing scripts to check for and read mail (Chapters 8 and 9), and to send replies (Chapter 10). By the end of that chapter, you'll be writing little mini applications that use Gmail as their remote processing system. Exciting? Oh yes!

in this part

Chapter 4
Skinning Gmail

Chapter 5
How Gmail Works

Chapter 6
Gmail and Greasemonkey

Chapter 7
Gmail Libraries

Chapter 8
Checking for Mail

Chapter 9
Reading Mail

Chapter 10
Sending Mail

Skinning Gmail

Being a web-based application, and written by people who understand modern practices, Gmail is skinnable using a user-side CSS file. This chapter analyzes Gmail's HTML layout, and shows you how to create and use CSS files that will give the application a whole new look. It won't change the way that Gmail works, only the way it looks, but you will learn a lot about the way Gmail has been built: knowledge that will prove invaluable in the following chapters.

Besides, it's really cool.

Deconstructing Gmail

In order to pack most of its functionality into a browser-side application, Gmail employs an extremely complex page structure. It does use CSS very heavily, happily making the styling of the page quite simple once you understand the names of the elements, but it also consists of at least nine iframes inside a frameset. To make things worse, much of the markup is dynamically created by JavaScript, meaning that just viewing the source won't help you.

Before you can get onto reskinning Gmail, then, you need to deconstruct it, and see how it is put together. Only then can you think about messing around with it.

To do that, you should use the Mozilla Firefox browser (at the time of this writing version 1.0), and the extremely popular Web Developer Extension, written by Chris Pederick. These are both highly recommended, and using them will help you to follow along at home with the rest of this section. Go to `www.mozilla.org` and `www.chrispederick.com/work/firefox/webdeveloper/`, respectively, and download the applications.

in this chapter

☑ Gmail's layout

☑ The user interface

☑ Changing colors

☑ Changing layout

Once you've downloaded the applications, you can start. Figure 4-1 shows my own Gmail Inbox with a single message inside.

The first thing to do is open up Firefox's DOM inspector, which tells you what the browser itself is seeing. Half expanded, it looks like Figure 4-2.

The figure shows you that the application is made up of a single document (obviously), containing a frameset and some markup. That tiny amount of markup, shown in Figure 4-2 as the NOSCRIPT section, is simply a message that displays only if you're trying to look at Gmail with JavaScript turned off, telling you that you're out of luck without JavaScript. The frameset is where it's at. It contains two frames, the first of which has 12 divs in its body, while the second frame has a large script element, but nothing of note in the body. Further exploration, not shown here, will point out that the second frame contains a vast amount of JavaScript and nothing else. That, as you will see in later chapters, makes up the real client-side workings of Gmail. For your purposes now, however, you can concentrate on the first frame.

So, working with the first frame, you see it is made up of 12 divs, each with its own class name, as illustrated in Figure 4-3.

FIGURE 4-1: A simple Gmail Inbox

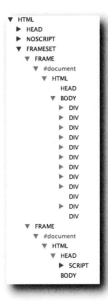

```
▼ HTML
  ▶ HEAD
  ▶ NOSCRIPT
  ▼ FRAMESET
    ▼ FRAME
      ▼ #document
        ▼ HTML
            HEAD
          ▼ BODY
            ▶ DIV
            ▶ DIV
            ▶ DIV
            ▶ DIV
            ▶ DIV
            ▶ DIV
            ▶ DIV
            ▶ DIV
            ▶ DIV
              DIV
            ▶ DIV
              DIV
    ▼ FRAME
      ▼ #document
        ▼ HTML
          ▼ HEAD
            ▶ SCRIPT
            BODY
```

FIGURE 4-2: What the DOM
inspector tells you about the Inbox

```
▼ HTML
    HEAD
  ▼ BODY
    ▶ DIV            d_conv
    ▶ DIV            d_conv2
    ▶ DIV            d_tlist
    ▶ DIV            d_tlist2
    ▶ DIV            d_clist
    ▶ DIV            d_clist2
    ▶ DIV            d_comp
    ▶ DIV            d_prefs
    ▶ DIV            d_hist
      DIV            md
    ▶ DIV            lo
      DIV            ind
```

FIGURE 4-3: The first frame's structure showing
class names

There's a great deal going on here, much of which will be revisited over the
course of this book. For now, you need to keep drilling down to the interface itself.

To see which of these divs is the mother lode, use the Web Developer Extension to Firefox to turn off the styling (click on the Disable menu, the first on the left, and then Disable Styles), outline the block level elements in red, and display their names. Doing this, you get the horrible Figure 4-4.

It's very plain from Figure 4-4 that the div called d_tlist2 is the one you're really interested in. It's the one that isn't empty, which is something of a giveaway. Using the DOM inspector, you can drill down further. Notice that d_tlist2 contains an iframe, called tlist, and that that iframe, when opened in a new DOM inspector, looks like Figure 4-5.

You can also see from the DOM inspector that the iframe that makes up this interface is addressed as follows: http://gmail.google. com/gmail?search=inbox&view=tl&start=0&init=1&zx=3177c401850460 90895581735.

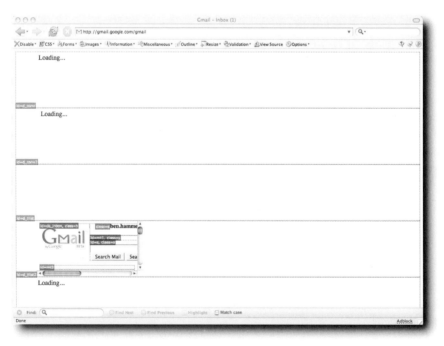

FIGURE 4-4: Gmail with no styling . . . quite ugly

FIGURE 4-5: Gmail's Inbox exposed in
the DOM inspector

Ferret that bit of information away for the moment. It will come in handy.
Meanwhile, back at the browser, you can dump the contents of this page from
the DOM inspector to a text editor. Remember that although this all seems a bit
long-winded, you cannot do it just by using View Source: Most of the markup is
created by JavaScript, and you'll get to see only some of the JavaScript if you do
that. You needed to use the DOM inspector to get to the actual code that the
browser is rendering and displaying on your screen. Rather than subject you, dear
readers, to the horrors of 14 pages of HTML here, I've placed the entire listing in
Appendix A. Before moving on to the style sheet's nuts and bolts, consider turning to Appendix A and perusing Listing A-1 first.

To make things a bit easier, let me strip out the JavaScript and isolate the style
sheet, tidy the whole thing up a bit, and walk through the document showing you
what each section does. From the top, then.

The Top Section

Figure 4-6 shows the top section of the Gmail Inbox, with the table elements arti-
ficially outlined with dotted lines.

FIGURE 4-6: The Gmail Inbox's top section, showing table elements

In the code, the top section of the Inbox is produced by the following HTML, shown in Listing 4-1.

Listing 4-1: The Top Section of the Gmail Inbox in HTML

```
<body>
<table width="100%" cellspacing="0" cellpadding="0">
<tbody>
<tr>
<td width="149" valign="top" rowspan="2">

<div id="ds_inbox" style="padding-top: 1ex;" class="h">
    <img width="143" height="59" src=
    "/gmail/help/images/logo.gif"></div></td>

<td valign="top" align="right">
<div class="s" style="padding-bottom: 2px; text-align:
right;">
<b>ben.hammersley@gmail.com</b> | <span id="prf_g" class=
"lk">Settings</span> | <a target="_blank" href="/support/"
    class="lc" id="help">Help</a> | <a target="_top" onclick=
    "return top.js._Main_OnLink(window,this,event)" class="lk"
href="?logout">Sign out</a></div></td></tr>

<tr>
<td valign="bottom">
<div class="s" id="mt1">
<table cellspacing="0" cellpadding="0">
<tbody>
<tr>
<td valign="bottom">
<form onsubmit="return top.js._MH_OnSearch(window,0)" style=
"padding-bottom: 5px; white-space: nowrap;" class="s" id="s">
<input value="" name="q" maxlength="2048" size="28">  
<input type="submit" value="Search Mail">  
        <input type="submit" onclick=
        "return top.js._MH_OnSearch(window,1)" value=
        "Search the Web">  </form></td>
<td>
<table cellspacing="0" cellpadding="0" style=
"vertical-align: top; padding-bottom: 4px;">
<tbody>
<tr>
<td><span id="mt_adv" style="font-size: 65%;" class=
"lk">Show search options</span>
  </td></tr>
<tr>
```

```
<td><span id="mt_cf1" style="font-size: 65%; vertical-align:
top;"
class=
"lk">Create a filter</span></td></tr></tbody></table
></td></tr></tbody></table></div>
<div style=
"height: 2.1ex; padding-right: 149px; visibility: hidden;"
    class="nt" id="nt1"></td></tr></tbody></table>
```

As you can see, the HTML uses tables, divs, and spans, and takes its styling from both the style sheet and some inline styling as well. This means that you must forcibly override some of their styling using the !important modifier. More on that in a few pages.

So, going from left to right, the Gmail logo is marked up with a div with an id of ds_inbox and a class of h. Looking in the style sheet, notice that this class merely changes the shape of your mouse pointer when you mouse over it. No styling there as such, but plenty of opportunity to remove the Gmail logo and add your own.

Moving over, my e-mail address and the links to the Settings, Help, and Sign Out buttons are all contained within an unnamed div, with a class of s. From the style sheet, you can see that s simply sets the font size to 80 percent. So there's scope here for styling, but not specifically this section. Nor can you really move it around.

That row is the top half of a table. The bottom half of the table has another table nesting inside it (and another nesting inside that one, as you shall see).

The outermost of those tables is split in two, with the left-hand side containing the search form, and the right-hand side containing the innermost table, which splits it into two rows. The top row, a span called mt_adv, acts as a link, showing the search options. The cunning way in which this JavaScript works is dealt with in Chapter 5.

The bottom row is another span called mt_cf1, which opens the filter creation box. After that, the code closes the table and the surrounding div.

The Navigation Menu

After two divs with no content, we come to the div called nav, which contains the entire navigation menu from the left of the screen, as in Figure 4-7.

Figure 4-7: The Gmail navigation menu

The code that produces this import part of the page is here, in Listing 4-2.

Listing 4-2: The HTML That Produces the Gmail Navigation Menu

```
<div style="padding-bottom: 1px;" id="mt2">
<div class="nt" id="nt2" style="display: none;">
<div id="nav" style="position: absolute; left: 1ex; width:
14ex;">
<div class="nl"><span id="comp" class="lk"><b>Compose
Mail</b></span></div>
<div style="padding-top: 9px;">
<table cellspacing="0" cellpadding="0" border="0" style=
"background: rgb(195, 217, 255) none repeat scroll 0%; -moz-
background-clip: initial; -moz-background-origin: initial;
-moz-background-inline-policy: initial;"
       class="cv">
<tbody>
<tr height="2">
<td width="8" class="tl"></tr>
<tr>
<td>
<td><span id="ds_inbox" class="lk b"><b>Inbox
(1)</b></span></td></tr>
<tr height="2">
<td class="bl"></tr></tbody></table>
<div class="nl"><span id="ds_starred" class="lk">Starred
     <img width="13" height="13" src=
     "/gmail/images/star_on_sm_2.gif" id="_ss"></span></div>
```

```
<div class="nl"><span id="ds_sent" class="lk">Sent
Mail</span></div>
<div class="nl"><span id="ds_drafts"
class="lk">Drafts</span></div>
<div class="nl"><span id="ds_all" class="lk">All
Mail</span></div>
<div class="nl"><span id="ds_spam"
class="lk">Spam</span></div>
<div class="nl"><span id="ds_trash" class=
"lk">Trash</span></div></div>
<div style="padding-top: 8px;">
<div class="nl"><span id="cont" class=
"lk"><b>Contacts</b></span></div></div>
<div id="nb_0" style="padding-top: 8px;">
<div style="width: 95%;">
<table width="100%" cellspacing="0" cellpadding="0" bgcolor=
"#B5EDBC">
<tbody>
<tr height="2">
<td class="tl">
<td class="tr"></tr></tbody></table>
<div style=
"padding: 0pt 3px 1px; background: rgb(181, 237, 188) none
repeat scroll 0%; -moz-background-clip: initial; -moz-
background-origin: initial; -moz-background-inline-policy:
initial;">
<div id="nt_0" class="s h"><img width="11" height="11" src=
"/gmail/images/opentriangle.gif"> Labels</div>
<table cellspacing="2" class="nb">
<tbody>
<tr>
<td>
<div align="right" id="prf_l" class="lk cs">
Edit labels</div></td></tr></tbody></table></div>
<table width="100%" cellspacing="0" cellpadding="0" bgcolor=
"#B5EDBC">
<tbody>
<tr height="2">
<td class="bl">
<td class="br"></tr></tbody></table></div></div>
<div id="nb_2" style="padding-top: 7px;">
<div style="padding-top: 7px;" class="s"><span style=
"color: rgb(170, 0, 0);" class="ilc" id="il">Invite 4
friends<br>
 to Gmail</span>  </div></div>
```

You'll notice when you read through this code that what look like links (the Inbox, Starred, Sent Mail, and so on) actually aren't. They're just plain text wrapped in spans that provide just enough styling to make them look like links: They're underlined, the mouse pointer changes, and so on. This is just another symptom of how cunning the Gmail application is. I'll be explaining all of this in Chapter 5. Just so you know.

The styling is simple here. After the Compose Message link (that's not, as I just said, a link in the sense of `<a href=""></a>` but rather just the plain text styled up to look like one), there's a table containing only the Inbox link and new mail count and then a succession of divs with class `nl`, containing spans with each of the menu options.

Then there's another non-link link to the Contacts functionality, and another table used to produce the label box. With labels defined, as you will see later, this table has more content. Finally, after the table, is a div called `il` containing the invitation link. (My bet is that `il` stands for Invitation Link, but ignorance of such things is the mark of the reverse engineer.) As you will have noticed by now, Gmail is built with very small names for all of the divs and spans. This is also true of the JavaScript functions covered in the next chapter. This is because Gmail is serving these pages millions of times a day, and the bandwidth saved by dropping everything down to one- or two-letter variable names is well worth the obfuscation.

Onward, then, to the real meat of the page.

The Activity Area

Right in the middle of the page, surrounded with a blue border, is what I'll call the *central activity area*. It's in this section that the majority of your work within Gmail is done: writing and reading mail, for example. It looks like Figure 4-8.

FIGURE 4-8: The central activity area

The central activity area is controlled by the code in Listing 4-3.

Listing 4-3: The Central Activity Area in HTML

```
<div style="margin-left: 14ex;" id="co">
<div id="tc_top">
<table width="100%" cellspacing="0" cellpadding="0" bgcolor=
"#C3D9FF">
<tbody>
<tr height="2">
<td class="tl">
<td class="tr"></tr></tbody></table>
<table width="100%" cellspacing="0" cellpadding="0" style=
"background: rgb(195, 217, 255) none repeat scroll 0%; -moz-
background-clip: initial; -moz-background-origin: initial;
-moz-background-inline-policy: initial;"
        class="th">
<tbody>
<tr>
<td width="8">
<td><button style="font-weight: bold;" id="ac_rc_^i"
class="ab"
type="button">Archive</button>    <button style=
"width: 8em; text-align: center;" id="ac_sp" class="ab"
        type="button">Report Spam</button>   <select
id=
        "tamu" onchange=
        "top.js._TL_OnActionMenuChange(window,this)" onfocus=
        "return
top.js._TL_MaybeUpdateActionMenus(window,this)"
        onmouseover=
        "return
top.js._TL_MaybeUpdateActionMenus(window,this)"
        style="vertical-align: middle;">
<option style="color: rgb(119, 119, 119);" id="mac">More
Actions
...</option>
<option style="color: rgb(119, 119, 119);" disabled id="nil">
--------</option>
<option style="color: rgb(119, 119, 119);" disabled
id="al">Apply
label:</option>
<option value="new">   New
label...</option></select>    <span id="refresh"
      class="lk">Refresh</span></td>
<td align="right">  <span style=
```

Continued

Listing 4-3 *(continued)*

```
"white-space: nowrap;"><b>1</b> - <b>1</b> of
<b>1</b></span></td>
<td width="4"></tr>
<tr>
<td>
<td valign="bottom" style="padding-top: 3px;"
colspan="2">Select:
<span id="sl_a" class="l">All</span> , <span id="sl_r" class=
"l">Read</span> , <span id="sl_u" class="l">Unread</span> ,
<span id="sl_s" class="l">Starred</span> , <span id="sl_t"
      class="l">Unstarred</span> , <span id="sl_n" class=
      "l">None</span></td></tr>
<tr height="3">
<td></tr></tbody></table></div>
<div style="border-left: 9px solid rgb(195, 217, 255);">
<div id="tbd">
<form target="hist" method="post" name="af" action=
"/gmail?search=inbox&amp;view=tl&amp;start=0"><input
type="hidden"
name="act"> <input type="hidden" name="at"> <input
type="hidden"
name="vp">
<table width="100%" cellspacing="0" cellpadding="1" id="tb"
      class="tlc">
<col style="width: 31px; text-align: right;">
<col style="width: 20px;">
<col style="width: 24ex;">
<col style="width: 2ex;">
<col>
<col style="width: 17px;">
<col style="width: 8ex;">
<tbody>
<tr id="w_0" class="ur">
<td align="right"><input type="checkbox"></td>
<td><img src="/gmail/images/star_off_2.gif"></td>
<td><span id="_user_ben@benhammersley.com"><b>Ben
Hammersley</b></span> (2)</td>
<td> </td>
<td><b>Skinning Gmail? That's so cool!</b> <span class="p">-
BEGIN
PGP SIGNED MESSAGE-- Hash: SHA1 la la la --BEGIN PGP
SIGNATURE--
Version: GnuPG v1 &hellip;</span></td>
<td> </td>
<td><b>2:29pm</b></td></tr></tbody></table></form>
```

```
<div style="padding: 0pt 20px;" class="s c"><br>
<br>
<br>
<br>
<br>
<br>
<br>
<br></div></div></div>
<img width="9" height="11" src="/gmail/images/chevron.gif"
     style="position: absolute; display: none;" id="ar">
<div id="tc_bot">
<table width="100%" cellspacing="0" cellpadding="0" style=
"background: rgb(195, 217, 255) none repeat scroll 0%; -moz-
background-clip: initial; -moz-background-origin: initial;
-moz-background-inline-policy: initial;"
        class="th">
<tbody>
<tr height="2">
<td></tr>
<tr>
<td width="8">
<td>Select: <span id="sl_a" class="l">All</span> , <span
id="sl_r"
class="l">Read</span> , <span id="sl_u"
class="l">Unread</span> ,
<span id="sl_s" class="l">Starred</span> , <span id="sl_t"
        class="l">Unstarred</span> , <span id="sl_n" class=
        "l">None</span></td></tr>
<tr height="4">
<td></tr>
<tr>
<td>
<td><button style="font-weight: bold;" id="ac_rc_^i"
class="ab"
type="button">Archive</button>    <button style=
"width: 8em; text-align: center;" id="ac_sp" class="ab"
        type="button">Report Spam</button>   <select
id=
        "bamu" onchange=
        "top.js._TL_OnActionMenuChange(window,this)" onfocus=
        "return
top.js._TL_MaybeUpdateActionMenus(window,this)"
        onmouseover=
        "return
top.js._TL_MaybeUpdateActionMenus(window,this)"
        style="vertical-align: middle;">
<option style="color: rgb(119, 119, 119);" id="mac">More
Actions
```

Continued

Listing 4-3 *(continued)*

```
...</option>
<option style="color: rgb(119, 119, 119);" disabled id="nil">
--------</option>
<option style="color: rgb(119, 119, 119);" disabled
id="al">Apply
label:</option>
<option value="new">   New
label...</option></select></td>
<td align="right"><span style="white-space: nowrap;"><b>1</b>
-
<b>1</b> of <b>1</b></span></td>
<td width="4"></tr></tbody></table>
<table width="100%" cellspacing="0" cellpadding="0" bgcolor=
"#C3D9FF">
<tbody>
<tr height="2">
<td class="bl">
<td class="br"></tr></tbody></table></div></div>
```

This code is also quite complicated, but working through it is just a matter of looking through the code for the class and id attributes and noting the tables in the middle. By now, you should be quite good at this, so you won't do that here. The next section, after all, provides a map of all of the classes and ids you need.

The Bottom Section

Now we come to the last remaining section of the Gmail screen: the bottom of the screen, as shown in Figure 4-9. Again, the drudgework is left out here; you see only the code. In the tradition of software textbooks, the figuring out of the names of the divs and spans within the bottom section is left as an exercise to the reader. Listing 4-4 shows you the code if you want to do this, or you can skip past Listing 4-4 to Figure 4-10, which outlines the whole page's structure in CSS.

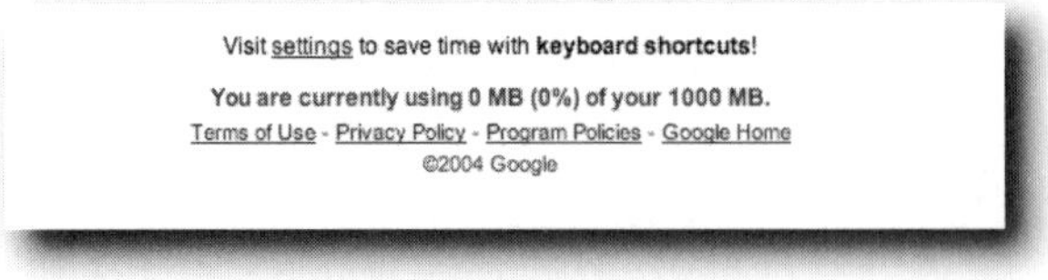

Visit settings to save time with **keyboard shortcuts**!

You are currently using 0 MB (0%) of your 1000 MB.

Terms of Use - Privacy Policy - Program Policies - Google Home

©2004 Google

FIGURE 4-9: The bottom section of the screen

Listing 4-4: The Bottom Section of the Screen in HTML

```
<div style="padding: 0ex 14ex;" id="ft">
<div style="margin-top: 20px;" class="c s">Use the <span
id="fsb"
style=
"color: rgb(0, 0, 204); text-decoration: underline; cursor:
pointer; white-space: nowrap;">
search</span> box or <span id="mt_adv" style=
"color: rgb(0, 0, 204); text-decoration: underline; cursor:
pointer; white-space: nowrap;">
search options</span> to find messages quickly!</div>
<div style="margin-top: 12px; color: rgb(0, 102, 51);" class=
"c s b">You are currently using 0 MB (0%) of your 1000
MB.</div>
<div style="margin-top: 4px;" class="c xs">
<div><a href="/gmail/help/terms_of_use.html" target="_blank"
   class="lc">Terms of Use</a> - <a href=
   "/gmail/help/privacy.html" target="_blank" class=
   "lc">Privacy Policy</a> - <a href=
   "/gmail/help/program_policies.html" target="_blank" class=
   "lc">Program Policies</a> - <a href=
   "http://www.google.com/" target="_blank" class="lc" id=
   "googh">Google Home</a></div>
<div style="color: rgb(68, 68, 68); margin-top: 4px;">
&copy;2004 Google</div></div></div>
<script type="text/javascript">
var fp='9cf0974955f546da';
</script><script type="text/javascript">
var loaded=true;D(['e']);
</script><script type="text/javascript">
try{top.js.L(window,45,'f4ba224ac4');}
catch(e){}

</script>
<div id="tip" style=
"border-style: outset; border-width: 1px; padding: 2px;
background: rgb(255, 255, 221) none repeat scroll 0%;
position: absolute; -moz-background-clip: initial; -moz-
background-origin: initial; -moz-background-inline-policy:
initial; left: 309px; top: 125px; display: none;">
<center><small>ben@benhammersley.com</small></center></div>
</body>
</html>
```

So, now you have worked your way through each of the separate sections of the Gmail layout, and you should have a good idea of the structure of the page and how it is produced by the HTML.

Why, you might ask have you just gone through 20 pages of gritty DOM inspection and poring over code? Because, and you have to trust me on this, Gmail's workings are almost entirely contained in that ungodly lump of framesets and JavaScript. Over the majority of the rest of the book, you will spend your time embedded in the depths of this code, so it's extremely useful to jump off into the deep end, as it were.

Applying a New Style

Now that you've slogged your way through the structure of the Gmail markup, you can use this knowledge to give the application a new look. First, however, you will need to install another extension to Firefox. You need the URIid extension written by Chris Neale, found at `http://extensionroom.mozdev.org/more-info/uriid`.

Once that is installed, go to your Profile folder. With Firefox, which is the browser I'm recommending for this chapter, the location of the Profile folder changes per operating system. Look at `www.mozilla.org/support/firefox/edit.html#profile` for the official reference. Once inside the Profile folder, you will be adding the CSS you are about to write to the `userContent.css` file inside the chrome subdirectory.

Open the `userContent-example.css` file, and rename it as `userContent.css`. You can now add any CSS you like, and have it affect the pages you are applying them to. You differentiate between the sites you want it to act upon by appending the base URL as a class. For example, to apply styles to Gmail, the ID gmail-google-com will be added to the body. The style sheet can then use the `#gmail-google-com` selector to apply styles only to that site. Once the CSS file is saved, restart Firefox, and your styles will take hold.

Creating Gmail Lite

During the course of my working day, I spend most of my time looking at my computer's screen. After a while, I yearn for calmer pages, with less to focus on. As I use Gmail a lot of the time, it's good to use the knowledge worked out in the preceding text to restyle the page into something easier to look at after a hard day. Figure 4-10 shows this newly styled Gmail, Gmail Lite.

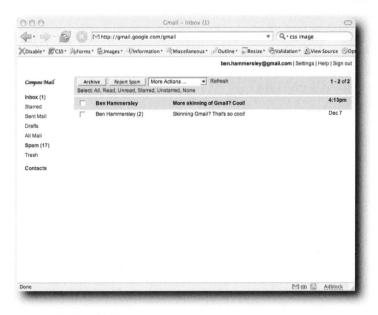

Figure 4-10: Gmail Lite

As you can see, it's a much simpler page layout, with no images, a muted color scheme, and without the labels, invitation link, and other superfluous material that just irritates after a day's writing. It's a minimalist Gmail whose styles are covered in the next section.

Walking Through the Style Sheet

The effects you see in Figure 4-10 are simple to achieve with a style sheet, and certainly much more impressive ones can be achieved by someone with more design skill than myself.

Begin with the following CSS:

```
body#gmail-google-com {
    background-color: #ffffff !important;
}

body#gmail-google-com img{
    display: none !important;
}

/* regular links */
```

```
body#gmail-google-com span.lk,
body#gmail-google-com a.lc,
body#gmail-google-com a.lk
{
     text-decoration: none !important;
     color: #191b4c !important;
}



/* The Search Form */
body#gmail-google-com  div#mt1 form{
display: none !important;
}

body#gmail-google-com  div#mt1 table{
display: none !important;
}
```

This code starts by declaring the background color of the whole page to be white, and then turning off any images by setting them to `display:none`. This CSS command is extremely useful for stripping sites of dullness, as you can see, after the section giving the links and pseudo-links on the page a nice dark blue color.

From the previous section, you already know that the Gmail logo and the search box are held in a table and a form, inside a div called `mt1`. By setting both of these to `display:none`, you remove them entirely.

The next section of CSS is as follows:

```
/*----------------------------------------------------------
*/
/*The Navigation Menu */


body#gmail-google-com span#comp {
font-family: cursive;
}



/* sidebar links */
body#gmail-google-com div#nav table.cv,
body#gmail-google-com div#nav table.cv td {
     background: #ffffff !important;
}

body#gmail-google-com table.cv td.tl,
body#gmail-google-com table.cv td.bl {
   height: 0 !important;
```

```
}

/* both current and other */
body#gmail-google-com table.cv td span.lk,
body#gmail-google-com div.nl span.lk{
    display: block !important;
    background: #ffffff !important;
    color: #191b4c;
    border: none !important;
    padding: 2px !important;
    margin-right: 5px !important;
}

/* Override the background color for the unselected options*/
body#gmail-google-com div.nl span.lk {
    background: #ffffff !important;
    border: none !important;
}


/* For the mouse-over color change */
body#gmail-google-com div.nl span.lk:hover {
    background: #d3cbb8 !important;
    border-color: #fef759 !important;
}

/* hide "New!" super-script */
body#gmail-google-com div#nav sup {
    display: none !important;
}


/* remove the colored left border of the inbox */
body#gmail-google-com div#co div {
    border: 0 !important;
}

/*--------------------------------------------------------*/
```

This section of the CSS file deals with the navigation sidebar. It did look like Figure 4-7, but now it's a great deal simpler. The link color change at the top of the CSS takes care of the color, so the first thing you do is restyle the font for the Compose Mail link. You know that this has an id of comp, so you set the font-family: cursive. This will, in compatible browsers, choose the default cursive typeface.

Next you override the background colors and borders of the menu items and finally remove the light blue edge of the application area that stretches from the active menu option in the normal view. It's much simpler now. Having manipulated these elements, consider this CSS:

```
/* labels */
body#gmail-google-com div#nb_0 {
display: none !important;
}


/* The Invitation Link */
body#gmail-google-com #il {
    display: none !important;
}


/* The footer */
body#gmail-google-com div#ft {
    display: none !important;
}
```

These three short sections turn off the labels, the invitation link, and the whole footer section. We're almost Zen-like now. Final stop: the application area:

```
/*----------------------------------------------------------
*/
/* THE APPLICATION AREA */

/* top bar */
body#gmail-google-com div#tc_top table,
body#gmail-google-com div#tc_top table td.tl,
body#gmail-google-com div#tc_top table td.tr,
body#gmail-google-com div#tc_top table.th,{
    background: #ffffff !important;
    border: none !important;
    padding: 2px !important;
    margin: 5px 0 5px 0 !important;
}


/* bottom bar*/
body#gmail-google-com div#tc_bot table,
body#gmail-google-com div#tc_bot table td.bl,
body#gmail-google-com div#tc_bot table td.br,
body#gmail-google-com div#tc_bot table.th{
    display: none !important;
}

/* selection links in bar */
body#gmail-google-com div#co div#tc_top span.l{
    color: #191b4c !important;
}
```

```
/* mailbox contents */
body#gmail-google-com div#co div#tbd {
    background: #ffffff !important;
    border: none !important;
    padding: 4px 0 4px 0 !important;
}


/* unread mail row inside the inbox */
body#gmail-google-com table.tlc tr.ur {
    background-color: #d7d7d7 !important;
    height: 30px;
}

/*read mail row inside the inbox */
body#gmail-google-com table.tlc tr.rr {
    background-color: #ffffff !important;
}

body#gmail-google-com table.tlc tr.ur td,
body#gmail-google-com table.tlc tr.rr td{
    border: 0 !important;
}

/* message hovering snippet expansion */
body#gmail-google-com table.tlc tr.ur:hover,
body#gmail-google-com table.tlc tr.rr:hover{
    background-color: #ffffff !important;
}

body#gmail-google-com table.tlc tr.ur:hover td,
body#gmail-google-com table.tlc tr.rr:hover td{
    border: none !important;
    vertical-align: top !important;
}

body#gmail-google-com table.tlc tr.ur:hover .sn,
body#gmail-google-com table.tlc tr.rr:hover .sn{
    display: block !important;
    white-space: normal !important;
}

/* and email address display */
body#gmail-google-com table.tlc tr.ur:hover td span,
body#gmail-google-com table.tlc tr.rr:hover td span {
    display: block; !important;
    color: #ff0000;
}

/* labels should still be inline */
```

```
body#gmail-google-com table.tlc tr.ur:hover td span.ct,
body#gmail-google-com table.tlc tr.rr:hover td span.ct{
    display: inline;
}

body#gmail-google-com table.tlc tr.ur:hover td span[id]:after,
body#gmail-google-com table.tlc tr.rr:hover td span[id]:after{
  content: attr(id);
  display: block;
  margin-left: -38px; /* hack to hide "user_" id prefix */
  color: #b6af9e;
}

/*---------------------------------------------------------
*/
```

The first thing to notice is that you turned off the bottom button bar. There's no need to have two, and you have one at the top already. Then you recolor the links within the top bar.

The next section colors the background of the application white and removes the solid borders. Then you have two bits of CSS: You define the background color of the rows for each message within the mailbox that is being viewed. Within the Inbox, these lines of CSS put a gray background behind unread mail, and a white background behind read mail (see Figure 4-11).

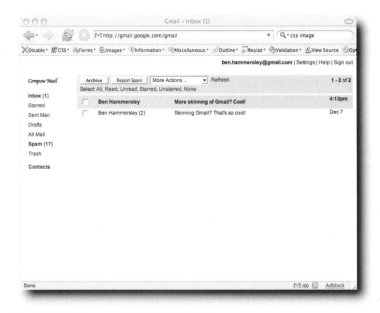

FIGURE 4-11: The new style sheet applied

The rest of the code deals with the physical layout of the application area, especially removing the borders. If you want to see the CSS listing in its entirety, flip to Appendix A and check out Listing A-2.

Thanks for the basis for this style sheet must go to Mihai Parparita, who released the original underneath the Creative Commons Attribution-ShareAlike license at `http://persistent.info/archives/2004/10/05/gmail-skinning`. Now that you have your new style sheet applied, you can get down to the business of ridding Gmail of advertising.

Removing Google's Advertising

Gmail is advertising-supported, and Google's advertising is in no way intrusive, and can be very useful. But if you're totally against the concept, and serene within your soul about the idea of using a service without the quid pro quo, it is entirely possible to remove the advertising using the techniques in this chapter. The advertising is contained entirely within a div called ad, so the code in Listing 4-5 turns off advertising.

 Warning I do not recommend you use this code to turn off advertising, but I include it regardless and leave the determination to you.

Listing 4-5: Turning Off Google's Advertising with CSS

```
/* Adverts */
body#gmail-google-com  div#ad {
display: none !important;
}
```

And Now . . .

In this chapter, you explored how Gmail is structured and saw that the entire interface is loaded into a complex selection of frames. You learned how to change the styling of this interface, and while doing so saw a lot of the interface code. You should be confident now that Gmail is not an enormously complex and incomprehensible application that instills fear into your heart: It's just very complex, slightly incomprehensible, and not at all scary.

So, now you've started to delve into Gmail's workings. The next chapter moves beyond the surface and shows you how your browser communicates with the Gmail server, how the interface is put together, and how Gmail actually works. You'll be using many of the same techniques as you did in this chapter but to a much greater depth. Put the kettle on, make some coffee, and let's go.

How Gmail Works

By now you've learned how to use Gmail with some flair, and you can change the way it looks to a certain extent. Now you have to look into exactly how it works. You already know that the majority of the Gmail functionality is enacted client-side — that is, on the browser, rather than at the server — and is done with JavaScript. This chapter describes exactly how this works and how you can exploit it.

What the Devil Is Going On?

Before revealing just what's happening, let's recap. In Chapter 4 you used the DOM inspector inside Firefox to help you dissect the HTML, and this will help you again. So, as before, open up Gmail in Firefox, and open the DOM inspector.

You already know that the main document is made of two frames, the first made of many subframes and the second one with nothing but a huge chunk of JavaScript. Figure 5-1 shows you that in the DOM inspector.

Using the DOM inspector's right-click menu Copy as XML function, you can grab the text of the script and copy it to a text editor. Ordinarily, I would include this code as a listing right here, but when I cut and pasted it into the manuscript of this book, it added another 120 pages in a single keystroke. This does not bode well, especially as Google has tried as hard as it can to format the JavaScript as tightly as possible. This saves bandwidth but doesn't help anyone else read what Google is doing. We'll reach that problem in a page or two.

in this chapter

☑ Getting at the code

☑ The interface

☑ XMLHttpRequest

☑ Packet sniffing

☑ Probing the interface

☑ Decoding the data

FIGURE 5-1: The location of the Gmail JavaScript shown with the DOM inspector

Back to the browser, then, and you find you have a very complicated page seemingly made up of close to 250KB of JavaScript, one iFrame you can see, and apparently ten or more that don't appear on the screen. Furthermore, the eagle-eyed in our midst will have noticed that the Gmail URL doesn't change very much when you're moving around the application. Changing from Inbox to All Mail for the subset of your mail you want to see on the screen changes the page but not the URL. For anyone used to, say, Hotmail, this is all very puzzling.

Preloading the Interface

What is actually happening is this: Gmail loads its entire interface into the one single HTML page. When you move around the application, you're not loading new pages, but triggering the JavaScript to show you other parts of the page you have already in your browser's memory. This is why it is so fast: There's no network connection needed to bring up the Compose window, or show the Settings page, as you've already loaded it. You can see this inside the DOM inspector. Figure 5-2 shows the section of the page with the various divs, each containing part of the interface.

You'll remember from Chapter 4 that the div d_tlist contains the majority of the interface for the Inbox. Well, further inspection shows that d_comp holds the Compose window, and d_prefs hold the Settings window, and so on.

This is all very interesting, but it doesn't really show how the application works. If anything, it asks a difficult question: if the page never refreshes, how does it send or receive any messages? The answer to this is in the JavaScript, and the use of one very clever function, XMLHttpRequest.

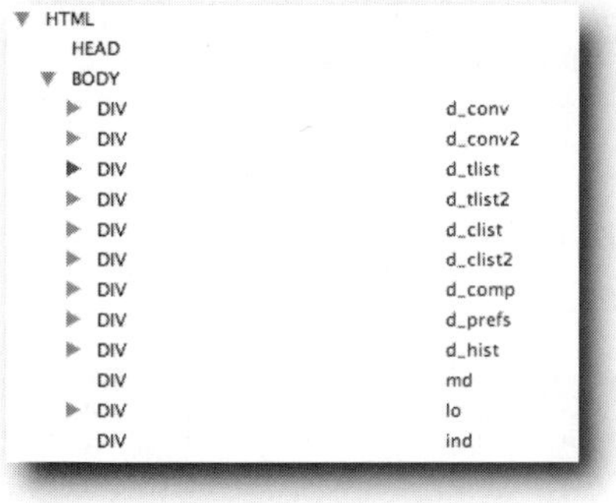

```
▼ HTML
    HEAD
  ▼ BODY
      ▶  DIV              d_conv
      ▶  DIV              d_conv2
      ▶  DIV              d_tlist
      ▶  DIV              d_tlist2
      ▶  DIV              d_clist
      ▶  DIV              d_clist2
      ▶  DIV              d_comp
      ▶  DIV              d_prefs
      ▶  DIV              d_hist
         DIV              md
      ▶  DIV              lo
         DIV              ind
```

FIGURE 5-2: The main interface divs

Introducing XMLHttpRequest

I like to think of this as quite a romantic story. JavaScript, you see, has had a bad rap over the years: it's commonly misconceived as a scrappy language for dodgy website effects circa 1999, and up there with the `<blink>` tag as something to be avoided by the truly righteous web developer. This is, of course, utter rot: Modern JavaScript is a rich and powerful language, and is rapidly regaining momentum. Perhaps since IE5 was launched, and certainly since Mozilla and Safari became mainstream, the majority of browsers have been capable of doing some very clever things in JavaScript. It's just that no one bothered to look.

One such function is `XMLHttpRequest`. Invented by Microsoft and now universally implemented, it allows a JavaScript program to communicate with a server in the background, without refreshing the page. This is very key for Gmail. It means that the JavaScript code can, upon a button push or any other trigger, send a tiny request to the Gmail server, parse the response, and throw it onto the screen, entirely without refreshing the page or causing any more traffic than is really necessary. It's blazingly fast, especially if you have a server optimized for just such a thing. Google, naturally, does.

Using XMLHttpRequest Yourself

To get an idea of just what is going on, it's a good idea to use `XMLHttpRequest` yourself. In this section you'll use it to create a little application of your own. You can skip this section if you're not interested in a deep understanding, but it's pretty cool stuff to play with anyway.

First, open up a directory on a website. You'll need to access it via a proper domain, you see. Create the directory, and make sure your browser can see it. In that directory, place a text file, called Listing.txt, and put the exclamation "Horrible!" inside the file. Bear with me.

Then create an HTML file, containing the code in Listing 5-1, and save this file to the directory you created earlier.

Listing 5-1: Listing.html — Showing XMLHttpRequest

```
<!DOCTYPE html PUBLIC "-//W3C//DTD XHTML 1.0 Transitional//EN"
"http://www.w3.org/tr/xhtml1/DTD/xhtml1-transitional.dtd">
<html>
<head>
<style></style>
<script type="text/javascript">

var xmlhttp=false;

try {
  xmlhttp = new ActiveXObject("Msxml2.XMLHTTP");
 } catch (e) {
  try {
   xmlhttp = new ActiveXObject("Microsoft.XMLHTTP");
  } catch (E) {
   xmlhttp = false;
  }
 }

if (!xmlhttp && typeof XMLHttpRequest!='undefined') {
  xmlhttp = new XMLHttpRequest();
}


function Listing1() {
 xmlhttp.open("GET", "Listing.txt",true);
 xmlhttp.onreadystatechange=function() {
  if (xmlhttp.readyState==4) {
   alert(xmlhttp.responseText)
  }
 }
 xmlhttp.send()
}

</script>
</head>

<body>

<h1>My Dog Has No Nose.</h1>
```

```
<a href="/" onclick="Listing1();return false;">How does it
smell?</a>
</body>
<html>
```

Open `Listing.html` in a browser and it should appear very much like Figure 5-3.

FIGURE 5-3: Ready to click on the link?

And when you click on the link, you should get a pop-up alert box similar to Figure 5-4.

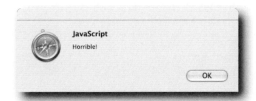

FIGURE 5-4: The result of an XMLHttpRequest function call

What has happened here? Well, the link in the code doesn't go anywhere, but clicking it sets the JavaScript going. Have a look at the first half of the code again:

```
<script type="text/javascript">

var xmlhttp=false;

try {
  xmlhttp = new ActiveXObject("Msxml2.XMLHTTP");
 } catch (e) {
  try {
   xmlhttp = new ActiveXObject("Microsoft.XMLHTTP");
  } catch (E) {
   xmlhttp = false;
  }
 }

if (!xmlhttp && typeof XMLHttpRequest!='undefined') {
  xmlhttp = new XMLHttpRequest();
}
```

Stepping through this from the beginning, you set up a variable called `xmlhttp` and set it to false. You use this variable to help check which browser you're using. The `XMLHttpRequest` object is called different things in different applications (Technically speaking, it's not a standard part of the JavaScript specification, so different people call it different things. Ho hum.). In Microsoft browsers, it's an Active X object called `Msxml2.XMLHTTP` or `Microsoft.XMLHTTP`, whereas in Mozilla, Safari, and others, it's a standard JavaScript function called `XMLHttpRequest`.

So the first half of the code goes through the alternatives, trying to define `xmlhttp` as an `XMLHttpRequest` object by calling each of the possible functions in turn. First it tries `Msxml2.XMLHTTP`, then `Microsoft.XMLHTTP`, and finally defaults to `XMLHttpRequest`. (Usually, of course, there's another test for no-JavaScript-support-at-all, but we'll skip that here for the sake of brevity.)

Now, go line by line through the second half of the code:

```
function Listing1() {
 xmlhttp.open("GET", "Listing.txt",true);
 xmlhttp.onreadystatechange=function() {
  if (xmlhttp.readyState==4) {
   alert(xmlhttp.responseText)
  }
 }
 xmlhttp.send()
}
```

The first line defines the name of the function: `Listing1`.

The second line sets up the `open` method of the `XMLHttpRequest` function you've placed into the `xmlhttp` object. `XMLHttpRequest` has six possible methods to call, as you'll see later. The `open` method takes three parameters: the HTTP call (such as `GET` or `POST`), the URL, and a flag of `true` or `false` to indicate if the request is asynchronous (set to `true`) or not (set to `false`). Asynchronous in this context means that the script continues processing while it is waiting for the server to reply. In this listing it's not a big deal, but in others this is very important: If you set the request to false, and the server takes a long time to get back to you, you can lock up the browser in the meantime.

The third line solves this problem. It sets up an `onreadystatechange` event handler, which waits for the `XMLHttpRequest` function's state to change before running the function it has defined. The possible values for `onreadystate change` are in Table 5-2, but in the meantime know that `readyState=4` means that the `XMLHttpRequest` function has completed its task. So, lines 3 and 4 mean "Wait until the function's state has changed, and if the state has changed to 'complete' then do the following; if not, keep waiting."

Line 5 is triggered if 3 and 4 come true. It displays an alert box, containing the result of the `responseText` method. This contains the contents of `Listing.txt`.

Lines 6 and 7 close off the functions prettily, and line 8 triggers the communication itself. Note the order this all comes in: You've set up the request ready to go. You've set up an Event Handler, watching for any request to come back and say it's done, and only then do you fire off the request itself.

So, now you've got a page with JavaScript code that can go out, fetch another file, and do something with its contents, all without refreshing the HTML. In our listing, it's a file with plain text, but it can be just about anything: XML, for example.

Before moving on to using this new knowledge to look into Gmail's code, have a look at Tables 5-1 and 5-2, which serve as a reference of the `XMLHttpRequest` functions, methods, and suchlike.

Table 5-1   XMLHttpRequest Object Methods

Method	Description
`abort()`	Stops the current request.
`getAllResponseHeaders()`	Returns complete set of headers (labels and values) as a string.

Continued

Table 5-1 *(continued)*

Method	Description
`getResponseHeader("headerLabel")`	Returns the string value of a single header label.
`open("method", "URL"[, asyncFlag[, "userName"[, "password"]]])`	Assigns the method, the URL, and the other optional attributes of a pending request.
`send(content)`	Sends the request, with an optional postable string or bit of DOM object data.
`setRequestHeader("label", "value")`	Assigns a label/value pair to the header to be sent with a request.

Table 5-2 contains some of the `XMLHttpRequest` object properties you'll likely need to use.

Table 5-2 Common XMLHttpRequest Object Properties

Property	Description
`onreadystatechange`	Event handler for an event. It fires whenever the state changes.
`readyState`	Object status integer: 0 = uninitialized 1 = loading 2 = loaded 3 = interactive 4 = complete
`responseText`	The data returned from the server, as a string.
`responseXML`	The data returned from the server, as a DOM-compatible document object.
`status`	Numeric http status code returned by server, such as 404 for "Not Found" or 200 for "OK."
`statusText`	Any string message accompanying the status code.

You should now feel confident that you understand how a simple HTML and JavaScript document can request data from a server in the background. There's no need for the page to reload in the browser for you to retrieve new information.

Finding XMLHttpRequest within the Gmail code

Don't take the presence of XMLHttpRequest within Gmail on trust. You can see this in action in Gmail's own code. Go back to the DOM inspector and open the second frameset — the one with all of the JavaScript in it. Copy the entire script into a text editor and save it, as you're going to refer to it a lot in this section. Once you've done that, search for the string xmlhttp. You'll find the function in Listing 5-2.

Listing 5-2: Gmail's XMLHttpRequest Function

```
function zd(){var R=null;if(da){var
vN=lJ?"Microsoft.XMLHTTP":"Msxml2.XMLHTTP";try{R=new
ActiveXObject(vN)}catch(f){C(f);alert("You need to enable active
scripting and activeX controls.")}}else{R=new
XMLHttpRequest();if(!R){;alert("XMLHttpRequest is not supported on
this browser.")}}return R}
```

As with all of the Gmail JavaScript, this is compressed and slightly confusing. Reformatted, it looks like Listing 5-3.

Listing 5-3: Gmail's XMLHttpRequest Function, Tidied

```
function zd(){
   var R=null;
   if(da){
      var vN=lJ?"Microsoft.XMLHTTP":"Msxml2.XMLHTTP";
      try{R=new ActiveXObject(vN)}
      catch(f){
      C(f);alert("You need to enable active scripting and
activeX controls.")}
      }else{
      R=new XMLHttpRequest();
      if(!R){
      ;alert("XMLHttpRequest is not supported on this
browser.")}
   }
return R}
```

This listing does exactly the same thing you did earlier: tries out the Microsoft Active X controls, then tries the more standard XMLHttpRequest and then, if all fails, bails with an error message. For future reference, and remember this because you'll need it later, the XMLHttpRequest object in the Gmail code is called R.

Sniffing the Network Traffic

So now that you understand how XMLHttpRequest works, you're led to some further questions: What is being sent and received using the XMLHttpRequest functions, and what are the URLs? Once you know the answers to these questions, you can write your own code to spoof these requests, and can then interface directly with the Gmail system. The rest of the book relies on this idea.

To find out what Gmail is saying to the browser, use a new tool: the packet sniffer. This is a generic term for a range of applications that can listen to raw network traffic, display it on the screen, log it, analyze it, and so on. What you're interested in is watching what your browser is doing in the background: what it is sending, where it is sending it to, and then the replies it is getting.

My packet sniffer of choice for this job is Jeremy Elson's Tcpflow, available at www.circlemud.org/~jelson/software/tcpflow/.

I use Marc Liyanage's OS X package, which you can download from www.entropy.ch/software/macosx/#tcpflow.

Tcpflow is available under the GPL, and can be compiled on most proper computing platforms. Windows users will need to look elsewhere, but the following techniques remain the same.

Firing Up Tcpflow

Install Tcpflow, and set it running inside a terminal window, monitoring port 80. On my machine, that means typing the following:

```
sudo tcpflow -c port 80
```

Then open a browser and request a page. Any will do: Figure 5-5 shows the start of a typical result.

As you can see from the figure and your own screen, Tcpflow captures all of the traffic flowing backward and forward across Port 80—all your web traffic, in other words. It shows the requests and the answers: headers, content, and all.

Tcpflow is perfect for the job. But there's a snag. Open up Gmail, and let it sit there for a while. After it settles down, you will notice that Tcpflow regularly burps up new traffic looking very similar to Listing 5-4. This is Gmail's heartbeat: checking for new mail. But it's very odd looking.

```
 ⊙⊙⊙                    tcpflow — tcsh (ttyp1) — ⌘1
[Ben-Hammersleys-Computer:~/WORK] ben%    sudo tcpflow -c port 80
Password:
tcpflow[13248]: listening on en0
192.168.016.050.59584-217.162.168.182.00080: GET /images/nav_pictures.gif HTTP/1.1
Host: www.entropy.ch
Connection: keep-alive
Referer: http://www.entropy.ch/software/macosx/
User-Agent: Mozilla/5.0 (Macintosh; U; PPC Mac OS X; en-us) AppleWebKit/125.5.5 (KHTML, li
ke Gecko) Safari/125.12
Accept: */*
Accept-Encoding: gzip, deflate;q=1.0, identity;q=0.5, *;q=0
Accept-Language: en-us, ja;q=0.62, de-de;q=0.93, de;q=0.90, fr-fr;q=0.86, fr;q=0.83, nl-nl
;q=0.79, nl;q=0.76, it-it;q=0.72, it;q=0.69, ja-jp;q=0.66, en;q=0.97, es-es;q=0.59, es;q=0
.55, da-dk;q=0.52, da;q=0.48, fi-fi;q=0.45, fi;q=0.41, ko-kr;q=0.38
Cookie: phpbb2mysql_data=aX3A0X3A%7B%7D


192.168.016.050.59585-217.162.168.182.00080: GET /images/nav_bottom.gif HTTP/1.1
Host: www.entropy.ch
Connection: keep-alive
Referer: http://www.entropy.ch/software/macosx/
User-Agent: Mozilla/5.0 (Macintosh; U; PPC Mac OS X; en-us) AppleWebKit/125.5.5 (KHTML, li
ke Gecko) Safari/125.12
Accept: */*
```

FIGURE 5-5: The start of a Tcpflow session

Listing 5-4: Gmail Checking for New Mail

```
216.239.057.107.00080-192.168.016.050.59607: HTTP/1.1 200 OK
Set-Cookie: SID=AfzuOeCbwFixNvWd6vNt7bUR2DpPxRz-
YhOB54dzyYwHeLIHjVq_eeHH5s6MYQbPE0hVUK_LMROFuRWkMhfSR-U=;
Domain=.google.com;Path=/;Expires=Tue, 06-Jan-2015 00:12:12 GMT
Set-Cookie: GBE=; Expires=Fri, 07-Jan-05 00:12:12 GMT; Path=/
Cache-control: no-cache
Pragma: no-cache
Content-Type: text/html; charset=utf-8
Content-Encoding: gzip
Transfer-Encoding: chunked
Server: GFE/1.3
Date: Sat, 08 Jan 2005 00:12:12 GMT

a
.........

216.239.057.107.00080-192.168.016.050.59607: 2c8
R...A{[uj...*..lQ...D.M.".h...}..."G...RD..7../}.c...K
H$g.....U.........M-.J
4......Y.......&....M.(.=.b..t...t.M.*...S!.....dZ.r.........
..w..iy....RQ.T.....n......n.*.sqK.0.e.Y.m..g...h....{.k[i.k...
..,d!....X..".. .Y.a..v......;...J.f29.4....E...Q..,gA.D.<....
l....r...n0X..z.]0...~g>o1.. x1,...U..f.VK....R++.6.
```

Continued

Listing 5-4 *(continued)*

```
.YG......Q...Y......V.O...v
Oh7.D.M.X..3{%f.6].N...V*j.....+.J....2z@..n..)8..?Z./o....j*o
.........3..
!=*.a.v.s.........."\..i{.;o..nh....K+q.\||...G.3]....x.;h.].r
...+..U?,...c.........s..PF.%!....i2...}..'+.zP._.
....M...a35u]9.........-A...2.].F|.=..eQK
..5k.qt.....Wt..@Wf{.y.I..
X..*;.D...<*.r.E>...?.uK9p...RC..c..C.~.<..<..0q..9..I.pg.>...
.
...x$..........
```

The headers are understandable enough, but the content is very strange indeed.
This is because your browser is taking advantage of Gzip encoding. Most modern
web servers can serve content encoded with the Gzip algorithm, and most modern browsers are happy to decode it on the fly. Human brains, of course, cannot, so
you need to force Gmail to send whatever it is sending over unencoded.

In the first few chapters of this book, you've been using Firefox, so return to that
browser again now. In the address bar, type the URL **about:config**.

You should see a page looking like Figure 5-6.

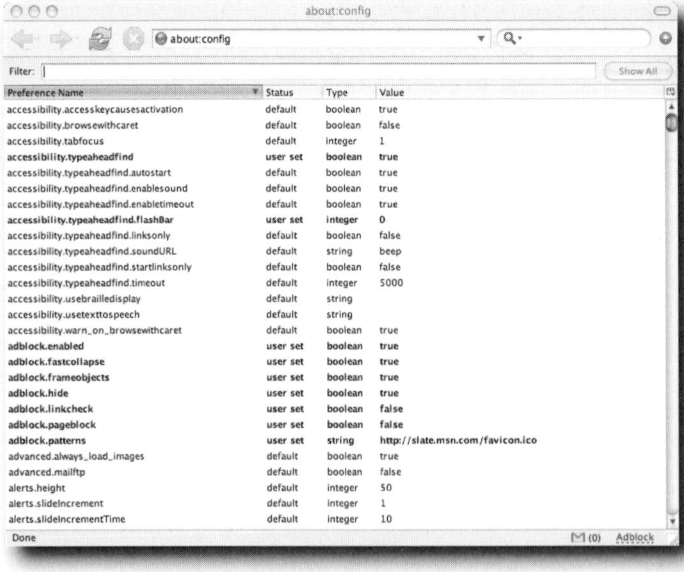

FIGURE 5-6: The Firefox secret settings page

This page allows you to change the more fundamental browser settings. You need to change only one. Scroll down to `network.http.accept-encoding` and click on the string. By default it reads `gzip/deflate`. Just delete that, and leave it blank, as shown in Figure 5-7.

network.hosts.smtp_server	default	string	mail
network.http.accept-encoding	user set	string	
network.http.accept.default	default	string	text/xml,application/xml,application/

FIGURE 5-7: The changed HTTP setting

Empty Firefox's cache to prevent a strange bug, and restart the browser for good measure. Now go back to Gmail and watch for the heartbeat. It will now look like Listing 5-5.

Listing 5-5: Gmail's Heartbeat, Unencoded

```
192.168.016.050.59622-216.239.057.107.00080: GET
/gmail?ik=344af70c5d&view=tl&search=inbox&start=0&tlt=1014fb79
f15&fp=54910421598b5190&auto=1&zx=24c4d6962ec6325a216123479
HTTP/1.1
Host: gmail.google.com
User-Agent: Mozilla/5.0 (Macintosh; U; PPC Mac OS X Mach-O;
en-GB; rv:1.7.5) Gecko/20041110 Firefox/1.0
Accept:
text/xml,application/xml,application/xhtml+xml,text/html;q=0.9
,text/plain;q=0.8,image/png,*/*;q=0.5
Accept-Language: en-gb,en;q=0.5
Accept-Charset: ISO-8859-1,utf-8;q=0.7,*;q=0.7
Keep-Alive: 300
Connection: keep-alive
Referer:
http://gmail.google.com/gmail?ik=344af70c5d&search=inbox&view=
tl&start=0&zx=24c4d6962ec6325a116384500
Cookie: GV=101014fb09ab5-af53c8c5457de50bec33d5d6436e82c6;
PREF=ID=2dfd9a4e4dba3a9f:CR=1:TM=1100698881:LM=1101753089:GM=1
:S=nJnfdWng4uY7FKfO; SID=AcwnzkuZa4aCDnqVeiG6-
pM487sZLlfXBz2JqrHFdjIueLIHjVq_eeHH5s6MYQbPE4wm3vinOWMnavqPWq3
SNNY=; GMAIL_AT=e6980e93d906d564-1014fb09ab7;
S=gmail=h7zPAJFLoyE:gmproxy=bnNkgpqwUAI; TZ=-60


216.239.057.107.00080-192.168.016.050.59622: HTTP/1.1 200 OK
```

Continued

Listing 5-5 *(continued)*

```
Set-Cookie:
SID=AbF6fUKA6tCIrC8Hv0JZuL5cLPt3vlO6qonGit87BAlMeLIHjVq_eeHH5s
6MYQbPE-F6IjzxJjnWuwgSIxPn3GQ=;Domain=.google.com;Path=/
Cache-control: no-cache
Pragma: no-cache
Content-Type: text/html; charset=utf-8
Transfer-Encoding: chunked
Server: GFE/1.3
Date: Sat, 08 Jan 2005 00:31:09 GMT

62
<script>var
loaded=true;</script><script>try{top.js.L(window,29,'18fd02c90
a
');}catch(e){}</script>
```

This you can recognize: The heartbeat had my browser requesting the following URL:

```
/gmail?ik=344af70c5d&view=tl&search=inbox&start=0&tlt=1014fb79f15&
fp=54910421598b5190&auto=1&zx=24c4d6962ec6325a216123479
```

Likewise, the heartbeat had my browser passing the following cookie:

```
Cookie: GV=101014fb09ab5-af53c8c5457de50bec33d5d6436e82c6;
PREF=ID=2dfd9a4e4dba3a9f:CR=1:TM=1100698881:LM=1101753089:GM=1:S=n
JnfdWng4uY7FKfO; SID=AcwnzkuZa4aCDnqVeiG6-
pM487sZLlfXBz2JqrHFdjIueLIHjVq_eeHH5s6MYQbPE4wm3vinOWMnavqPWq3SNNY
=; GMAIL_AT=e6980e93d906d564-1014fb09ab7;
S=gmail=h7zPAJFLoyE:gmproxy=bnNkgpqwUAI; TZ=-60
```

The browser then received a new cookie:

```
SID=AbF6fUKA6tCIrC8Hv0JZuL5cLPt3vlO6qonGit87BAlMeLIHjVq_eeHH5s6MYQ
bPE-F6IjzxJjnWuwgSIxPn3GQ=;Domain=.google.com;Path=/
```

Along with the new cookie, my browser also received a snippet of JavaScript as the contents of the page:

```
<script>var
loaded=true;</script><script>try{top.js.L(window,29,'18fd02c90a

');}catch(e){}</script>
```

What can you tell from all of this? Well, you now know how Gmail on your browser communicates with the server, and you know how to listen in on the conversation. Two things remain in this chapter, therefore: collecting as many of these phrases as possible and then working out what they mean.

Prodding Gmail to Hear It Squeak

The technique to further learn Gmail's secrets is obvious. Use it — sending mail, receiving mail, and so on — and watch what it does in the background. From these clues, and the JavaScript listing you already have, you can piece together a complete picture of the Gmail server's interface. And it's that interface that you ultimately want to deal with directly.

To get a clear idea of what is going on, you need to capture everything that happens when Gmail is loaded, when it sits idle, and when you perform the common actions with it.

Preparing to Watch the Gmail Boot Sequence

To start the process with gusto, open up Firefox again, and clear all of the caches. Then open up a terminal window, and set Tcpflow running, and save its output to a text file, like so:

```
sudo tcpflow -c '(port 80 or 443)' >> login_capture.txt
```

This records everything that goes over HTTP or HTTPS. Then log in to Gmail until you get to a nice, calm, idle Inbox like the placid Inbox shown in Figure 5-8.

FIGURE 5-8: A nice, calm Inbox at the end of the boot sequence

You'll be referring back to this figure in a page or two.

Now, stop the Tcpflow application with a judicious Control+c and open up the `login_capture.txt` file.

Cleaning Up the Log

Before looking through the log properly, it needs to be cleaned up a bit. There's a lot of information that you don't need. For instance, every request sent by my browser has this code, which is superfluous to your needs:

```
User-Agent: Mozilla/5.0 (Macintosh; U; PPC Mac OS X Mach-O;
en-GB; rv:1.7.5) Gecko/20041110 Firefox/1.0
Accept:
text/xml,application/xml,application/xhtml+xml,text/html;q=0.9
,text/plain;q=0.8,image/png,*/*;q=0.5
Accept-Language: en-gb,en;q=0.5
Accept-Charset: ISO-8859-1,utf-8;q=0.7,*;q=0.7
Keep-Alive: 300
Connection: keep-alive
```

Search for this code and replace it with a single new line. Next, toward the end, line 1862 in my working version is a whole collection of requests and responses for image files. You're not interested in these at all, so you can reduce them until they look like so:

```
192.168.016.053.64150-216.239.057.106.00080: GET
/gmail/help/images/logo.gif 216.239.057.106.00080-
192.168.016.053.64150: HTTP/1.1 200 OK
```

This makes things much more readable. Now, between lines 394 and 1712 (more or less, it may be slightly different in your log file) is the serving of the one enormous JavaScript file. Strip the code out, and replace it with your own comment.

Finally, right at the beginning, are a few pages going backward and forward that seem to be made of utter nonsense. These are encrypted. So, again, strip them out and replace them with a comment.

You should now have around 500 lines of traffic between your browser and Gmail. It's time to step through it and see what is going on. To see the entire boot sequence log, flip to Appendix A and look through Listing A-3.

Stepping Through the Gmail Boot Sequence

To be able to write an API, you need to know how the login works, so we shall start there. In all of the following, my machine has the IP address 192.168.016.053.

This Is Going to Break

During the writing of this book, the Gmail login sequence has changed at least three times. Not massively so, it must be said, but enough to break code until I worked out just what had changed. This section, and the chapters following, therefore, must be taken as guides to reverse engineering the thing yourself, and not as a definitive reference to the Gmail login sequence. If what I describe here no longer matches reality completely, I apologize. Take solace in the fact that I have no idea what Google is up to either.

Logging In

Start by requesting the page `http://gmail.google.com`. Whereupon, Gmail replies back with an http 302 redirect to `https://gmail.google.com/?dest=http%3A%2F%2Fgmail.google.com%2Fgmail`, which the browser automatically follows, switching to encrypted traffic:

```
192.168.016.053.64142-216.239.057.106.00080: GET / HTTP/1.1
Host: gmail.google.com


216.239.057.106.00080-192.168.016.053.64142: HTTP/1.1 302
Moved Temporarily
Location:
https://gmail.google.com/?dest=http%3A%2F%2Fgmail.google.com%2
Fgmail
Cache-control: private
Content-Length: 0
Content-Type: text/html
Server: GFE/1.3
Date: Sun, 16 Jan 2005 17:11:18 GMT

192.168.016.053.64143-216.239.057.106.00443
LOTS OF ENCRYPTED TRAFFIC CLIPPED OUT FROM THIS SECTION
```

Because the login page is encrypted—the traffic flows over HTTPS not HTTP—you can't follow what it does using the log. You need to use a script to follow the URLs until you get back to the trace. I used the following snippet of Perl code to pretend to be a browser to see what is going on:

```
#!/usr/bin/perl -w

use LWP::UserAgent;
use HTTP::Request;
```

```
use Crypt::SSLeay;

my $ua = LWP::UserAgent->new();

$ua -> agent("Mozilla/4.0 (compatible; MSIE 6.0; Windows NT
5.1; .NET CLR 1.1.4322)");

my $request = HTTP::Request->new(GET =>
'https://gmail.google.com/');

my $result = $ua->request($request);

if ($result->is_success) {
        print $result->content;
                            } else {
                            print $result->status_line;
                            }
```

You can infer from actually doing it, or by using a script like the one above, that the page continues with another redirect (or perhaps more than one), finally ending up at https://www.google.com/accounts/ServiceLogin? service=mail&continue=http%3A%2F%2Fgmail.google.com%2Fgmail, as you can see in Figure 5-9.

FIGURE 5-9: The Gmail login screen

Viewing source on this page shows you two important things. First, there is the username and password form itself and second some JavaScript that sets a cookie. Deal with the form first. Listing 5-6 gives a cleaned-up version of the code, with the styling removed.

Listing 5-6: The Gmail Login Form

```
<form action="ServiceLoginAuth" id="gaia_loginform"
method="post">

<input type="hidden" name="continue"
value="http://gmail.google.com/gmail">

<input type="hidden" name="service" value="mail">

Username: <input type="text" name="Email" value="" size="18">

Password: <input type="password" name="Passwd"
autocomplete="off" size="18">

<input type="checkbox" name="PersistentCookie" value="yes">
Don't ask for my password for 2 weeks.

<input type="submit" name="null" value="Sign in">
</form>
```

From this we can see that the URL the page POSTs towards to log in is produced as follows, split here for clarity.

```
https://www.google.com/accounts/ServiceLoginBoxAuth/continue=h
ttps://gmail.google.com/gmail
&service=mail
&Email=XXXXX
&Passwd=XXXXX
&PersistentCookie=yes
&null=Sign%20in
```

You will need this later on, but now, the cookie setting.

The First Cookie

The relevant sections of the JavaScript listing inside the login page appear in Listing 5-7.

Listing 5-7: Cookie-Setting Code from the Gmail Login

```
function SetGmailCookie(name, value) {
  document.cookie = name + "=" + value +
";path=/;domain=google.com";
}

// This is called when the user logs in to gmail.
// We set a GMAIL_LOGIN2 cookie with the initial timings.
// The first letter "T" in the cookie value means that the
login is not
// completed yet. The main JS will complete logging the
timings and update
// the GMAIL_LOGIN2 cookie. See main.js
function lg() {
  var now = (new Date()).getTime();

  // use start_time as a place holder for login_box_time until
we've
  // completely rolled out html-only login
  var cookie = "T" + start_time + "/" + start_time + "/" +
now;
  SetGmailCookie("GMAIL_LOGIN2", cookie);
}

var login_box_time;
function IframeOnLoad() {
  if (!login_box_time) {
    login_box_time = (new Date()).getTime();
  }
}

function el(id) {
  if (document.getElementById) {
    return document.getElementById(id);
  }
  return null;
}

var ONE_PX = "https://gmail.google.com/gmail/images/c.gif?t="
+
            (new Date()).getTime();

function LogRoundtripTime() {
  var img = new Image();
  var start = (new Date()).getTime();
  img.onload = GetRoundtripTimeFunction(start);
```

```
    img.src = ONE_PX;
}

function GetRoundtripTimeFunction(start) {
  return function() {
    var end = (new Date()).getTime();
    SetGmailCookie("GMAIL_RTT2", (end - start));
  }
}

function OnLoad() {
  var form = document.getElementById("gaia_loginform");
  form.onsubmit = lg;
  CheckBrowser();
  LogRoundtripTime();
}
```

This JavaScript sets two cookies. The first, GMAIL_LOGIN2, is set with a value of Tstart_time/start_time/now where both start_time and now are the date-time exactly then. As you can see from the comments in the code, Google intends to replace this in the future.

The second cookie is called GMAIL_RTT2 and contains the time it takes to retrieve a 1-pixel image file from the Gmail servers. RTT, presumably, stands for Round Trip Time.

You won't look at it in this book, but the rest of the JavaScript code on that page presents a very nice listing of a browser check that removes the login window if the browser isn't capable of using Gmail.

If you watch the Gmail login sequence from your own browser, you will see that it goes through more redirects before it settles into HTTP again, and you can see what is going on from the Tcpflow trace file.

Hitting stop on the browser at just the right time (and that is, to quote the fine words of my editor, a total crapshoot), gives you this URL:

```
https://www.google.com/accounts/CheckCookie?continue=http%3A%2F
%2Fgmail.google.com%2Fgmail%3F_sgh%3D8a6d8ffbb159f1c7c9246bd4f4
9e78a1&service=mail&chtml=LoginDoneHtml
```

Viewing source on that page gives you Listing 5-8.

Listing 5-8: The Gmail Cookie Check

```
<html>
<head>
<title>Redirecting</title>
<meta content="0;
url=http://gmail.google.com/gmail?_sgh=8a6d8ffbb159f1c7c9246bd
4f49e78a1" http-equiv="refresh"></head>
<body alink="#ff0000" text="#000000" vlink="#551a8b"
link="#0000cc" bgcolor="#ffffff">
<script type="text/javascript" language="javascript"><!--
location.replace("http://gmail.google.com/gmail?_sgh=8a6d8ffbb
159f1c7c9246bd4f49e78a1")
//--> </script>
</body>
</html>
```

This HTML forces you onto the next page, in this case `http://gmail.google.com/gmail?_sgh=8a6d8ffbb159f1c7c9246bd4f49e78a1`.

You have seen this sort of URL before: Look back again at Listing A-3, after the second excised block of encrypted code. So now you know that between the form submission and the page you get in Listing 5-8, something else happens. You can also guess that something happens to the cookie you set on the first page — it is being checked for something. Considering that those cookies do not contain anything but the time they were set, I am guessing that this step is to ensure that the connection is current and not the result of caching from someone's browser. It's to ensure a good, fresh session with Gmail on the part of the browser application and the user himself. Or so I would guess.

Either way, the boot sequence continues from here automatically, with everything in standard HTTP. You will see within the trace that the boot sequence loads the Inbox next. So that's what the next section considers.

Loading the Inbox

As you come to the end of the boot sequence you have nothing to do but load in the Inbox and address book. This section deals specifically with the Inbox loading. The output from the Tcpflow program earlier in this chapter doesn't contain enough mail to be of use in this regard, but if you do the trace again, only this time with a few more messages in the Inbox, you can see what is going on. Figure 5-10 shows the new Inbox, loaded with messages.

A Summary of the Login Procedure

As I have said before, the login procedure for Gmail seems to be changing on a very regular basis. Check with the libraries examined in Chapter 6 for the latest news on this. Basically, however, the login procedure goes like this, with each step moving on only if the previous was reported successful.

1. Request the Gmail page.

2. Set the two cookies.

3. Send the contents of the form.

4. Request the cookie check page.

5. Request the Inbox.

FIGURE 5-10: Gmail with some new, unread messages

Listing 5-9 shows the new trace.

Listing 5-9: The Inbox with More Messages Within

```
192.168.016.051.59905-064.233.171.107.00080: GET
/gmail?ik=&search=inbox&view=tl&start=0&init=1&zx=vzmurwe44cpx
6l HTTP/1.1
Host: gmail.google.com
User-Agent: Mozilla/5.0 (Macintosh; U; PPC Mac OS X Mach-O;
en-GB; rv:1.7.5) Gecko/20041110 Firefox/1.0
Accept:
text/xml,application/xml,application/xhtml+xml,text/html;q=0.9
,text/plain;q=0.8,image/png,*/*;q=0.5
Accept-Language: en-gb,en;q=0.5
Accept-Charset: ISO-8859-1,utf-8;q=0.7,*;q=0.7
Keep-Alive: 300
Connection: keep-alive
Referer: http://gmail.google.com/gmail/html/hist2.html
Cookie: GV=1010186d43b2b-b6b21a87a46b00d1bc5abf1a97357dd7;
PREF=ID=0070250e68e17190:CR=1:TM=1106068639:LM=1106068639:S=O1
Nivj_xqk7kvdGK;
GMAIL_LOGIN=T1106068635841/1106068635841/1106068648645;
SID=DQAAAGoAAAC06FIY2Ix4DJlCk7ceaOnWPvpK4eWn9oV6xpmOT4sNhdBPkZ
2npQE8Vi8mWY9RybWVwJet9CHeRBw99oUdRqQHvBb8IWxhLcurTBFZJstXoUbW
FDZTmxZKt55eUxnspTHLane119LsAU1wqHcHhlHI7;
GMAIL_AT=5282720a551b82df-10186d43b2e;
S=gmail=WczKrZ6s5sc:gmproxy=UMnFEH_hYC8; TZ=-60


064.233.171.107.00080-192.168.016.051.59905: HTTP/1.1 200 OK
Set-Cookie:
SID=DQAAAGoAAAC06FIY2Ix4DJlCk7ceaOnWPvpK4eWn9oV6xpmOT4sNhdBPkZ
2npQE8Vi8mWY9RybWVwJet9CHeRBw99oUdRqQHvBb8IWxhLcurTBFZJstXoUbW
FDZTmxZKt55eUxnspTHLane119LsAU1wqHcHhlHI7;Domain=.google.com;Pa
th=/
Cache-control: no-cache
Pragma: no-cache
Content-Type: text/html; charset=utf-8
Transfer-Encoding: chunked
Server: GFE/1.3
Date: Tue, 18 Jan 2005 17:17:36 GMT


936
<html><head><meta content="text/html; charset=UTF-8" http-
equiv="content-type"></head><script>D=(top.js&&top.js.init)?fu
nction(d){top.js.P(window,d)}:function(){};if(window==top){top
.location="/gmail?ik=&search=inbox&view=tl&start=0&init=1&zx=v
zmurwe44cpx6l&fs=1";}</script><script><!--
D(["v","15b3e78585d3c7bb","33fc762357568758"]
);
D(["ud","ben.hammersley@gmail.com","{\"o\":\"OPEN\",\"/\":\"SE
ARCH\",\"\\r\":\"OPEN\",\"k\":\"PREV\",\"r\":\"REPLY\",\"c\":\
```

```
"COMPOSE\",\"gc\":\"GO_CONTACTS\",\"gd\":\"GO_DRAFTS\",\"p\":\
"PREVMSG\",\"gi\":\"GO_INBOX\",\"m\":\"IGNORE\",\"a\":\"REPLYA
LL\",\"!\":\"SPAM\",\"f\":\"FORWARD\",\"u\":\"BACK\",\"ga\":\"
GO_ALL\",\"j\":\"NEXT\",\"y\":\"REMOVE\",\"n\":\"NEXTMSG\",\"g
s\":\"GO_STARRED\",\"x\":\"SELECT\",\"s\":\"STAR\"}","344af70c
5d","/gmail?view=page&name=contacts&ver=50c1485d48db7207"]
);
D(["su","33fc762357568758",["l","/gmail/help/images/logo.gif",
"i","Invite a friend to Gmail","j","Invite PH_NUM friends to
Gmail"]
]
);
D(["p",["bx_hs","1"]
,["bx_show0","1"]
,["bx_sc","0
064.233.171.107.00080-192.168.016.051.59905: "]
,["bx_pe","1"]
,["bx_ns","1"]
]
);
D(["ppd",0]
);
D(["i",6]
);
D(["qu","1 MB","1000 MB","0%","#006633"]
);
D(["ft","Search accurately with <a style=color:#0000CC
target=_blank
href=\"/support/bin/answer.py?ctx=gmail&answer=7190\">operator
s</a> including <b>from:</b>  <b>to:</b>
 <b>subject:</b>."]
);
D(["ds",2,0,0,0,0,16,0]
);
D(["ct",[["Heads",0]
,["Knees",0]
,["Shoulders",0]
,["Toes",0]
]
]
);
D(["ts",0,50,3,0,"Inbox","10186d450f9",3,]
);

//--></script><script><!--
D(["t",["101865c04ac2427f",1,0,"<b>4:06pm</b>","<span
id=\'_user_ben@benhammersley.com\'><b>Ben
Hammersley</b></span>","<b>&raquo;</b> ","<b>This is the
third message</b>",,[]
```

Continued

Listing 5-9 *(continued)*

```
,"","101865c04ac2427f",0,"Tue Jan 18 2005_7:06AM"]
,["101865b95fc7a35a",1,0,"<b>4:05pm</b>","<span
id=\'_user_ben@benhammersley.com\'><b>Ben
Hammersley</b></span>","<b>&raquo;</b> ","<b>This is the
second message</b>",,[]
,"","101865b95fc7a35a",0,"Tue Jan 18 2005_7:05AM"]
,["101480d8ef5dc74a",0,1,"Jan 6","<span
id=\'_user_ben@benhammersley.com\'>Ben
Hammersley</span>","<b>&raquo;</b> ","Here\'s a nice
message.",,["^t","Heads"]
,"","101480d8ef5dc74a",0,"Thu Jan 6 2005_4:44AM"]
]
);
D(["te"]);

//--></script><script>var
fp='341d292f3e55766f';</script><script>var
loaded=true;D(['e']);</script><script>try{top.js.L(window,45,'
cb803471f1');}catch(e){}</script>
```

What to make of these traces? First, you can see that to call the contents of the Inbox, the browser requests two URLs. First, this one:

```
/gmail?ik=&search=inbox&view=tl&start=0&init=1&zx=z6te3fe41hmsjo
```

And next, this one:

```
/gmail?ik=&search=inbox&view=tl&start=0&init=1&zx=781ttme448dfs9
```

And second, it appears that the real workings of the Inbox are contained in the JavaScript function that starts D(["t"]), as Listings 5-10 and 5-11 show.

Listing 5-10: With One Message

```
D(["t",["101480d8ef5dc74a",0,0,"Jan 6","<span
id=\'_user_ben@benhammersley.com\'>Ben
Hammersley</span>","<b>&raquo;</b> ","Here\'s a nice
message.",,[]
,"","101480d8ef5dc74a",0,"Thu Jan 6 2005_4:44AM"]
]
);
```

Listing 5-11: With Three Messages

```
D(["t",["101865c04ac2427f",1,0,"<b>4:06pm</b>","<span
id=\'_user_ben@benhammersley.com\'><b>Ben
Hammersley</b></span>","<b>&raquo;</b> ","<b>This is the
third message</b>",,[]
,"","101865c04ac2427f",0,"Tue Jan 18 2005_7:06AM"]
,["101865b95fc7a35a",1,0,"<b>4:05pm</b>","<span
id=\'_user_ben@benhammersley.com\'><b>Ben
Hammersley</b></span>","<b>&raquo;</b> ","<b>This is the
second message</b>",,[]
,"","101865b95fc7a35a",0,"Tue Jan 18 2005_7:05AM"]
,["101480d8ef5dc74a",0,1,"Jan 6","<span
id=\'_user_ben@benhammersley.com\'>Ben
Hammersley</span>","<b>&raquo;</b> ","Here\'s a nice
message.",,["^t","Heads"]
,"","101480d8ef5dc74a",0,"Thu Jan 6 2005_4:44AM"]
]
);
```

From looking at these listings, you can deduce that the Inbox structure consists of one or more of the following arrays (I've added in line breaks for clarity):

```
[
"101480d8ef5dc74a",
0,
0,
"Jan 6",
"<span id=\'_user_ben@benhammersley.com\'>Ben
Hammersley</span>",
"<b>&raquo;</b> ",
"Here\'s a nice message.",
,[]
,""
,"101480d8ef5dc74a"
,0
,"Thu Jan 6 2005_4:44AM"
]
```

From further deduction, where I sent different types of e-mail to Gmail and watched what it did — I'll omit all of that here for the sake of brevity, but you should have the idea — you can see that the array consists of the following:

```
[
"101480d8ef5dc74a",          -> The message id.
0,                           -> Unread=1, Read=0
0,                           -> Starred=1, plain=0
```

```
"Jan 6",                          -> The date displayed
"<span id=\'_user_ben@benhammersley.com\'>Ben
Hammersley</span>",               -> Who sent it
"<b>&raquo;</b> ",           -> The little icon in the inbox
"Here\'s a nice message.",        -> The subject line
,[]                               -> Labels
,""                               -> Attachments
,"101480d8ef5dc74a"               -> The message ID
,0                                -> Unknown
,"Thu Jan 6 2005_4:44AM"          -> The full date and time

]
```

You now know how to decode the Gmail mail listing. You can also see how to request this data structure — by calling the URL, and parsing the returned JavaScript function. You can do this in simple regular expressions, a topic explored in Chapter 7.

Storage Space

The detail of the mail in the Inbox isn't the only information sent when you request that URL. Look above the `mail` function and you can see the following:

```
D(["qu","1 MB","1000 MB","0%","#006633"]
```

This line of data sent from Gmail's servers clearly corresponds to the display at the bottom of the screen giving your mailbox usage statistics:

- **D(["qu",:** The name of the Gmail function that deals with the usage information.
- **"1 MB",:** The amount of storage used.
- **"1000 MB",:** The maximum amount available.
- **"0%",:** The percentage used.
- **"#006633":** The hex value for a nice shade of green.

Labels

In Figure 5-10 I have added some labels to the Gmail system. Spotting them in the Tcpflow is easy:

```
D(["ct",[["Heads",0],["Knees",0],["Shoulders",0],["Toes",0]]]);
```

You can deduce straight away that the function starting with `D(["ct"` contains the names and an unknown value (perhaps it's a Boolean, perhaps it's a string, you don't know as yet) of the Labels. You can more easily harvest this data when you come to write your own API.

Reading an Individual Mail

Fire up Tcpflow again, and click one of the messages in the Inbox in Figure 5-10. The trace resulting from this action is shown in Listing 5-12.

Listing 5-12: Trace from Reading a Message

```
192.168.016.051.59936-064.233.171.105.00080: GET
/gmail?ik=344af70c5d&view=cv&search=inbox&th=101865c04ac2427f&
lvp=-1&cvp=0&zx=9m4966e44e98uu HTTP/1.1
Host: gmail.google.com
User-Agent: Mozilla/5.0 (Macintosh; U; PPC Mac OS X Mach-O;
en-GB; rv:1.7.5) Gecko/20041110 Firefox/1.0
Accept:text/xml,application/xml,application/xhtml+xml,text/htm
l;q=0.9,text/plain;q=0.8,image/png,*/*;q=0.5
Accept-Language: en-gb,en;q=0.5
Accept-Charset: ISO-8859-1,utf-8;q=0.7,*;q=0.7
Keep-Alive: 300
Connection: keep-alive
Referer:
http://gmail.google.com/gmail?ik=&search=inbox&view=tl&start=0
&init=1&zx=iv37tme44d1tx5
Cookie: GV=1010186dcc455-ce01891ce232fa09b7f9bcfb46adf4e7;
PREF=ID=0070250e68e17190:CR=1:TM=1106068639:LM=1106068659:GM=1
:S=3jNiVz8ZpaPf0GW0; S=gmail=WczKrZ6s5sc:gmproxy=UMnFEH_hYC8;
TZ=-60; SID=DQAAAGoAAACm_kF5GqnusK0rbFcAlLKoJUx2616np-
H5Een1P_hN--yWqycLWSJUZt3G9Td_Cgw_ZK1naS891aWxZ6IkbNiBFN1J41mO
COTvOn7r3bnYjWlOqB6netb06ByuEf56Cd12ilfgika0MxmuamO3FWzw;
GMAIL_AT=29a3f526e2461d87-10186dcc456; GBE=d-540-800


064.233.171.105.00080-192.168.016.051.59936: HTTP/1.1 200 OK
Set-Cookie: SID=DQAAAGoAAACm_kF5GqnusK0rbFcAlLKoJUx2616np-
H5Een1P_hN--yWqycLWSJUZt3G9Td_Cgw_ZK1naS891aWxZ6IkbNiBFN1J41mO
COTvOn7r3bnYjWlOqB6netb06ByuEf56Cd12ilfgika0MxmuamO3FWzw;Domai
n=.google.com;Path=/

Set-Cookie: GBE=; Expires=Mon, 17-Jan-05 18:00:37 GMT; Path=/
Cache-control: no-cache
Pragma: no-cache

Content-Type: text/html; charset=utf-8
Transfer-Encoding: chunked

Server: GFE/1.3
```

Continued

Listing 5-12 *(continued)*

```
Date: Tue, 18 Jan 2005 18:00:37 GMT



4d5

<html><head><meta content="text/html; charset=UTF-8" http-
equiv="content-type"></head><script>D=(top.js&&top.js.init)?fu
nction(d){top.js.P(window,d)}:function(){};if(window==top){top
.location="/gmail?ik=344af70c5d&view=cv&search=inbox&th=101865
c04ac2427f&lvp=-
1&cvp=0&zx=9m4966e44e98uu&fs=1";}</script><script><!--
D(["v","15b3e78585d3c7bb","33fc762357568758"]
);
D(["i",6]
);
D(["qu","1 MB","1000 MB","0%","#006633"]
);
D(["ft","Compose a message in a new window by pressing
\"Shift\" while clicking Compose Mail or Reply."]
);
D(["ds",1,0,0,0,0,16,0]
);
D(["ct",[["Heads",0]
,["Knees",0]
,["Shoulders",0]
,["Toes",0]
]
]
);
D(["cs","101865c04ac2427f","This is the third message","This
is the third message","",["^i"]
,[]
,0,1,"h3ttlgu1hqiz9324trq5kp5qo7wa96s",,"101865c04ac2427f"]
);
D(["mi",0,1,"101865c04ac2427f",0,"0","Ben
Hammersley","ben@benhammersley.com","me","4:05pm (2&frac12;
hours ago)",["Ben Hammersley <ben.hammersley@gmail.com>"]
,[]
,[]
,[
064.233.171.105.00080-192.168.016.051.59936: ]
,"Tue, 18 Jan 2005 16:05:17 +0100","This is the third
message","",[]
,1,,,"Tue Jan 18 2005_7:05AM"]
```

```
);
D(["mb","3rd! THREE! THIRD!<br><br>",0]
);
D(["ce"]);

//--></script><script>var
loaded=true;D(['e']);</script><script>try{top.js.L(window,70,'
1
ab915da64');}catch(e){}</script>
```

First thing first: the URL. Requesting this message caused Gmail to load this URL:

```
/gmail?ik=344af70c5d&view=cv&search=inbox&th=101865c04ac2427f&l
vp=-1&cvp=0&zx=9m4966e44e98uu.
```

Or, to put it more understandably:

```
/gmail?
ik=344af70c5d
&view=cv
&search=inbox
&th=101865c04ac2427f
&lvp=-1
&cvp=0
&zx=9m4966e44e98uu
```

As you can see, `th` is the message ID of the message I clicked on. But the others are mysterious at the moment.

At this point in the proceedings, alarms went off in my head. Why, I was thinking, is the variable for message ID `th` — when that probably stands for thread. So, I sent a few mails back and forth to create a thread, and loaded the Inbox and the message back up again under Tcpflow. Listing 5-13 shows the resulting trace. It is illuminating.

Listing 5-13: Retrieving a Thread, Not a Message

```
THE INBOX LOADING:

D(["t",["10187696869432e6",1,0,"<b>9:00pm</b>","<span
id=\'_user_ben@benhammersley.com\'>Ben</span>, <span
id=\'_user_ben.hammersley@gmail.com\'>me</span>, <span
id=\'_user_ben@benhammersley.com\'><b>Ben</b></span>
(3)","<b>&raquo;</b> ","<b>This is the third
message</b>",,[]
```

Continued

Listing 5-13 *(continued)*

```
,"","10187696869432e6",0,"Tue Jan 18 2005_12:00PM"]
,["101865b95fc7a35a",1,0,"<b>4:05pm</b>","<span
id=\'_user_ben@benhammersley.com\'><b>Ben
Hammersley</b></span>","<b>&raquo;</b> ","<b>This is the
second message</b>",,[]
,"","101865b95fc7a35a",0,"Tue Jan 18 2005_7:05AM"]
,["101480d8ef5dc74a",0,1,"Jan 6","<span
id=\'_user_ben@benhammersley.com\'>Ben
Hammersley</span>","<b>&raquo;</b> ","Here\'s a nice
message.",,["^t","Heads"]
,"","101480d8ef5dc74a",0,"Thu Jan 6 2005_4:44AM"]
]
);
D(["te"]);
```

THE GETTING MESSAGE EXCHANGE

```
192.168.016.051.61753-216.239.057.105.00080: GET
/gmail?ik=344af70c5d&view=cv&search=inbox&th=10187696869432e6&
lvp=-1&cvp=0&zx=241f19e44iyx7g HTTP/1.1

Host: gmail.google.com

User-Agent: Mozilla/5.0 (Macintosh; U; PPC Mac OS X Mach-O;
en-GB; rv:1.7.5) Gecko/20041110 Firefox/1.0

Accept:
text/xml,application/xml,application/xhtml+xml,text/html;q=0.9
,text/plain;q=0.8,image/png,*/*;q=0.5

Accept-Language: en-gb,en;q=0.5

Accept-Charset: ISO-8859-1,utf-8;q=0.7,*;q=0.7

Keep-Alive: 300

Connection: keep-alive

Referer:
http://gmail.google.com/gmail?ik=&search=inbox&view=tl&start=0
&init=1&zx=cs149e44iu4pd

Cookie: GV=101018770f6a0-36b4c5fcaa4913584af2219efa21740e;
SID=DQAAAGoAAACTZryXzUYHgTI4VWtHGXDY5J8vchRrqp_Ek4XjEgdZYQwBUE
```

pXOuyokCt-EOOmsaL8J8_bQ3jkrMfskffoH8Mb6GvEJJPAhS6noKP8IjnR-
EcWN8MTvIPeqOYYoxE52oLva00EWdOrsGhtCy18RphU;
GMAIL_AT=aa5dcfedda2d8658-1018770f6a2; S=gmail=p-
114BJCt_4:gmproxy=c9z4V0uxx2o; TZ=-60; GMAIL_SU=1;
PREF=ID=e38a980ef675b953:TM=1106078936:LM=1106078936:GM=1:S=T0
D_V1EFUHr7faSw; GBE=d-540-800

216.239.057.105.00080-192.168.016.051.61753: HTTP/1.1 200 OK

Set-Cookie:
SID=DQAAAGoAAACTZryXzUYHgTI4VWtHGXDY5J8vchRrqp_Ek4XjEgdZYQwBUE
pXOuyokCt-EOOmsaL8J8_bQ3jkrMfskffoH8Mb6GvEJJPAhS6noKP8IjnR-
EcWN8MTvIPeqOYYoxE52oLva00EWdOrsGhtCy18RphU;Domain=.google.com
;Path=/

Set-Cookie: GBE=; Expires=Mon, 17-Jan-05 20:12:34 GMT; Path=/

Set-Cookie: GMAIL_SU=; Expires=Mon, 17-Jan-05 20:12:34 GMT;
Path=/

Cache-control: no-cache

Pragma: no-cache

Content-Type: text/html; charset=utf-8

Transfer-Encoding: chunked

Server: GFE/1.3

Date: Tue, 18 Jan 2005 20:12:34 GMT

b23

<html><head><meta content="text/html; charset=UTF-8" http-
equiv="content-type"></head><script>D=(top.js&&top.js.init)?fu
nction(d){top.js.P(window,d)}:function(){};if(window==top){top
.location="/gmail?ik=344af70c5d&view=cv&search=inbox&th=101876
96869432e6&lvp=-
1&cvp=0&zx=241fl9e44iyx7g&fs=1";}</script><script><!--
D(["su","33fc762357568758",["l","/gmail/help/images/logo.gif",
"i","Invite a friend to Gmail","j","Invite PH_NUM friends to
Gmail"]

Continued

Listing 5-13 *(continued)*

```
]
);
D(["v","15b3e78585d3c7bb","33fc762357568758"]
);
D(["i",6]
);
D(["qu","1 MB","1000 MB","0%","#006633"]
);
D(["ft","Automatically <span style=\"color:#0000CC;text-
decoration:underline;cursor:pointer;cursor:hand;white-space:no
wrap\" id=\"prf_d\"><b>forward</b></span> your Gmail messages
to another email account.   <a style=color:#0000CC
target=_blank
href=\"/support/bin/answer.py?ctx=gmail&answer=10957\">Learn&n
bsp;more</a>"]
);
D
216.239.057.105.00080-192.168.016.051.61753:
(["ds",1,0,0,0,0,16,0]
);
D(["ct",[["Heads",0]
,["Knees",0]
,["Shoulders",0]
,["Toes",0]
]
]
);
D(["cs","10187696869432e6","This is the third message","This
is the third message","",["^i"]
,[]
,0,3,"g6yz3b2a3jhoga7fql7qx3yo6l9gvyf",,"10187696869432e6"]
);
D(["mi",2,1,"101865c04ac2427f",0,"0","Ben
Hammersley","ben@benhammersley.com","me","4:05pm (5 hours
ago)",["Ben Hammersley <ben.hammersley@gmail.com>"]
,[]
,[]
,[]
,"Tue, 18 Jan 2005 16:05:17 +0100","This is the third
message","3rd! THREE! THIRD!",[]
,1,,,"Tue Jan 18 2005_7:05AM"]
);

//--></script><script><!--
```

```
D(["mi",2,2,"101876847addcbd1",0,"0","Ben
Hammersley","ben.hammersley@gmail.com","Ben","8:59pm (13
minutes ago)",["Ben Hammersley <ben@benhammersley.com>"]
,[]
,[]
,["Ben Hammersley <ben.hammersley@gmail.com>"]
,"Tue, 18 Jan 2005 20:59:13 +0100","Re: This is the third
message","And this is a reply back On Tue, 18 Jan 2005
16:05:17 +0100, Ben Hammersley &lt;...",[]
,1,,,"Tue Jan 18 2005_11:59AM"]
);
D(["mi",0,3,"10187696869432e6",0,"0","Ben
Hammersley","ben@benhammersley.com","me","8:59pm (12 minutes
ago)",["Ben Hammersley <ben.hammersley@gmail.com>"]
,[]
,[]
,[]
,"Tue, 18 Jan 2005 20:59:40 +0100","Re: This is the third
message","",[]
,1,,,"Tue Jan 18 2005_11:59AM"]
);
D(["mb","And this is another reply back yet again<br>",1]
);
D(["mb","<div><div class=ea><span id=e_10187696869432e6_1>-
Show quoted text -</span></div><span class=e
216.239.057.105.00080-192.168.016.051.61753:
id=q_10187696869432e6_1><br>On 18 Jan 2005, at 20:59, Ben
Hammersley wrote:<br><br>&gt; And this is a reply
back<br>&gt;<br>&gt;<br>&gt; On Tue, 18 Jan 2005 16:05:17
+0100, Ben Hammersley<br>&gt; &lt;<a onclick=\"return
top.js.OpenExtLink(window,event,this)\"
href=\"mailto:ben@benhammersley.com\">ben@benhammersley.com</a
>&gt; wrote:<br>&gt;&gt; 3rd! THREE!
THIRD!<br>&gt;&gt;<br>&gt;&gt;<br><br></span></div>",0]
);
D(["ce"]);

//--></script><script>var
loaded=true;D(['e']);</script><script>try{top.js.L(window,32,'
9
36bba732b');}catch(e){}</script>
```

As you can deduce, th does indeed stand for thread. In Gmail, it turns out, you do not just retrieve single messages. Rather, you retrieve the requested message and also the entire set of headers for the rest of the messages in the thread. You can see this quite clearly in the example above. The lines in bold type show the headers for all three messages, and the whole thing finishes with the entire content of the requested message.

You then allow the JavaScript code to wrangle the interface afterward. This is a clever trick: it allows the interface to be very quick at the point the user wants it to be — when you're reading through a thread — instead of loading each message individually.

So, you now know how to retrieve messages. But how do you read them?

Listing 5-14 shows the relevant bit of JavaScript.

Listing 5-14: The Message Itself

```
D(["mi",0,3,"10187696869432e6",0,"0","Ben
Hammersley","ben@benhammersley.com","me","8:59pm (12 minutes
ago)",["Ben Hammersley <ben.hammersley@gmail.com>"]
,[]
,[]
,[]
,"Tue, 18 Jan 2005 20:59:40 +0100","Re: This is the third
message","",[]
,1,,,"Tue Jan 18 2005_11:59AM"]
);
D(["mb","And this is another reply back yet again<br>",1]
);
D(["mb","<div><div class=ea><span id=e_10187696869432e6_1>-
Show quoted text -</span></div><span class=e
id=q_10187696869432e6_1><br>On 18 Jan 2005, at 20:59, Ben
Hammersley wrote:<br><br>&gt; And this is a reply
back<br>&gt;<br>&gt;<br>&gt; On Tue, 18 Jan 2005 16:05:17
+0100, Ben Hammersley<br>&gt; &lt;<a onclick=\"return
top.js.OpenExtLink(window,event,this)\"
href=\"mailto:ben@benhammersley.com\">ben@benhammersley.com</a
>&gt; wrote:<br>&gt;&gt; 3rd! THREE!
THIRD!<br>&gt;&gt;<br>&gt;&gt;<br><br></span></div>",0]
);
```

From this you can see that the message is sent in three JavaScript arrays. `D(["mi"` contains the header information — its status, the message ID, who sent it, and so on — and then there are two arrays starting with `D(["mb"` that contain the first line and the whole rest of the message, respectively, marked up in HTML. Parsing this out, as you will in Chapter 8, will be easy. So you now know how to request a message and read it.

And Now . . .

In this chapter, you learned how Gmail works, and you looked at the techniques you would use to probe the system for the knowledge you need to communicate with the Gmail server directly. You can log in, request mail, read mail, and access label titles and other sorts of information. In the next chapter, however, you will look at the existing APIs for Gmail — both confirming what you have learned here — and learn how to put your new expertise to use.

Gmail and Greasemonkey

in this chapter

☑ What is Greasemonkey?

☑ Using userscripts

☑ Customizing the Gmail experience

Another phenomenon to hit the web at the same time as Gmail was the Firefox browser. Indeed, the growth of this open source application easily rivaled Gmail for shocking explosiveness. Apart from the additional security benefits and tasty user interface advantages that Firefox gives, the browser is also open to a considerable amount of hacking in itself. One of the key hacks for Firefox was Greasemonkey. In this chapter, you learn how Greasemonkey and Firefox can be used to radically improve your Gmail experience, and how the understanding you now have about the workings of Gmail will enable you to build your own Greasemonkey scripts.

What Is Greasemonkey?

Greasemonkey allows the user to assign snippets of JavaScript code to run automatically whenever a certain page is loaded. The upshot of this is that you can write JavaScript code that will customize those web pages, modifying layout, adding new features, or removing extraneous parts of the page. Greasemonkey has been used to remove advertising, rewrite links, add new links to other sites, and even add completely new menus to sites. Gmail, being one huge hunk of burning JavaScript, is beautifully positioned to be taken advantage of by Greasemonkey.

To use Greasemonkey, you have to install it first. Do that by getting the latest version from `http://greasemonkey.mozdev.org/`.

The snippets of JavaScript used by Greasemonkey are called *userscripts*. They need to be installed into Firefox for the application to work. You do that like this: Go to the page with the userscript in it. It will look really ugly, with lots of JavaScript, and the top 20 or so lines preceded by double forward-slashes, as in Figure 6-1.

Click Tools, and then Install User Script. Check that everything looks okay. (Nothing red and scary? Good, carry on.) That's it. You're done.

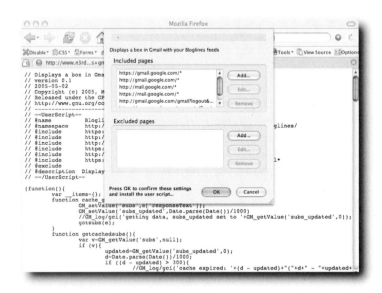

The Userscripts

Now that you know how to install userscripts, you can start to use them. Ordinarily, you wouldn't have to type the code in, seeing as you just point your browser to the site and let fly with the installation procedure, as detailed in the preceding text, but you can learn a lot from looking at the code. For the next few examples, therefore, you shall take a look. There are techniques to be learned, and inspiration to be had, here.

Displaying Bloglines Within Gmail

Bloglines — shown in Figure 6-2 — is another great web-based application. It's an RSS reader — you can use it to keep track of hundreds of sites' content by subscribing to each of the sites' feeds. Many users, myself included, keep close to a hundred sites in their Bloglines subscription. Some have many more. Indeed, the regular trawl of unread news items in Bloglines is close to as important as the regular checking of my Inbox.

FIGURE 6-2: The Bloglines Greasemonkey extension in action

Martin Sersale's beautiful code, which can be installed from
`http://www.n3rds.com.ar/greasemonkey/bloglines+gmail.user.js`,
allows you to combine the two. First, the listing, and then we shall talk about the
more interesting sections. The whole thing is listed here, in Listing 6-1, as it's full
of very useful stuff.

Listing 6-1: Displaying Bloglines with Gmail

```
// Displays a box in Gmail with your Bloglines feeds
// version 0.1
// 2005-05-02
// Copyright (c) 2005, Martin Sarsale -
martin@malditainternet.com
// Released under the GPL license
// http://www.gnu.org/copyleft/gpl.html
// ----------------------------------------------------------
---------
// ==UserScript==
// @name          Bloglines
// @namespace
http://martin.malditainternet.com/greasemonkey/gmail+bloglines
/
// @include       https://gmail.google.com/*
```

Continued

Listing 6-1 *(continued)*

```
// @include      http://gmail.google.com/*
// @include      http://mail.google.com/*
// @include      https://mail.google.com/*
// @include      http://gmail.google.com/gmail?logout&hl=en
// @include
https://www.google.com/accounts/ServiceLogin?service=mail*
// @exclude
// @description  Displays a box in Gmail with your Bloglines
feeds
// ==/UserScript==

(function(){
    var __items={};
    function cache_gotsubs(e){
        GM_setValue('subs',e['responseText']);
        GM_setValue('subs_updated',Date.parse(Date())/1000)
        //GM_log/gci('getting data, subs_updated set to
'+GM_getValue('subs_updated',0));
        gotsubs(e);
    }
    function getcachedsubs(){
        var v=GM_getValue('subs',null);
        if (v){
            updated=GM_getValue('subs_updated',0);
            d=Date.parse(Date())/1000;
            if ((d - updated) > 300){
                //GM_log/gci('cache expired: '+(d -
updated)+"("+d+" - "+updated+")");
                return false;
            }else{
                return v;
            }
        }
        return false;
    }
    function getsubs(){
        v=getcachedsubs();
        if (v){
            gotsubs(v);
            return true;
        }
        getsubs();
    }
    function _getsubs(){

GM_xmlhttpRequest({'method':'GET','url':"http://rpc.bloglines.
com/listsubs",'onload':cache_gotsubs});
```

```
        }
    function parsesubs(r){
        parser=new DOMParser();
        dom=parser.parseFromString(r,'text/xml');
        outlines=dom.getElementsByTagName('outline');
        subs=new Array();
        for(i=0; i<outlines.length; i++){
            if (outlines[i].getAttribute('type') != undefined
){
                d={ 'title':outlines[i].getAttribute('title'),
'htmlUrl':outlines[i].getAttribute('htmlUrl'),
'type':outlines[i].getAttribute('type'),
'xmlUrl':outlines[i].getAttribute('xmlUrl'),
'BloglinesSubId':outlines[i].getAttribute('BloglinesSubId'),
'BloglinesUnread':outlines[i].getAttribute('BloglinesUnread')
};
                subs[subs.length]=d;
            }
        }
        return subs;
    }
    function gotsubs(response){
        if (typeof(response)=='object'){
            data=response['responseText'];
        }else{
            data=response;
        }
        r=parsesubs(data);
        r.sort(function(a,b){; var r=a['BloglinesUnread'] >
b['BloglinesUnread']; if(r){return -1}else{return 1} });
        addsubhtml_init();
        for(i=0; i<r.length; i++){
            addsubhtml(r[i]);
        }
        addsubhtml_end();
    }
    function addsubhtml_end(){
        ul=document.getElementById('bloglines_subs');
        if (ul){
            GM_setValue('subs_cached_html',ul.innerHTML);
        }
    }
    function createbutton(str){
            a=document.createElement('div');
            a.appendChild(document.createTextNode(str))
            a.style.backgroundColor='#dddddd';
            a.style.borderStyle='outset';
            a.style.borderColor='#eeeeee';
```

Continued

Listing 6-1 *(continued)*

```
                    a.style.borderWidth='2px';
                    a.style.width='10px';
                    a.style.height='10px';
                    a.style.lineHeight='10px';
                    a.style.verticalAlign='middle';
                    a.style.textAlign='center';
                    a.style.fontSize='x-small';
                    a.style.fontWeight='bold';
                    a.style.position='absolute';
                    a.style.top='0px';
                    a.style.right='0px';
                    return a;
        }
        function addsubhtml_init(){
            ul=document.getElementById('bloglines_subs');
            ul.innerHTML='';
            if (!document.getElementById('bloglines_reload')){
                a=createbutton('R');
                a.addEventListener('click',_getsubs,false);
                a.id='bloglines_reload';
                ul.parentNode.appendChild(a);
            }

        }
        function addsubhtml(d){
            ul=document.getElementById('bloglines_subs');
            li=document.createElement('li');
            li.className='nl';
            li.style.padding='0px';
            li.style.margin='0px';
            li.style.width='100%';
            li.style.overflow='hidden';

            a=document.createElement('a');
            a.id=d['BloglinesSubId'];


a.href='http://www.bloglines.com/myblogs_display?sub='+d['Blog
linesSubId']+'&site=0';
            a.target='_blank';
            txt=d['title']
            a.style.fontSize='small';
            if (d['BloglinesUnread']>0){
                a.style.fontWeight='bold';
                txt=txt+" ("+d['BloglinesUnread']+")";
```

```
        }
        a.appendChild(document.createTextNode(txt));
        li.appendChild(a);
        ul.appendChild(li);
    }
    function getsub(e){
        id=e.target.id;


GM_xmlhttpRequest({'method':'GET','url':"http://rpc.bloglines.
com/getitems?n=0&s="+id,'onload':gotsub});

    }
    function gotsub(r){
        var d=parsesub(r['responseText']);
        for(var i=0; i<d.length; i++){
            item=d[i];

items[getText(item.getElementsByTagName('guid')[0])]=item;
        }
        for(i=0; i<d.length; i++){
            item=d[i];
            displaysubhtml(item);
        }
    }
    function displaysubhtml(item){
        li=document.createElement('li');
        b=document.getElementById('items');

        a=document.createElement('a');
        a.id=getText(item.getElementsByTagName('guid')[0]);
        a.addEventListener('click',displayitem,false);

a.appendChild(document.createTextNode(getText(item.getElements
ByTagName('title')[0])));
        li.appendChild(a);
        b.appendChild(li);
    }
    function displayitem(e){
        id=e.target.id;
        var item=__items[id];
        displayitemhtml(item);
    }
    function displayitemhtml(item){
        i=document.getElementById('item');

i.innerHTML=getText(item.getElementsByTagName('description')[0
]);
```

Continued

Listing 6-1 *(continued)*

```
    }
    function getText(e){
        nodes=e.childNodes;
        for (var i=0; i<nodes.length; i++){
            if (nodes[i].nodeValue != null){
                return nodes[i].nodeValue;
            }
        }
    }
    function parsesub(r){
        parser=new DOMParser();
        dom=parser.parseFromString(r,'text/xml');
        r=dom.getElementsByTagName('item');
        return r;
    }
    function checkifpresenthtml(){
        d=document.getElementById('nt_9');
        if (!d){
            inithtml();
            getsubs();
        }
    }
    function switch_labels(){
        for(i=0; i<window.labels_readed.length; i++){
            label=window.labels_readed[i];
            if (label.style.display != 'none'){
                label.style.display='none';
            }else{
                label.style.display='block';
            }
        }
    }
    function inithtml(){
        bar=document.getElementById('nav');
        if (bar){

document.styleSheets[0].insertRule('ul#bloglines_subs>li>a{tex
t-decoration:none}',document.styleSheets[0].length);

            v=getcachedsubs();
            if (v){
                data=GM_getValue('subs_cached_html','');
            }else{
                data='';
```

```
                }

                invite=document.getElementById('nb_1');
                if (invite){ invite.style.display='none'; }

document.getElementById('ds_spam').parentNode.style.display='n
one';

document.getElementById('ds_all').parentNode.style.display='no
ne';

document.getElementById('ds_trash').parentNode.style.display='
none';

document.getElementById('comp').parentNode.style.display='none
';

                div=document.createElement('div');
                div.style.paddingTop='0px';
                div.id='nb_9';
                html="<div style='width:
95%;padding:0px;position:relative'><table width='100%'
style='margin-top:0px;' cellspacing='0' cellpadding='0'
bgcolor='#c3d9ff'> <tbody> <tr height='2'> <td class='tl'>
</td> <td class='tr'> </td> </tr> </tbody> </table> <div
style='padding: 0pt 3px 1px; background: rgb(195, 217, 255)
none repeat scroll 0%; -moz-background-clip: initial; -moz-
background-origin: initial; -moz-background-inline-policy:
initial;'> <div id='nt_9' class='s h'> <table cellspacing='0'
cellpadding='0'> <tbody> <tr> <td style='vertical-align: top;'
class='s h'> <img width='11' height='11'
src='/gmail/images/opentriangle.gif' /> </td> <td class='s'>
Bloglines</td></tr></tbody> </table> </div> <table
cellspacing='2' class='nb'> <tbody> <tr> <td><ul
id='bloglines_subs' style='width:100%; margin:0px;
padding:0px; list-style-type:none'>"+data+"</ul></td> </tr>
</tbody> </table> </div> <table width='100%' cellspacing='0'
cellpadding='0' bgcolor='#c3d9ff'> <tbody> <tr height='2'> <td
class='bl'> </td> <td class='br'> </td> </tr> </tbody>
</table></div>";
                div.innerHTML=html;
                bar.appendChild(div);
                return true;
            }
        return false;
    }
    function init(){
        return inithtml();
```

Continued

Listing 6-1 *(continued)*

```
    }
    if
(window.location.href=='http://gmail.google.com/gmail?logout&h
l=en' || window.location.href.substr(0,57) ==
'https://www.google.com/accounts/ServiceLogin?service=mail' ){
        //GM_log/gci('logout');
        GM_setValue('subs',null);
        GM_setValue('subs_update',null);
        GM_setValue('subs_cached_html',null);
    }else{
        if(init()){
            getsubs();
            setInterval(checkifpresenthtml,1000);
        }
    }
})()
```

How It Works

Have a read through the preceding code. From the knowledge you have from the chapters on skinning CSS and how the JavaScript within Gmail works, you should be able to glean a little inkling into how it works. For the sake of brevity, I won't repeat all of the functions here, but to walk through, the first interesting things are the _getsubs (note the plural and underscore) and parsesubs functions. _getsubs uses the same xmlhttprequest system that Gmail does. _getsubs requests your list of subscriptions from Bloglines.

Once the subs have been got by _getsubs, the script goes through a series of functions to cache them. That is all at the top of the script, and causes the subscriptions list to be collected only once an hour. (At the bottom of the script, the very last function, is code to check if the page Greasemonkey can see is the one you get only if the user has logged out of Gmail. If that page is hit, the cache is emptied as well.)

A freshly retrieved list of subs is then passed through the parsesubs function. This parses the XML of the subscription list into an array.

Note here that this is, so far, very useful stuff. Many sites provide information feeds in XML, and all you have here really is a script that pulls in a feed (after checking it's not in a cache) and parses it. You can reuse that structure to pull in data from just about anywhere. Indeed, if an ordinary website has no feed, but is well-formed XHTML, you can even use this same technique to screenscrape something and display that information within a page.

Even better, the script then has to go use the data in the subs list, which is placed inside an array. In the `getsub` function (note the singular, and lack of underscore), the script retrieves the XML of the feed. Once you have that, use the functions `displaysubhtml` and `inithtml` to convert the XML of the feed into HTML and display it on the page. From Chapter 4, even if you know no JavaScript, you should be able decipher the meaning of lines such as this:

```
document.getElementById('ds_spam').parentNode.style.display='none';
```

They prevent the browser from displaying that particular div, making space for the HTML it then adds onto the screen.

To go more deeply into this script would require another book, on JavaScript and Greasemonkey at the very least, but I hope by reading through it you can see how it works. It's very hackable — have a go at converting it to displaying information from other XML-providing sources. The weather forecasts available at `http://weather.gov/xml/` are a good starting point. For extra inspiration, consider displaying the weather at the location of a new mail's sender. Tricky one, that.

Add a Delete Button

Not content with grabbing data from other sources and chucking it all over the site like some crazed mash-up DJ, you can also use Greasemonkey to add additional user interface elements. Anthony Lieuallen's script at `www.arantius.com/article/arantius/gmail+delete+button/` adds a Delete button to the menu, as shown in Figure 6-3.

FIGURE 6-3: The added
Delete button

Without such a button, as you know, you have to move the message to trash. Not much of a change, admittedly, but a nice UI improvement. Listing 6-2 shows the code.

Listing 6-2: Adding the Delete Button

```
// ==UserScript==
// @name          Gmail Delete Button
// @namespace
http://www.arantius.com/article/arantius/gmail+delete+button/
// @description   Add a "Delete" button to Gmail's interface.
// @include       http*://*mail.google.com/*mail*?*
// @version       2.9.1
// ==/UserScript==

//
// Version 2.91:
//   - Japanese and Hungarian translation
// Version 2.9:
//   - Compatibility upgrade, works in GM 0.6.2 in Firefox 1.5
Beta 1
// Version 2.8.3:
//   - Polish translation
// Version 2.8.2:
//   - Russian translation
// Version 2.8.1:
//   - Bulgarian translation
// Version 2.8:
//   - Cleaned up bits of the code.  No more global scope
objects.
//   - Deer Park compatible.
// Version 2.7.2:
//   - Better i81n, file encoded as unicode, to be compatible
with newer
//     versions of greasemonkey.
// Version 2.7:
//   - Internationalization.  If you speak a language other
than english,
//     please check the existing text (if there) and/or suggest
the right
//     word to mean 'Delete' in your language.
//   - A change to the default include path.
// Version 2.6:
//   - Add button into starred and sent mail section as per
user request.
//   - Rework logic to use events (mouse click and key press)
instead of
//     timers to further ameliorate lockouts.  I've recieved at
least one
//     report that it was fixed by 2.3, and others that it was
not at 2.5.
```

```
//    Perhaps it was fixed and the timing of reports was off,
but this
//    should make things more certain.  I always welcome
constructive
//    bug reports, I have never had a problem so I need
information from
//    those who have to change anything.
// Version 2.5:
//  - Change default include pattern to match a change in
Gmail's code.
// Version 2.4:
//  - Remove red text.  You may restore the red color by un-
commenting
//    the proper line in _gd_make_dom_button.
//  - Do not show for a message in the spam folder.
//  - Minor tweaks.
// Version 2.3:
//  - Add/change code to track down/eliminate error
conditions.
//  - Display error when there are no selected messages to
delete.
//  - Include delete button in all labels and 'All Mail'
section.
// Version 2.2:
//  - Patched to work with GreaseMonkey 0.3.3
//
// -------------------------------------------------------------
---------
// Originally written by Anthony Lieuallen of
http://www.arantius.com/
// Licensed for unlimited modification and redistribution as
long as
// this notice is kept intact.
// -------------------------------------------------------------
---------
//
// If possible, please contact me regarding new features,
bugfixes
// or changes that I could integrate into the existing code
instead of
// creating a different script.  Thank you
//

(function(){

function _gd_dumpErr(e) {
    var s='Error in Gmail Delete Button:\n';
    s+='  Line: '+e.lineNumber+'\n';
```

Continued

Listing 6-2 *(continued)*

```
        s+='   '+e.name+': '+e.message+'\n';
        dump(s);
}

function _gd_element(id) {
    try {
        var el=window.document.getElementById(id);
    } catch (e) {
        gd_dumpErr(e);
        return false;
    }
    if (el) return el;
    return false;
}

function _gd_gmail_delete(e) {
    dump('Called _gd_gmail_delete()...\n');
    //find the command box
    var delete_button=e.target;
    var
command_box=delete_button.parentNode.getElementsByTagName('sel
ect')[0];
    command_box.onfocus();

    //find the command index for 'move to trash'
    var delete_index=-1;
    for (var i=0; i<command_box.options.length; i++) {
        if ('tr'==command_box.options[i].value &&
!command_box.options[i].disabled ) {
            delete_index=i;
            break;
        }
    }

    //don't try to continue if we can't move to trash now
    if (-1==delete_index) {
        var box=_gd_element('nt1');
        if (box) {
            try {
                //if we find the box put an error message in
it
                box.firstChild.style.visibility='visible';

box.getElementsByTagName('td')[1].innerHTML='Could not delete.
Make sure at least one conversation is selected.';
```

```
            } catch (e) {
                gd_dumpErr(e);
            }
        }
        return;
    }

    //set the command index and fire the change event
    command_box.selectedIndex=delete_index;
    command_box.onchange();
    //command_box.dispatchEvent('click');
    //var evt=createEvent();
}

function _gd_make_dom_button(id) {
    var delete_button=window.document.createElement('button');
    delete_button.setAttribute('class', 'ab');
    delete_button.setAttribute('id', '_gd_delete_button'+id);
    delete_button.addEventListener('click', _gd_gmail_delete,
false);

    //uncomment (remove the two leading slashes) from the next
line for red text
    //delete_button.style.color='#EE3311';

    //this is a little hack-y, but we can find the code for
the language here
    var lang='';
    try {
        var
urlToTest=window.top.document.getElementsByTagName('frame')[1]
.src;
        var
m=urlToTest.match(/html\/([^\/]*)\/loading.html$/);
        if (null!=m) lang=m[1];
    } catch (e) {
        gd_dumpErr(e);
    }
    //now check that language, and find the right word!
    var buttonText='Delete'; //the default text for the
button, overriden
                             //in the switch below if we know
the right word
    switch (lang) {
    case 'it': buttonText='Elimina'; break;
    case 'es': buttonText='Borrar'; break;
    case 'fr': buttonText='Supprimer'; break;
    //case 'pt-BR': buttonText='Supress&#227;o'; break;
```

Continued

Listing 6-2 *(continued)*

```
    //it was suggested by a user that 'Apaga' is more proper
for this language
    case 'pt-BR': buttonText='Apaga'; break;
    case 'de': buttonText='L&#246;schen'; break;
    case 'bg':
buttonText='&#1048;&#1079;&#1090;&#1088;&#1080;&#1081;';
break;
    case 'ru':
buttonText='&#1059;&#1076;&#1072;&#1083;&#1080;&#1090;&#1100;'
; break;
    case 'pl': buttonText='Usu&#324;'; break;
    case 'ja':
buttonText='\u30b4\u30df\u7bb1\u3078\u79fb\u52d5'; break;
    case 'hu': buttonText='T&#246;r&#246;l'; break;
    }

    delete_button.innerHTML='<b>'+buttonText+'</b>';
    return delete_button;
}

function _gd_insert_button(insert_container, id) {
    if (!insert_container) return false;
    if (_gd_element('_gd_delete_button'+id)) {
        return false;
    }

    //get the elements
    var spacer, delete_button;
    delete_button=_gd_make_dom_button(id);

spacer=insert_container.firstChild.nextSibling.cloneNode(false
);

    //pick the right place to put them
    var insert_point=insert_container.firstChild;  //this is
default
    if (2==id || 3==id) {
        // 2 and 3 are inside the message and go at a
different place
        insert_point=insert_point.nextSibling.nextSibling;
    }
    if (window.document.location.search.match(/search=query/))
{
        //inside the search page we go yet different places
with different spacers
```

```
        if (0==id) {

spacer=insert_container.firstChild.nextSibling.nextSibling.clo
neNode(false);

insert_point=insert_container.firstChild.nextSibling.nextSibli
ng.nextSibling;
        }
        if (1==id)
spacer=window.document.createElement('span'); //no space
really needed here
    } else if
(window.document.location.search.match(/search=sent/)) {
        //inside the sent page we go yet different places with
different spacers
        if (0==id) {

//spacer=insert_container.firstChild.nextSibling.nextSibling.c
loneNode(false);

//insert_point=insert_container.firstChild.nextSibling.nextSib
ling.nextSibling;
        spacer=window.document.createTextNode(' ');

insert_point=insert_container.firstChild.nextSibling.nextSibli
ng;
        }
        if (1==id)
spacer=window.document.createElement('span'); //no space
really needed here
    }

    //put them in
    insert_container.insertBefore(spacer, insert_point);
    insert_container.insertBefore(delete_button, spacer);
}

function _gd_place_delete_buttons() {
    if (!window || !window.document || !window.document.body)
return;
    var top_menu=_gd_element('tamu');  if (top_menu)
_gd_insert_button(top_menu.parentNode, 0);
    var bot_menu=_gd_element('bamu');  if (bot_menu)
_gd_insert_button(bot_menu.parentNode, 1);
    var mtp_menu=_gd_element('ctamu'); if (mtp_menu)
_gd_insert_button(mtp_menu.parentNode, 2);
    var mbt_menu=_gd_element('cbamu'); if (mbt_menu)
_gd_insert_button(mbt_menu.parentNode, 3);
```

Continued

Listing 6-2 *(continued)*

```
}

function _gd_button_event() {
    try{
        setTimeout(_gd_place_delete_buttons, 333);
        gd_place_delete_buttons();
    } catch(e) {
        gd_dumpErr(e);
    }
}

var s=window.document.location.search;
dump('Load gmail page: '+s+'\n');
if (s.match(/\bsearch=(inbox|query|cat|all|starred|sent)\b/)
||
    ( s.match(/view=cv/) && !s.match(/search=(trash|spam)/) )
) {
    dump('==== Apply Gmail Delete Button to: ====\n'+s+'\n');
    //put the main button in
    try{_gd_place_delete_buttons();}catch(e){dump(e.message);}

    //set events to try adding buttons when the user does
things
    //because gmail might create new places to need buttons.
    window.addEventListener('mouseup', _gd_button_event,
false);
    window.addEventListener('keyup', _gd_button_event, false);
}

})();
```

Again, without going into JavaScript too deeply, there are two things to note here. The first is how it draws a new button into the page. The second is that the script checks the language the interface is being displayed in and labels the button accordingly. Very pleasingly done.

GmailSecure

Mark Pilgrim's userscript, GmailSecure, found at `http://userscripts.org/scripts/show/1404` and in Listing 6-3, has a simple function: to force Gmail to use HTTPS instead of HTTP.

It is ridiculously simple, consisting simply of only one line of actual code (the rest, to the chagrin of those of us who print on dead trees, is simply the license under which the code is released, which has to be included). Here's the line. Brace yourself:

```
location.href = location.href.replace(/^http:/, 'https:');
```

Because Gmail works via either HTTP or HTTPS, all the userscript needs to do is make sure that every time a hyperlink starts with `http:` that part of the URL is replaced with `https:`.

Greasemonkey does this by invoking the `location.href.replace` function.

Listing 6-3: The Ludicrously Simple GmailSecure

```
// GMailSecure
// version 0.3 BETA!
// 2005-06-28
// Copyright (c) 2005, Mark Pilgrim
// Released under the GPL license
// http://www.gnu.org/copyleft/gpl.html
//
// ------------------------------------------------------------
---------
//
// This is a Greasemonkey user script.
//
// To install, you need Greasemonkey:
http://greasemonkey.mozdev.org/
// Then restart Firefox and revisit this script.
// Under Tools, there will be a new menu item to "Install User
Script".
// Accept the default configuration and install.
//
// To uninstall, go to Tools/Manage User Scripts,
// select "GMailSecure", and click Uninstall.
//
// ------------------------------------------------------------
---------
//
// ==UserScript==
// @name          GMailSecure
// @namespace
http://diveintomark.org/projects/greasemonkey/
// @description   force GMail to use secure connection
// @include       http://mail.google.com/*
// ==/UserScript==

/* BEGIN LICENSE BLOCK
```

Continued

Listing 6-3 *(continued)*

```
Copyright (C) 2005 Mark Pilgrim

This program is free software; you can redistribute it and/or
modify it under the terms of the GNU General Public License
as published by the Free Software Foundation; either version 2
of the License, or (at your option) any later version.

This program is distributed in the hope that it will be
useful,
but WITHOUT ANY WARRANTY; without even the implied warranty of
MERCHANTABILITY or FITNESS FOR A PARTICULAR PURPOSE.  See the
GNU General Public License for more details.

You can download a copy of the GNU General Public License at
http://diveintomark.org/projects/greasemonkey/COPYING
or get a free printed copy by writing to the Free Software
Foundation,
Inc., 51 Franklin Street, Fifth Floor, Boston, MA 02110-1301,
USA.
END LICENSE BLOCK */

location.href = location.href.replace(/^http:/, 'https:');

//
// ChangeLog
// 2005-07-08 - 0.3 - MAP - added license block
// 2005-06-28 - 0.2 - MAP - changed GMail URL
//
```

This idea, rewriting URLs, can be very powerfully used. With Mark Pilgrim's technique of using `location.href.replace`, you can do this by brute force. With the next example, "Mailto Compose in Gmail," you will see the more radical version of this.

MailtoComposeInGmail

Perhaps the biggest issue that hits Gmail users, if they start to use the application as their primary e-mail tool, is that `mailto:` links found within e-mails do not trigger Gmail, but rather cause your operating system to load up what it thinks is the default e-mail application. One moment of thoughtless clicking, and Outlook Express starts appearing all over the screen. Nausea and discomfort result.

Julien Couvreur's MailtoComposeInGmail userscript solves this issue. It applies itself to every site apart from Gmail, rewriting the `mailto:` links it finds into a link that opens the Gmail compose page, with the `to:` and `subject:` lines already filled in.

Listing 6-4 elucidates the userscript. Afterwards, you will see how it works.

Listing 6-4: MailtoComposeInGmail

```
// MailtoComposeInGMail
// version 0.1
// 2005-03-28
// Copyright (c) 2005, Julien Couvreur
// Released under the GPL license
// http://www.gnu.org/copyleft/gpl.html
// ----------------------------------------------------------
---------
//
// This is a Greasemonkey user script.
//
// To install, you need Greasemonkey:
http://greasemonkey.mozdev.org/
// Then restart Firefox and revisit this script.
// Under Tools, there will be a new menu item to "Install User
Script".
// Accept the default configuration and install.
//
// To uninstall, go to Tools/Manage User Scripts,
// select "Mailto Compose In GMail", and click Uninstall.
//
// Aaron Boodman also has a similar script, at:
//     http://youngpup.net/userscripts/gmailto.user.js
// In his approach, the links are re-written at the time that
you click
//     on them. One benefit is that the link still looks like
mailto:x
//     when you hover over it.
// ----------------------------------------------------------
---------
//
// WHAT IT DOES:
// After the page is loaded, look for "mailto:" links and
hooks their onclick
//  event to go to GMail's compose page, passing all the usual
parameters
//  (to, cc, subject, body,...).
```

Continued

Listing 6-4 *(continued)*

```
// ------------------------------------------------------------
---------
//
// ==UserScript==
// @name            Mailto Compose In GMail
// @namespace
http://blog.monstuff.com/archives/000238.html
// @description     Rewrites "mailto:" links to GMail compose
links
// @include         *
// @exclude         http://gmail.google.com
// ==/UserScript==

(function() {

    var processMailtoLinks = function() {
        var xpath = "//a[starts-with(@href,'mailto:')]";
        var res = document.evaluate(xpath, document, null,

XPathResult.UNORDERED_NODE_SNAPSHOT_TYPE, null);

        var linkIndex, mailtoLink;
        for (linkIndex = 0; linkIndex < res.snapshotLength;
linkIndex++) {
            mailtoLink = res.snapshotItem(linkIndex);
            //alert(mailtoLink.href);

            var m = mailtoLink.href;
            var matches =
m.match(/^mailto:([^\?]+)(\?([^?]*))?/);
            var emailTo, params, emailCC, emailSubject,
emailBody;

            emailTo = matches[1];
            //alert("Found to=" + emailTo);

            params = matches[3];
            if (params) {
                var splitQS = params.split('&');
                var paramIndex, param;

                for (paramIndex = 0; paramIndex <
splitQS.length; paramIndex++) {
                    param = splitQS[paramIndex];
                    nameValue = param.match(/([^=]+)=(.*)/);
```

```
                      if (nameValue && nameValue.length == 3) {
                        // depending on name, store value in a
pre-defined location
                        switch(nameValue[1]) {
                          case "to":
                            emailTo = emailTo + "%2C%20" +
nameValue[2];
                            break;
                          case "cc":
                            emailCC = nameValue[2];
                            //alert("Found CC=" +
emailCC);
                            break;
                          case "subject":
                            emailSubject = nameValue[2];
                            //alert("Found subject=" +
emailSubject);
                            break;
                          case "body":
                            emailBody = nameValue[2];
                            //alert("Found body=" +
emailBody);
                            break;
                        }
                      }
                    }
                  }

          mailtoLink.href =
"https://mail.google.com/mail?view=cm&tf=0" +
              (emailTo ? ("&to=" + emailTo) : "") +
              (emailCC ? ("&cc=" + emailCC) : "") +
              (emailSubject ? ("&su=" + emailSubject) : "")
+
              (emailBody ? ("&body=" + emailBody) : "");
          // mailtoLink.onclick = function() { location.href
= newUrl; return false; };
        }
    }

    window.addEventListener("load", processMailtoLinks,
false);

})();
```

Instead of rewriting the `mailto:` links directly, as Mark Pilgrim's script does to
make HTTP links into HTTPS, this script adds a JavaScript `onclick` function

to the link instead. When you click such a link, Firefox fires off the JavaScript function instead of following the link. The `onclick` function, in turn, opens the page in Gmail that allows a mail to be composed. Because `mailto:` links can contain the recipients, message subject, and body text, the userscript has to retrieve these and add them to the Gmail compose page. You already know that the compose mail URL can be built up in this way, so it's pretty easy to do that. Here's the code that does it:

```
mailtoLink.href = "https://mail.google.com/mail?view=cm&tf=0"
+
                (emailTo ? ("&to=" + emailTo) : "") +
                (emailCC ? ("&cc=" + emailCC) : "") +
                (emailSubject ? ("&su=" + emailSubject) : "")
+
                (emailBody ? ("&body=" + emailBody) : "");
            // mailtoLink.onclick = function() { location.href
= newUrl; return false; };
        }
```

When you run on a link that points to `mailto:ben.hammersley@gmail.com`, this will produce the URL `https://mail.google.com/mail?view=cm&tf=0?&to-ben@benhammersley.com`.

Perfect. Using this code, you can compose other messages. Perhaps you might like to use it to produce an "e-mail this to me" userscript, populating the message body with the contents of the page.

Other Userscripts

Greasemonkey continues to recruit happy developers, and the number of userscripts is ever increasing. Here are some more scripts that provide additional functionality to Gmail. More still can be found at `http://userscripts.org`.

As ever, of course, you must remember that Gmail's interface is an ever-changing mélange of weirdness, and these userscripts may well fade in and out of functionality. If one stops working, check its coder's website for updates.

Mark Read Button

Documentation: `http://userscripts.org/scripts/show/689`

Userscript: `http://userscripts.org/scripts/source/689.user.js`

Jim Lawton's userscript creates a button that, when mails are selected, allows them to be marked as read, en masse. Very useful in itself, it also provides the core code for acting on a large number of mails in one go: handy for your own scripts, perhaps.

Multiple Signatures

Documentation: `http://userscripts.org/scripts/show/1592`

Userscript: `http://userscripts.org/scripts/source/1592.user.js`

This is a very smart script indeed. Using the ability to change the `reply-to:` address within Gmail, it allows the user to change both their e-mail signature, their `reply-to:` address, and — brilliantly — Gmail's color scheme at the same time. This allows you to use Gmail for multiple mail accounts without getting them mixed up in the heat and fury of a working day. Very clever.

Hide Invites

Documentation: `http://userscripts.org/scripts/show/673`

Userscript: `http://userscripts.org/scripts/source/673.user.js`

A very simple use of Greasemonkey. This userscript simply hides the box that holds the facility to send Gmail invitations to your friends. As you have already looked at the way Gmail is constructed, you can modify this userscript yourself to stop the display of any section of the interface.

Random Signatures

Documentation: `http://userscripts.org/scripts/show/1704`

Userscript: `http://userscripts.org/scripts/source/1704.user.js`

Robson Braga Araujo's userscript adds a random tagline to the bottom of your Gmail signature and also creates an option in the Settings menu to edit the taglines and control how the userscript operates.

And Now . . .

In this chapter, you saw that Gmail's interface and workings are even more customizable than you might have first thought. By using Greasemonkey, you can seriously improve the Gmail experience. And by looking at the way the scripts work, you can learn how to write your own.

Gmail Libraries

In the previous chapters, you discovered how Gmail works: how it loads into your browser, and how it handles your mail through a series of JavaScript tricks and the passing of data in the background. You can use this newfound knowledge to take control of the application from within your own programs.

To do that, you need to use a *library*—a piece of code that encapsulates the nitty gritty of the interaction between your program and Gmail itself in such a way that it makes writing that program very easy. Instead of, for example, having to write code that requests the Inbox's JavaScript array, parses it, finds the message identity, requests the thread, parses that, and finally displays it on the screen, you can simply run the function to download the next unread mail.

This approach, of wrapping complex activities up into their own simpler-to-use functions, is one of the bases of software engineering, so it's not surprising that there are already many such modules for Gmail. This chapter examines examples for PHP, Perl, and Python.

Warning

As with all of the code in this book, these libraries are dependent on Gmail's code standing still for a while. Google, on the other hand, likes to keep improving things. You may find that the APIs don't quite work when you try them. Usually this is because Google has changed the login procedure to Gmail, or something simple like that. Give it a few days, and you will probably find that the API's authors or user community has hacked up a run-around.

PHP — Gmailer

Yin Hung Gan's Gmailer library is the obvious choice for PHP coders. Gan wrote it so that he could build a simplified interface for Gmail, and check his mail from his PDA. It is really two projects: the Gmailer library and Gmail-Lite, which uses the library to give Gan his simple HTML interface.

Getting and Installing the Library

Gmailer can be downloaded from `http://gmail-lite.sourceforge.net/`. At the time of this writing, Gmailer is at version 0.6.9a. The Gmailer homepage looks like Figure 7-1.

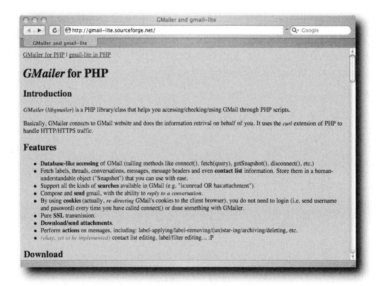

FIGURE 7-1: The Gmailer homepage

Once downloaded, you need only unpack it into the directory your script will run in. You will also need cURL, from `http://curl.haxx.se/`, and the OpenSSL package from `www.openssl.org/`, but it is very likely that you will already have those installed as a matter of course. If not, follow the instructions on their websites to download and install them properly. To save time, worry about those only if any error messages tell you to.

How to Use It

Gmailer provides a series of methods that can be used to log in to Gmail and perform the usual functions. Table 7-1 gives the complete rundown of the methods.

Table 7-1   Gmailer's Methods

Method	Function
void setSessionMethod (GM_CONSTANT method) [0.6.4]	To set the session handling method before connect. If you want PHP to handle it with cookies, set it to GM_USE_PHPSESSION| GM_USE_COOKIE; if you want PHP to handle it but without using cookies, set it to !GM_USE_COOKIE|GM_USE_ PHPSESSION; if you do not want PHP to handle it, set it to GM_USE_COOKIE| !GM_USE_PHPSESSION. It will set to GM_USE_PHPSESSION|GM_USE_COOKIE by default.
void setLoginInfo string name, string password, int GMT_timezone)	To set the login information before connect.
void setProxy(string hostname, string username, string password) [0.6.4]	To set the proxy information if necessary. If your proxy server does not require login, set both username and password to ""
bool connect()	To connect to Gmail. It will use header() to set cookies at the client-side browser. So you shouldn't output anything before calling this method, or use connectNoCookie() otherwise. It returns 1 if it succeeds, 0 otherwise.
bool connectNoCookie()	To connect to Gmail without storing any cookies at the client-side browser. It returns 1 if it succeeds, 0 otherwise.
bool isConnected()	To check if connected.
bool fetch(string query)	To fetch the URL query result from Gmail. It is intended to be used internally (private method). Use fetchBox() instead.
bool fetchBox GM_CONSTANT type, string box, int position)	To fetch a result from Gmail by given: type: Gmailer constant, such as GM_LABEL. box: name of box (such as Inbox, your_label) position: cursor for paged result.
bool fetchContact()	To fetch the contact list.

Continued

Table 7-1 *(continued)*

Method	Function
`GMailSnapshot get Snapshot(GM_CONSTANT type)`	To get a snapshot, an object (see GMailSnapshot below) for you to access the query result at ease.
`bool getAttachment (string attachment_id, string message_id, string filename)`	To download an attachment of a message.
`array getAttachmentsOf (array GMailSnapshot-> conv, string path_to_ store_files)`	To download all files attached to a conversation. The full path of downloaded files will be returned (as array).
`bool send(string to, string subject, string body, string cc, string bcc, string message_replying, string thread_replying, array attachments)`	To send Gmail. `to`, `cc`, and `bcc` are comma-separated addresses. `attachments` is an array of names of files to be attached.
`bool performAction (GM_CONSTANT action_ type, array message_id, string label)`	To perform an action on a message. `message_id` can be a string if only one message is to be acted.
`void disconnect()`	To disconnect from Gmail. Any cookies set at the client-side browser by `libgmailer` will be removed.
`string dump(string query)`	To dump all it gets from the *URL query* string, including headers.
`array getStandardBox()`	To get an array of names of the standard box (Inbox, Starred, and so on).

Logging in with Gmailer

Logging into Gmail with the Gmailer library is very simple. First you point your script to the library itself:

```
require("libgmailer.php");
```

Then you invoke the new Gmailer object:

```
$gm = new GMailer();
```

Then you set the `setLoginInfo` method, giving the username, password, and time zone from GMT:

```
$gm->setLoginInfo($name, $pwd, $tz);
```

Finally, you tell Gmailer to connect:

```
$gm->connect();
```

You need to use `setLoginInfo` only once — Gmailer saves your Gmail cookies, so once you've logged in, you only need to use the `connect()` method to pass more commands.

Putting that all together, then, you arrive at Listing 7-1, which gets you logged in to Gmail, ready for some more code.

Listing 7-1: Logging in to Gmail with PHP

```php
<?php

require("libgmailer.php");

$gm = new GMailer();
$name = "username";
$pwd = "password";
$tz = "0";
$gm->setLoginInfo($name, $pwd, $tz);

    if ($gm->connect()) {

        /** THE REST OF YOUR CODE GOES IN HERE **/

    }

$gm->disconnect();

?>
```

The `disconnect()` method logs you out again.

Retrieving the Inbox

Once you are logged in, retrieving a thread is simple and is a good example to show the deeper functions available from the Gmailer library.

Assuming you're logged in, request the Inbox like so:

```
$gm->fetchBox(GM_STANDARD, Inbox, 0);
```

Then parse it into an object called a `Snapshot`, like so:

```
$snapshot = $gm->getSnapshot(GM_STANDARD);
```

Once you have the Inbox loaded into a `Snapshot`, you can query that `Snapshot` and get all of the information out of it. You'll have noticed, however, two things not yet covered: the phrase `GM_STANDARD` and the properties that `Snapshots` themselves have.

The Constants

`GM_STANDARD` is a *constant*. Gmailer has 20 constants available, each representing a different feature of the Gmail system: the Inbox, the Labels, the Contacts, and so on. To work with Gmail, you need to use a method to retrieve one of the constants, and then you create a `Snapshot` of it, and finally query that `Snapshot`. This two-stage process is really all there is to the Gmailer library, so once you understand it, you are good to go.

Table 7-2 gives the constants available to the programmer.

Table 7-2   Gmailer's Constants

Constant	Description
GM_STANDARD	All the information about a standard box (Inbox, Sent, All, Starred, Spam, Trash).
GM_LABEL	All the information about the labels.
GM_CONVERSATION	All the information about a particular conversation.
GM_QUERY	All about a search query.
GM_CONTACT	All about the contact list.
GM_ACT_APPLYLABEL GM_ACT_REMOVELABEL	Apply or remove label from message.
GM_ACT_STAR GM_ACT_UNSTAR	Star or unstar a message.
GM_ACT_SPAM GM_ACT_UNSPAM	Mark or unmark a message as spam.
GM_ACT_READ GM_ACT_UNREAD	Mark a message as read or unread.
GM_ACT_ARCHIVE GM_ACT_INBOX	Move a message away from or to the Inbox.

Constant	Description
GM_ACT_TRASH GM_ACT_UNTRASH	Move message to or away from the Trash.
GM_ACT_DELFOREVER	Delete message forever.
GM_USE_PHPSESSION [0.6.4]	Use PHP session to handle Gmail-lite session.
GM_USE_COOKIE [0.6.4]	Use cookie to handle Gmail-lite session.

Table 7-3 gives special properties available for each constant's Snapshot.

Table 7-3   The Data Available via a Snapshot

Properties available to all Snapshot types except GM_CONTACT

Property	Description
gmail_ver	Version of Gmail JavaScript core program.
quota_mb	Mailbox quota in MB.
quota_per	Mailbox quota in percentage.
std_box_new	*Number-indexed array.* Number of unread mails in each standard box. You may call GMailer::getStandardBox() to get an array of names of standard boxes.
have_invit	Number of invites you have. 0 = no invitation, and so forth.
label_list	*Number-indexed array.* An array of label names.
label_new	*Number-indexed array.* Number of unread mails in each label. (A 1-to-1 mapping of label_list.)

Properties available to Snapshot types GM_STANDARD, GM_LABEL, and GM_QUERY

Property	Description
box_name	Name of the standard box or label, or query string currently viewing.
box_total	Total number of conversations in current mailbox.
box_pos	Current starting position (for paged results).
	Number-indexed array. An array of conversations in the current mailbox. Each conversation is a *text-indexed array* of the following:

Continued

Table 7-3 *(continued)*

	Index	Description
	Id	Conversation ID.
	is_read	0 = read; 1 = not read yet.
	is_starred	0 = not starred; 1 = starred.
	Date	Arrival date/time of the most recent message.
	sender	Senders of message in this conversation.
	Flag	Flag.
	Subj	Subject of this conversation.
	snippet	Snippet, or preview, of this conversation.
	Labels	*Number-indexed array*. Name of labels that this conversation is bearing.
	attachment	*Number-indexed array*. Name of all attaching files of this conversation.
	Msgid	Message ID of the most recently received message of this conversation.

For example, in order to get the subject of the sixth conversation of the current viewing box you write $snapshot->box[5]["subj"].

Properties available to Snapshot type GM_CONVERSATION

Property	Description
conv_title	Subject (title) of this conversation.
conv_total	Total number of messages in this conversation.
conv_id	Conversation ID.
conv_labels	*Number-indexed array*. Name of labels that this conversation is bearing.
conv_starred [0.6.4]	Is the conversation starred? This is true if any of the messages of a conversation are starred.

Number-indexed array. An array of messages of the current conversation. Each message is a *text-indexed array* of the following:

Index	Description
index	Index.
id	Message ID.
sender	Name of sender of this message.
sender_email	E-mail address of the sender.
recv	Name of receiver of this message.

Index	Description
`recv_email`	E-mail address of the receiver.
`reply_email`	Replying address of this message.
`dt_easy`	Arrival date/time of this message in easy format, such as 9 Aug (2 days ago).
`dt`	Arrival date/time of this message in long format, such as Mon, 9 Aug 2004 19:34:03 +0800.
`subj`	Subject of this message.
`is_starred` `[0.6.4]`	Is the message starred?
`snippet`	Snippet, or preview, of this message.
`body`	Message body.
`attachment`	Number-indexed array. An array of attachment information, which is a text-indexed array of the following:

	Index	Description
	`id`	Attachment ID.
	`filename`	Filename of this attaching file.
	`type`	File type (such as JPG, GIF, PDF) of this attaching file.
	`size`	Size in bytes of this file.

Example: `$snapshot->conv[3]["attachment"][1]["size"]` (size of the 2nd attaching file of the 4th messages of current conversation)

Properties available to Snapshot type GM_CONTACT

Property	Description
`contacts_all`	*Number-indexed array*. Array of *entries* (see the table that follows) of your All address book.
`contacts_freq`	*Number-indexed array*. Array of *entries* of your frequently mailed address book:

	Index	Description.
	`name`	Name (nickname).
	`email`	E-mail address.
	`notes`	Notes.
	`is_freq`	0 = not frequently mailed; 1 = frequently mailed.

Once you've requested the Inbox and created a Snapshot, you can query that Snapshot for details. To print out the number of threads within the Inbox, you can say this:

```
echo "Threads in the inbox:" . $snapshot->box_total;
```

In order to get the Thread ID of the first thread in the Inbox, you can do this:

```
$threaded    = $snapshot->box[0]["id"];
```

As you can see from the code and the preceding tables, it's really quite a straightforward interface. You'll be using the interface in later chapters, but to finish, Listing 7-2 shows PHP code using the Gmailer library to log in and display the contents of the first message in the first thread in the Inbox.

Listing 7-2: Reading the First Message in the Inbox

```php
<?php

require("libgmailer.php");

$gm = new GMailer();
$name = "username";
$pwd = "password";
$tz = "0";
$gm->setLoginInfo($name, $pwd, $tz);

    if ($gm->connect()) {

        $gm->fetchBox(GM_STANDARD, Inbox, 0);
        $snapshot = $gm->getSnapshot(GM_STANDARD);

        $threaded    = $snapshot->box[0]["id"];

        $gm->fetchBox(GM_CONVERSATION, $threaded, 0);
        $snapshot = $gm->getSnapshot(GM_CONVERSATION);

        echo "The first message reads" . $snapshot-
>conv[0]["body"];

    }

$gm->disconnect();


?>
```

You return to this library in later chapters.

Perl — Mail::Webmail::Gmail

CPAN, the directory of Perl modules, lists quite a few Gmail-related modules, one of which is shown in Figure 7-2. But at time of this writing, the only one working is Allen Holman's Mail::Webmail::Gmail.

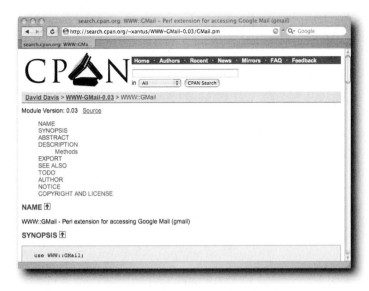

FIGURE 7-2: A CPAN search resulting in a Gmail module

Getting and Installing the Library

Mail::Webmail::Gmail is available from CPAN. You can download it directly from http://search.cpan.org/~mincus/ or use the command line like this:

```
sudo perl -MCPAN -e 'install Mail::Webmail::Gmail'
```

However installed, the module has a few dependencies that you will need to have installed already:

- LWP::UserAgent
- HTTP::Headers
- HTTP::Cookies
- HTTP::Request::Common
- Crypt::SSLeay
- Exporter

Using the Library

The Mail::Webmail::Gmail module is remarkably simple to use and very thorough. You'll be using it extensively in the next few chapters, so here we shall just summarize the options.

Logging In

The standard call for logging into Gmail session is:

```
my $gmail = Mail::Webmail::Gmail->new(username => 'username',
password => 'password', );
```

That call can also take some optional arguments. If given the details, you can use a proxy server, and you can also encrypt the entire session as opposed to just the login sequence. Call them all like so:

```
my $gmail = Mail::Webmail::Gmail->new(
username => 'username',
password => 'password',
proxy_username => 'proxy_username',
proxy_password => 'proxy_password',
proxy_name => 'proxy_server',
encrypt_session => 1
);
```

Once logged in, you can make requests for data and pass methods on the Gmail Inbox. There are lots of methods that you can use.

The Other Functions

This chapter provides only a table of the available functions (see Table 7-4). They are more fully explained as you use them in the rest of the book.

Table 7-4   The Functions Within Mail::Gmail::Webmail

Function	What It Does
get_labels()	Retrieves an array of the labels in the account.
edit_labels (label=> 'label_name', action => 'create');	Creates the label 'label name'.
edit_labels(label => 'label_name', action => 'rename', new_name => 'renamed_label');	Renames the label 'label_name' to 'renamed_label'.

Function	What It Does

`edit_labels( label =>`
`'label_name', action =>`
`'delete' );`
	Deletes the label `'label_name'`.

`edit_labels( label =>`
`'label_name', action =>`
`'add', msgid =>`
`$message_id );`
	Adds a label to a message.

`$gmail->edit_labels`
`( label => 'label_name',`
`action => 'remove',`
`msgid => $message_id );`
	Removes a label from a message.

`update_prefs`
`( indicators => 0,`
`reply_to =>`
`'test@test.com' );`
	Sets preferences inside Gmail. The available options are:
	`keyboard_shortcuts = ( 0, 1 )`
	`indicators = ( 0, 1 )`
	`snippets = ( 0, 1 )`
	`max_page_size = ( 25, 50, 100 )`
	`display_name = ( '', string value up to 96`
	`characters )`
	`reply_to = ( '', string value up to 320`
	`characters )`
	`signature = ( '', string value up to 1000`
	`characters )`

`edit_star( action =>`
`'add', 'msgid' =>`
`$msgid );`
	Stars a message.

`edit_star( action =>`
`'remove', 'msgid' =>`
`$msgid );`
	Unstars the message.

`edit_archive( action =>`
`'archive', 'msgid' =>`
`$msgid );`
	Archives the message.

`edit_archive( action =>`
`'unarchive', 'msgid' =>`
`$msgid );`
	Unarchives the message.

Continued

Table 7-4 *(continued)*

Function	What It Does
`$gmail->get_messages ( label => 'work' );`	Retrieves a reference to an array of hashes for the messages within the stated label. Or you can use the Gmail standard folder names 'INBOX', 'STARRED', 'SPAM', or 'TRASH' get_messages(label => $Mail::Webmail::Gmail::FOLDERS{ 'INBOX' }); The array of hashes looks like this: `$indv_email{ 'id' }` `$indv_email{ 'new' }` `$indv_email{ 'starred' }` `$indv_email{ 'date_received' }` `$indv_email{ 'sender_email' }` `$indv_email{ 'subject' }` `$indv_email{ 'blurb' }` `@{ $indv_email{ 'labels' } }` `@{ $indv_email{ 'attachments' } }`
`size_usage();`	Returns a scalar value with the amount of megabytes remaining to use.
`get_indv_email( id => $msgid)`	Retrieves a hash of hashes containing an individual message in this format: `$indv_email{ 'id' }` `$indv_email{ 'sender_email' }` `$indv_email{ 'sent' }` `$indv_email{ 'to' }` `$indv_email{ 'read' }` `$indv_email{ 'subject' }` `@{ $indv_email{ 'attachments' } }`
`get_mime_email( msg => $msgid )`	Retrieves the message as a string, in MIME format.
`get_contacts();`	Retrieves an array of hashes containing the Gmail address book. The array of hashes is in the following format: `$indv_contact{ 'id' }` `$indv_contact{ 'name1' }` `$indv_contact{ 'name2' }` `$indv_contact{ 'email' }` `$indv_contact{ 'note' }`

Function	What It Does
send_message(to => 'user@domain.com', subject => 'Test Message',	Sends a message to a single recipient. To send to multiple users, send an arrayref containing all of the users: msgbody => 'This is a test.'); my $email_addrs = ['user1@domain.com', 'user2@domain.com', 'user3@domain.com',]; $gmail->send_message(to => $email_addrs, subject => 'Test Message', msgbody => 'This is a test.');
send_message(to => 'user@domain.com', subject => 'Test Message', msgbody => 'This is a test.', file0 => ["/tmp/ foo"], file1 => ["/tmp/ bar"]);	Sends a message with an attachment.
delete_message (msgid => $msgid, del_ message => 0);	Sends a message to the Trash.
delete_message(msgid => $msgid);	Permanently deletes the message.

The rest of this module is covered in Chapter 8 onwards.

Python—Libgmail

The trifecta of scripting languages beginning with P ends with ython, and is completed by Libgmail, the Python bindings for Gmail access.

Getting and Installing the Library

Libgmail is hosted on Sourceforge at http://Libgmail.sourceforge.net/ and can be downloaded directly from there. The authors of Libgmail advise using the version from CVS if possible, as it is more likely to work with whatever changes Google has made to the service lately. Figure 7-3 gives the traditional screenshot of the project's homepage.

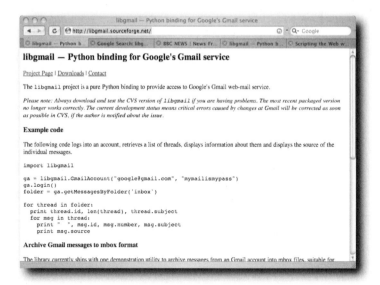

FIGURE 7-3: Python's Libgmail binding

You should follow the instructions on their website to install the latest version. As mentioned before, if Libgmail stops working, it may just be a matter of time before a new version restores functionality.

How to Use It

Libgmail comes with some sample code, but no real documentation at the moment. There are currently 15 methods available, which offer the vast majority of the functionality that Gmail can give. Start by logging in.

login

To log in, import the Libgmail bindings, create a new `GmailAccount` object, and use the `login` method on it, like so:

```
import Libgmail

ga = Libgmail.GmailAccount("google@gmail.com",
"mymailismypass")
ga.login()
```

Now that you're logged in, you want to retrieve the messages from a folder.

getMessagesByFolder

The `getMessagesByFolder` method takes the name of the folder, and an optional True/False flag to indicate selecting every page of that folder's listing. (Remember that these libraries interact with Gmail by scraping the pages it returns, effectively, so you still have to consider the information as it is meant for the real Gmail interface, not just yours).

Leaving the flag off sets it to the default `False`. To place the details of the Inbox into an object called `folder`, you do the following:

```
folder= ga.getMessagesByFolder('inbox')
```

This returns a `GmailSearchResult` instance that you can query.

getMessageByLabel

The `getMessageByLabel` method works in exactly the same way as `getMessagesByFolder` but replaces the folder with a label. It returns a `GmailSearchResult` instance, which is examined in two paragraphs' time.

getMessagesByQuery

The `getMessagesByQuery` method works in exactly the same way as `getMessagesByFolder` but does so with a search query instead of the name of the mailbox. For example:

```
messages = ga.getMessagesByQuery('ransom  note')
```

This query will also return a `GmailSearchResult` instance.

All this talk of `GmailSearchResult` instances begs the question: What exactly is a `GmailSearchResult` instance? A `GmailSearchResult` instance is a *thread* object. This contains details of the thread, plus one or more `msg` objects, corresponding to the messages within. These can be queried like so:

```
for thread in folder:
  print thread.id              # the id of the thread
  print len(thread)            # the number of messages
  print thread.subject         # the subject of the thread
  for msg in thread:
    print msg.id               # the id of the message
    print msg.number           # the number within the thread
    print msg.subject          # the message subject
    print msg.source           # the raw source of the message
```

Keeping Your Powder Dry

The remaining methods—`sendMessage`, `trashMessage`, `trashThread`, `getLabelNames`, `createLabel`, `deleteLabel`, `renameLabel`, and `storeFile`—are, apart from being self-explanatorily named, covered in great detail in the remainder of this book.

---

getQuotaInfo

The `getQuotaInfo` method allows you to retrieve information on how much storage you are taking up inside Gmail. It returns an array of megabytes used, total megabytes available, and percentage of storage used.

getUnreadMsgCount

When invoked, the `getUnreadMsgCount` method returns an integer equal to the number of unread messages within the Inbox:

```
new_messages = ga.getUnreadMsgCount()
```

Reading the First Message in the Inbox

Putting together the methods discussed so far, you can display the messages in the Inbox, and information about the amount of storage you have left, with the code in Listing 7-3.

Listing 7-3: Using Python to Display the First Message in the Inbox

```
#!/usr/bin/python2.3

import Libgmail

ga = Libgmail.GmailAccount("google@gmail.com",
"mymailismypass")
ga.login()
folder = ga.getMessagesByFolder('inbox')

for thread in folder:
  print thread.id, len(thread), thread.subject
  for msg in thread:
    print "Message ID:", msg.id
    print "Message Number:", msg.number
    print "Message Subject:", msg.subject
    print msg.source
```

```
quotaInfo = ga.getQuotaInfo()
quotaMbUsed = quotaInfo[QU_SPACEUSED]
quotaMbTotal = quotaInfo[QU_QUOTA]
quotaPercent = quotaInfo[QU_PERCENT]
print "%s of %s used. (%s)\n" % (quotaMbUsed, quotaMbTotal,
quotaPercent)
```

Setting Yourselves Up for the Remaining Chapters

To aid you in your coding over the next few chapters, you shall also need a small Perl module of your own, which tidies up the boring things such as logging in. Listing 7-4 gives the script Utils.pm, which you should place within the directory in which you wish to work. You will need to place your own username and password in the place indicated.

Listing 7-4: Utils.pm

```perl
package Utils;

require Mail::Webmail::Gmail;

require Exporter;
@ISA    = qw(Exporter);
@EXPORT = qw(login strip_bold);

sub login {
    return Mail::Webmail::Gmail->new(
        username => "USERNAME",
        password => "PASSWORD"
    );
}

# get rid of <b> and </b> in subjects
sub strip_bold {
    my $str = shift;
    $str =~ s/<b>(.*)<\/b>/$1/;
    return $str;
}

1;
```

You will also need the following Perl modules installed:

- libwww-perl: `http://search.cpan.org/~gaas/libwww-perl-5.803/`
- MIME-Base64: `http://search.cpan.org/~gaas/MIME-Base64-3.05/`
- MIME-tools: `http://search.cpan.org/~dskoll/MIME-tools-5.417/`
- MailFolder: `http://search.cpan.org/~kjohnson/MailFolder-0.07/`
- MD5: `http://search.cpan.org/~gaas/MD5-2.03/`

And Now . . .

In this chapter, you worked through a quick overview of the most popular Gmail libraries available for the most popular scripting languages. As you have seen, the libraries are at varying stages of completeness and simplicity but are nevertheless extremely useful.

In the next few chapters, you will use the Perl library to perform the basic Gmail functions and start to produce Gmail-based applications of your own.

Checking for Mail

Now that you've been introduced to the Gmail libraries, you can them to use with a simple script to tell you when you have new mail. In this chapter, you go through the first stage of this code in all of the languages and then build on it in Perl to make a standalone application.

Warning As previously discussed, the APIs upon which this code is based may cease to work every so often, as Google changes the way that Gmail operates. If that's the case, your knowledge gained in Chapter 5 should help you help the API's author to fix things.

The Basics in Perl

Using the Mail::Webmail::Gmail module to check for mail is simplicity itself. You need to set up the modules and then log in:

```
use Mail::Webmail::Gmail;

my $gmail = Mail::Webmail::Gmail->new(
    username => "ben.hammersley\@gmail.com",
    password => "XXXXXXXX",
);
```

After that, retrieve the Inbox and step through the list of messages in it. Within the Perl library, using the `get_messages` method gives you an array of hashes, with the value of `'new'` being the read/unread flag. So all you need to do is count the number of messages with a true value in that reference, like so:

in this chapter

☑ Checking for new mail with Perl, PHP, and Python

☑ Instant Messenger alerts

☑ Alerts to your mobile phone

```perl
my $new_msgs = 0;

if ( defined($messages) ) {
    foreach ( @{$messages} ) {
        if ( $_->{'new'} ) {
                $new_msgs++;
        }
    }
}
```

This leaves you with the variable `$new_msgs` to give you the number of unread messages in the Inbox. Listing 8-1 gives an entire working script to display this.

Listing 8-1: Checking the New Mail Count in Perl

```perl
#!/usr/bin/perl

use warnings;
use strict;
use Mail::Webmail::Gmail;

my $gmail = Mail::Webmail::Gmail->new(
    username => "ben.hammersley\@gmail.com",
    password => "XXXXXXXX",
);

my $messages =
  $gmail->get_messages( label =>
$Mail::Webmail::Gmail::FOLDERS{'INBOX'} );

my $new_msgs = 0;

if ( defined($messages) ) {
    foreach ( @{$messages} ) {
        if ( $_->{'new'} ) {
                $new_msgs++;
        }
    }
}

print "you have $new_msgs new messages in your inbox\n";
```

Obviously, from here you can build out to produce all sorts of interesting alerts, as you shall do later on in this chapter.

An alternative and easier way of doing this can be found in Listing 8-2.

Listing 8-2: An Even Easier Way to Check Mail

```
use Utils;

$gmail = login();

$messages = $gmail->get_messages();      # simply get all
messages
$count    = 0;
foreach ( @{$messages} ) {               # and iterate through
them
    if ( $_->{"new"} ) {                 # if message is new
        $count++;
    }
}
print "Number of unread messages: " . $count . "\n";
```

This uses the Utils module you created in Chapter 7 — Listing 7-4 to be precise. That module encapsulates the login process into one simple `login()` function, allowing the script to be even simpler than before.

The Basics in PHP

PHP, too, provides a simple interface to check for new mail in Gmail. The libgmailler library, as you saw in Chapter 6, handles it perfectly well. First, you need to log in:

```
$gm->setLoginInfo($name, $pwd, $tz);

if ($gm->connect()) {
```

Then you fetch the Inbox and create the `Snapshot` object:

```
$gm->fetchBox(GM_STANDARD, "Inbox", 0);

$snapshot = $gm->getSnapshot(GM_STANDARD);
```

After that, loop through all of the messages in the Inbox, incrementing a variable by one for every unread mail you see:

```
if ($snapshot) {
    for ($i = 0;$i < $snapshot->box_total ; $i++ )
        {
    if ($snapshot->box[$i]["is_read"] == 1)
        { $new++;
                        }

        }
```

Listing 8-3 gives you a complete script, printing to the screen a count of the new mail in your account.

Listing 8-3: Checking for New Mail in PHP

```PHP
<?PHP

require("libgmailer.php");
$gm = new GMailer();

$name = "USERNAME";
$pwd  = "PASSWORD";
$tz   = "0";
$new  = 0;

$gm->setLoginInfo($name, $pwd, $tz);

if ($gm->connect()) {

    $gm->fetchBox(GM_STANDARD, "Inbox", 0);

    $snapshot = $gm->getSnapshot(GM_STANDARD);

if ($snapshot) {
    for ($i = 0;$i < $snapshot->box_total ; $i++ )
        {
    if ($snapshot->box[$i]["is_read"] == 1)
        { $new++;
                        }
            }

echo "You have". $new . "new messages";

}
}
?>
```

The Basics in Python

Python's libgmail provides the simplest method to get a new mail count: There's a specific function that you can use.

So, as usual, you first need to log in and check for errors there:

```
ga = libgmail.GmailAccount(username, password)
try:
    ga.login()
except:
    new_messages =  "login failed"
```

Then run the `getUnreadMsgCount` function:

```
else:
    new_messages = ga.getUnreadMsgCount()
```

Take the result of that function and display it. Listing 8-4 gives a complete script to do this and gives grammatically correct display as well.

Listing 8-4: Checking for New Mail in Python

```
#!/usr/bin/env python

import libgmail

username = "user"
password = "pass"

ga = libgmail.GmailAccount(username, password)
try:
    ga.login()
except:
    new_messages =  "login failed"
else:
    new_messages = ga.getUnreadMsgCount()

if new_messages == "login failed":
    print "Login "

elif int(new_messages) == 0:
    print "You have no new messages"

elif int(new_messages) == 1:
    print "You have 1 new message."

else:
    print "You have " + new_messages + " new messages."
```

Building on the Basics

Now that you have seen the basics for retrieving the number of unread messages, you can look at new and interesting ways of displaying that number. You saw desktop applications that do this in Chapter 2, so this section concentrates on the more unusual ways of seeing the number.

New Mail Count in RSS

It's a fair bet that the majority of the readers of a book like this one will also be heavy users of RSS. The XML-based family of syndication technologies is now very popular indeed, and presents a lot of opportunities for keeping track of many different types of information. I personally use the following technique to keep tabs on Gmail accounts that I use on an infrequent basis: for accounts where checking them manually is too much bother but where a desktop alert is too intrusive.

Start off, in the normal way, by loading the core Perl modules. In this case, you will need Mail::Webmaiil::Gmail, as ever, and the commonly used XML::RSS module to help produce the RSS feed, and the ubiquitous CGI module to deal with the incoming parameters and the correct serving of the feed. XML::RSS is a little out of the scope of this book, and is nevertheless very simple to understand from its own documentation.

Then take the username and password from parameters in the URL, and set up the WWW::Gmail object like so:

```
use CGI qw(standard);

use Mail::Webmail::Gmail;

my $username = param("username");
my $password  = param("password");


my $gmail = Mail::Webmail::Gmail->new(
    username => $username,
    password => $password,
);
```

And then it's the usual matter of downloading the Inbox and counting the unread messages:

```perl
my $messages =
  $gmail->get_messages( label =>
$Mail::Webmail::Gmail::FOLDERS{'INBOX'} );

my $new_msgs = 0;

if ( defined($messages) ) {
    foreach ( @{$messages} ) {
        if ( $_->{'new'} ) {
                $new_msgs++;
        }
    }
}
```

Once you have the unread message count, you need to use the XML::RSS module to produce the feed. Listing 8-5 gives the entire script an airing and shows how this works.

Listing 8-5: Producing a New Mail Count in an RSS Feed

```perl
#!/usr/bin/perl -w
use strict;
use XML::RSS;


use CGI qw(standard);

use Mail::Webmail::Gmail;

my $username = param("username");
my $password    = param("password");


my $gmail = Mail::Webmail::Gmail->new(
    username => $username,
    password => $password,
);

my $messages =
  $gmail->get_messages( label =>
$Mail::Webmail::Gmail::FOLDERS{'INBOX'} );

my $new_msgs = 0;

if ( defined($messages) ) {
    foreach ( @{$messages} ) {
        if ( $_->{'new'} ) {
```

```
                    $new_msgs++;
        }
    }
}

my $rss = new XML::RSS (version => '0.91');

$rss->channel(  title  => "Unread mail count for $username",
                link => "http://gmail.google.com/",
                description => "The unread mail count for
$username",
                   language => "en",
                );

 $rss->add_item(
                title   => "You have $new_msgs messages"),
                link    => "http://gmail.google.com"),
                );

print header('application/xml+rss'), $rss->as_string;
```

Installing this script on a web server and pointing your newsreader at the URL produces a single-item RSS feed showing the number of unread messages in your Inbox. It's simple and unobtrusive in that way. The URL should be structured like so:

```
http://www.example.com/gmail2rss.cgi?username=USERNAME&password=
PASSWORD
```

You build upon this script in later chapters.

New Mail Count to AOL Instant Messenger

As well as an RSS reader, you might also have an AOL Instant Messenger (AIM) application running. In this section, you build two ways of receiving new mail notification via AIM. The first is by using a script very similar to that in Listing 8-4. This one checks for mail, logs in to AIM, and sends you a message with the number. You just need to set the script to run on a schedule, and it keeps you up to date in a relatively painless way.

To do this, you first log in and check for new mail, as per the preceding scripts, and then use the Net::AOLIM module to send the message. Like so:

```
my $aim_user = "";
my $aim_password = "";
my $aim_destuser = "";
```

```perl
my $message = "Your Gmail inbox, $username, has a new message
count of $new_msg";

$aim = Net::AOLIM->new('username' => $aim_user,
                       'password' => $aim_password,
                       );

$aim->signon or die "Cannot sign on to AIM";
$aim->toc_send_im($aim_destuser, $message);
```

Listing 8-6 shows the entire code for this script.

```perl
#!/usr/bin/perl -w
use strict;
use XML::RSS;


use CGI qw(standard);

use Mail::Webmail::Gmail;
use Net::AOLIM;

my $username = param("username");
my $password  = param("password");


my $gmail = Mail::Webmail::Gmail->new(
    username => $username,
    password => $password,
);

my $messages =
  $gmail->get_messages( label =>
$Mail::Webmail::Gmail::FOLDERS{'INBOX'} );

my $new_msgs = 0;

if ( defined($messages) ) {
    foreach ( @{$messages} ) {
        if ( $_->{'new'} ) {
                $new_msgs++;
        }
    }
}
```

```
my $aim_user = "";
my $aim_password = "";
my $aim_destuser = "";

my $message = "Your Gmail inbox, $username, has a new message
count of $new_msg";

$aim = Net::AOLIM->new('username' => $aim_user,
                       'password' => $aim_password,
                       );

$aim->signon or die "Cannot sign on to AIM";
$aim->toc_send_im($aim_destuser, $message);
```

To use this script, place your Gmail and AIM username and passwords in the variables at the top. (You will need a separate AIM account for the script itself, which you can sign up for at www.aol.com) and then use cron to schedule it to run at the desired interval.

A good introduction to cron can be found at www.unixgeeks.org/security/newbie/unix/cron-1.html, but I set mine for this script to the following:

```
1 * * * *  /usr/bin/perl ~/code/gmail2AIM.pl
```

The preceding code should give you an idea of how you should set up cron.

The second and perhaps more fun way of sending Gmail new mail counts over AIM is to create an AIM bot. This is a script that logs in as an AIM user and replies when you "talk" to it. In this case, it's not going to be particularly clever in what it says — it will merely reply with the latest count.

To create a bot, start off by logging in to AIM as you did before and then permitting anyone to send you a message:

```
$aim = Net::AOLIM->new("username" => $aim_user,
                       "password" => $aim_password,
                       "callback" => \&reply,
                       "allow_srv_settings" => 0,
                       "login_timeout" => 2 );

$aim->im_permit_all();

$aim -> sign_on();
```

Once that is in place, set the script on a loop, waiting for an incoming message. This is done with the Net::AOLIM's ui_dataget function, like so:

```
while (1)
{
    last unless defined($foo->ui_dataget(undef));
}
```

When Net::AOLIM receives a message, it hands the script off to the subroutine called `reply`. `reply` must check if the incoming message is a direct Instant Message, not an internal error message. Once it has done that, it retrieves the buddy name of the person who sent it.

```
sub reply
{

    my $params = $_[ARG1];

    my $aim_event_type = $params->[0];

    if($aim_event_type eq 'IM_IN') {

    my $aimdestuser = $params->[1];
```

And all that remains to be done is to check Gmail for new mail and reply to the message sender with a nice answer. Once that is done, the script returns to its loop. Listing 8-7 shows all.

Listing 8-7: A New Mail Count AIM Bot

```
#!/usr/bin/perl -w

use warnings;
use strict;
use Mail::Webmail::Gmail;
use Net::AOLIM;

my $gmail_user ="";
my $gmail_password = "";

my $aim_user = "";
my $aim_password = "";
my $aim_destuser = "";

$aim = Net::AOLIM->new("username" => $aim_user,
                "password" => $aim_password,
                "callback" => \&reply,
                "allow_srv_settings" => 0,
                "login_timeout" => 2 );
```

```perl
$aim->im_permit_all();

$aim -> sign_on();

while (1)
{
    last unless defined($foo->ui_dataget(undef));
}

sub reply
{

    my $params = $_[ARG1];

    my $aim_event_type = $params->[0];

    if($aim_event_type eq 'IM_IN') {

    my $aimdestuser = $params->[1];

    my $gmail = Mail::Webmail::Gmail->new(
    username => $gmail_user,
    password => $gmail_password,
);

my $messages =
  $gmail->get_messages( label =>
$Mail::Webmail::Gmail::FOLDERS{'INBOX'} );

my $new_msgs = 0;

if ( defined($messages) ) {
    foreach ( @{$messages} ) {
        if ( $_->{'new'} ) {
                $new_msgs++;
        }
    }
}

    my $message = "$gmail_user has a new message count of
$new_msg";
    $aim->toc_send_im($aim_destuser, $message);


    }
}
s
```

Run this as a background application by typing the following command:

```
./google2rssbot.pl &
```

You can kill it with a judicious control-c.

There are many ways to extend this script — allowing different people to check different accounts depending on their buddy name, and so on. It should be clear from the listing how to do this.

And Now . . .

So now you have seen how to check for new mail in three languages, and how to create some interesting applications to repurpose that data. In all, quite simple stuff but a good starting point. In the next chapter, you move on to the next logical stage: reading the mail.

Reading Mail

In Chapter 7, you built scripts and applications to tell you that you had new mail. In this chapter, you move on to the next logical step and retrieve that mail from Gmail so you can read it.

Reading an individual mail from Gmail is unlike reading individual mails from a POP3 or IMAP server. In the more common e-mail systems, an e-mail is identified by a number and can be retrieved directly. In Gmail, as you found in Chapter 6, this isn't possible: You have to retrieve the entire thread and then retrieve the message from that. In an ideal world, a Gmail library would hide this horrible fact, and they all do this to a lesser or greater extent.

in this chapter

☑ Locating the mail

☑ Retrieving the message source

☑ Parsing the message source

Reading Mail with Perl

The process with Mail::Webmail::Gmail is remarkably easy. You log in, retrieve the contents of the Inbox, find the thread with the message you require, retrieve it, find the message within that thread, and parse out the contents.

The Basics

Logging in and retrieving the contents of the Inbox, as ever, looks like this:

```
my $gmail = Mail::Webmail::Gmail->new(
    username => "ben.hammersley\@gmail.com",
    password => "XXXXXXX",
);

my $messages =
  $gmail->get_messages( label =>
$Mail::Webmail::Gmail::FOLDERS{'INBOX'} );
```

Now you have a reference to an array of hashes containing the contents of the Inbox. You can loop through this array of hashes, and pull out the details of the messages with the et_indv_email function. This function can either take the message ID or, as in this case, take the reference to the specific message, like this:

```
foreach ( @{ $messages } ) {
        my $message = $gmail->get_indv_email( msg => $_ );
        print "$message->{ $_->{ 'id' } }->{ 'body' }\n";
    }
```

Of course, spinning through your Inbox and printing out all of the bodies might be fun to do once, but it's not very useful.

Accessing All the Data of a Message

Mail::Webmail::Gmail can, of course, give you all of the information within a message. However, relying on addressing the data directly within your script is a recipe for trouble. Even as I type this sentence, the Gmail UI seems to be changing and rendering bits of Mail::Webmail::Gmail out of date until either Gmail changes back or the library is fixed. To make sure that your own code isn't entirely broken by such changes, do something like this:

```
foreach ( @{ $messages } ) {
        my $message = $gmail->get_indv_email( msg => $_ );

        my $to = $message->{ $_->{ 'id' } }->{ 'to'} || "To
irretrievable";
        my $sender_email = $message->{ $_->{ 'id' } }->{
'sender_email'} || "Sender_email irretrievable";
        my $sent = $message->{ $_->{ 'id' } }->{ 'sent'} ||
"To irretrievable";
        my $subject = $message->{ $_->{ 'id' } }->{ 'subject'}
|| "Subject irretrievable";
        my $body = $message->{ $_->{ 'id' } }->{ 'body'} ||
"Body irretrievable";

        print "$to \n $sender_email \n $sent \n $subject \n
$body";

    }
```

Tip The double pipe at the end of the variable setting lines basically means, "If this call to the API returns empty, make it this value instead." This is a simple catch to make sure that, at least, your script doesn't just fail on you.

Listing the Mail and Displaying a Chosen Message

So, with that all fully understood, you can put your knowledge, and that of Chapter 7, to use. Listing 9-1 shows code that logs in, displays the mail you have in your account in a list, and then lets you select the one you want to read. Select that, and it displays it. Easy and useful.

Listing 9-1 follows, and then I'll walk you through it. It uses the Utils.pm module from Chapter 7 to deal with the login procedure.

Listing 9-1: Mail Listing and Display

```
use Utils;

$gmail = login();

$messages = $gmail->get_messages(); # simply get all messages
$id = 1;
$num = 0;
@nums;
foreach (@{$messages}) { # and iterate through them
    if ($_->{"new"}) {
........print $id . "\t" . $_->{"sender_email"} . "\t" .
strip_bold($_->{"subject"}) . "\n"; # output message data
........push(@nums, $num);
........$id++;
    }
    $num++;
}

print "\n";
print "enter message number to retrieve it\n";
$num = <>;
print "\n";

$message = @{$messages}[$nums[$num - 1]];
$msgid = $message->{"id"};
if ($msgid) { # check if message id is OK
    my $full_message = $gmail->get_indv_email(msg =>
$message); # and retrive full message (including body but not
attachments - if we need them as well - we need to use
get_attachment method)
    print "sender:  " . $full_message->{$id}->{"sender"} .
"\n";
```

Continued

Listing 9-1 *(continued)*

```
    print "sent:      " . $full_message->{$id}->{"sent"} . "\n";
    print "to:        " . $full_message->{$id}->{"to"} . "\n";
    print "subject: " . strip_bold($full_message->{$id}-
>{"subject"}) . "\n";
    print $full_message->{$id}->{"body"} . "\n\n";
}
```

So how does this work? First you use the Utils.pm module you made at the end of
Chapter 7 and have it log you in:

```
use Utils;
$gmail = login();
```

Now that you're logged in, you need to retrieve the messages and loop through
each one, numbering it and printing the sender and subject line.

```
$messages = $gmail->get_messages(); # simply get all messages
$id = 1;
$num = 0;
@nums;
foreach (@{$messages}) { # and iterate through them
    if ($_->{"new"}) {
........print $id . "\t" . $_->{"sender_email"} . "\t" .
strip_bold($_->{"subject"}) . "\n"; # output message data
........push(@nums, $num);
........$id++;
    }
    $num++;
}
```

Now you give the option to enter the number (as printed in the preceding code)
of the message you want to see.

```
print "\n";
print "enter message number to retrieve it\n";
$num = <>;
print "\n";
```

Once a number has been entered, retrieve the message and print it on the screen.

```
$message = @{$messages}[$nums[$num - 1]];
$msgid = $message->{"id"};
if ($msgid) { # check if message id is OK
    my $full_message = $gmail->get_indv_email(msg =>
$message); # and retrive full message (including body but not
```

```
attachments - if we need them as well - we need to use
get_attachment method)
    print "sender:  " . $full_message->{$id}->{"sender"} .
"\n";
    print "sent:    " . $full_message->{$id}->{"sent"} . "\n";
    print "to:      " . $full_message->{$id}->{"to"} . "\n";
    print "subject: " . strip_bold($full_message->{$id}-
>{"subject"}) . "\n";
    print $full_message->{$id}->{"body"} . "\n\n";
}
```

Now, as you can see from the in-code comments, this code can't deal with attachments. It's time you learned how. Oh. Look . . .

Dealing with Attachments

Gmail's enormous storage capacity gives you the opportunity to use it for very large attachments. There are many possibilities for this feature, but first you need to know how to retrieve the attachments themselves.

You retrieve an attachment in a way very closely connected to the method you used in the RSS script in Listing 9-1. First, retrieve the list of messages and then loop through them, pulling out the data on each message. Here you differ — you're looking for an attachment, so you test to see if one is present, and if so you go on to do something about it. The first part of a script after logging in, therefore, is:

```
my $messages = $gmail->get_messages();

foreach ( @{$messages} ) {
    my $email = $gmail->get_indv_email( msg => $_ );
    if ( defined( $email->{ $_->{'id'} }->{'attachments'} ) )
{
        foreach ( @{ $email->{ $_->{'id'} }->{'attachments'} }
) {

            # Here do something with each attachment

        }
    }
}
```

Making an RSS Feed of Your Inbox

So now you know how to gather the mail from a specific folder and print it out. Let's do something more useful with it, as an exercise. How about an RSS feed of your Inbox? In Chapter 7 you already made a feed that displays the unread message count. Do the same here, only displaying the messages instead.

Listing 9-2 shows the code, which is followed by a walkthrough.

Listing 9-2: Gmail Inbox to RSS

```perl
#!/usr/bin/perl

use warnings;
use strict;
use XML::RSS;
use Mail::Webmail::Gmail;
use CGI qw(standard);

my $username = param("username");
my $password = param("password");

my $gmail = Mail::Webmail::Gmail->new(
    username => $username,
    password => $password,
);

my $messages =
  $gmail->get_messages( label =>
$Mail::Webmail::Gmail::FOLDERS{'INBOX'} );

my $rss = new XML::RSS( version => '2.0' );

foreach ( @{$messages} ) {

    my $message = $gmail->get_indv_email( msg => $_ );

    my $messageid = $_->{'id'};

    my $sender_email = $message->{ $_->{'id'} }-
>{'sender_email'}
        || "Sender_email irretrievable";

    my $sent = $message->{ $_->{'id'} }->{'sent'}
        || "To irretrievable";

    my $subject = $message->{ $_->{'id'} }->{'subject'}
        || "Subject irretrievable";
```

```
    my $body = $message->{ $_->{'id'} }->{'body'}
        || "Body irretrievable";

    $rss->add_item(
        title => "$subject",
        link =>
"http://gmail.google.com/gmail/h/abcde12345/?th=$messageid&v=c
",
        author       => "$sender_email",
        description => "$body",
    );

}


$rss->channel(
    title => "The Gmail inbox for $username",
    link  => "http://gmail.google.com/",
);

print header('application/xml+rss');
print $rss->as_string;
```

The first thing to notice is that this script is very simple indeed. That's because of the Perl module — the whole point of these modules is to abstract away this sort of thing. So, the first thing you do is load the modules up and log in as usual:

```
use XML::RSS;
use Mail::Webmail::Gmail;
use CGI qw(standard);

my $username = param("username");
my $password = param("password");

my $gmail = Mail::Webmail::Gmail->new(
    username => $username,
    password => $password,
);
```

Because you want the script to return an RSS feed, you've made it into a CGI script, to be called from, and run by, a server. The easiest way to make this useful is to take the Gmail account's username and password from parameters in the script's URL. Saving this script as gmailinboxtorss.cgi would allow you to subscribe to the following URL:

```
http://www.example.com/gmailinboxtorss.cgi?username=USERNAME&passw
ord=PASSWORD
```

By this point in the script, you have logged in. Now to retrieve the messages in the Inbox:

```
my $messages =
  $gmail->get_messages( label =>
$Mail::Webmail::Gmail::FOLDERS{'INBOX'} );
```

This places the contents of the Inbox into $messages as a reference to an array of hashes, which contains the messages within the Inbox. Before looping through this array and creating an RSS item from each one, first you need to create the object that creates the RSS feed. Do that with this line:

```
my $rss = new XML::RSS( version => '2.0' );
```

Now for the real workings. You have an array where each member is a hash, containing a single message and all its details. To get to these details, you need to be able to address them with the hash's key. So, loop through the array, take the name of the hash, use that as its key, and grab out the values:

```
foreach ( @{$messages} ) {

    my $message = $gmail->get_indv_email( msg => $_ );

    my $messageid = $_->{'id'};

    my $sender_email = $message->{ $_->{'id'} }-
>{'sender_email'}
        || "Sender_email irretrievable";

    my $sent = $message->{ $_->{'id'} }->{'sent'}
        || "To irretrievable";

    my $subject = $message->{ $_->{'id'} }->{'subject'}
        || "Subject irretrievable";

    my $body = $message->{ $_->{'id'} }->{'body'}
        || "Body irretrievable";
```

Noting, again, the double pipe in the statement that gives the variable a value even if the Mail::Webmail::Gmail module cannot. This protects you a little from Gmail's evolution breaking the module and hence your scripts.

Next, create the RSS item for the message:

```
    $rss->add_item(
        title => "$subject",
        link =>
"http://gmail.google.com/gmail/h/abcde12345/?th=$messageid&v=c
",
```

```
    author      => "$sender_email",
    description => "$body",
);
```

That's all quite self-explanatory, except for the line that creates the item's `link` element. There you can see a long URL that is completed with the message ID number. This produces a link to the HTML-only version of the Gmail interface, but you will have to wait until Chapter 12 to see that fully explained. Skip ahead if you're curious.

The only thing left to do here is serve the feed, so you do this:

```
$rss->channel(
    title => "The Gmail inbox for $username",
    link  => "http://gmail.google.com/",
);

print header('application/xml+rss');
print $rss->as_string;
```

To install and run this script, place it in a CGI-enabled directory on your server, and remember to CHMOD it to executable.

This script highlights a simple method of gathering messages and doing something with them. As you saw in the previous chapter, you can easily direct the `get_messages()` function, which above retrieves the array of hashes from the Inbox. You can grab the messages from the Starred folder, for example, by changing the line in Listing 9-1 to the following:

```
my $messages = $gmail->get_messages( label =>
$Mail::Webmail::Gmail::FOLDERS{ 'STARRED' } );
```

Moving messages around the labels and default folders is examined in Chapter 10. There you will also look at finding which labels and folders you have.

And Now . . .

In this chapter, then, you've learned how to retrieve e-mails from Gmail using Perl. You should now be able to access the data of any mail you wish and use it within your programs. As you will see in the later chapters, this opens many new opportunities. In the next chapter, you learn how to send mail via Gmail.

Sending Mail

Now that you know how to read the mail in your Inbox with your own programs, it's time to move on to replying to those mails by sending your own messages.

Sending Mail with Gmail SMTP

The first thing to remember is that Gmail provides its own SMTP server. This offers two major features. First, you can use the SMTP server from your own e-mail application, which is a great help if you're traveling and your usual e-mail provider is unreachable. The second use is that every single scripting language you might have a desire to use has standard SMTP support available as a library, and the support for TLS encryption, which you need to connect to Gmail, is being added apace.

First, though, the settings you'll need:

- **Server name:** smtp.google.com
- **Username:** yourgmailname@gmail.com
- **Password:** Your Gmail password
- **Security:** Yes, using TLS

One thing to note about this technique is that Gmail will rewrite your e-mail headers. It replaces the From: and Reply-to: lines with your Gmail address because Gmail also automatically adds the so-called Domain Keys to their outgoing e-mails, allowing spam-hit system administrators to block fake Gmail mail from their servers. Without the Domain Keys this wouldn't work, but Gmail can't send mail with a different From: or Reply-to: address without breaking the Domain Key.

One other advantage of using the Gmail SMTP client is that any mail sent via the SMTP gateway is automatically stored within your Gmail account.

Using the SMTP Server Programmatically

If you want to talk directly to the SMTP server instead of using the APIs featured in the rest of this chapter, then you will need to use a library that can deal with TLS encryption. There is no standard module to do this within Perl or PHP at the time of this writing, but Python users can use the standard smtplib, which comes with the Python distribution.

Sending Mail with Perl

The Mail::Webmail::Gmail module encapsulates mail sending in one single function, `send_message`. The basic method to send a message is:

```
$gmail->send_message(
to => 'user@domain.com',
subject => 'Test Message',
msgbody => 'This is a test.'
);
```

To send to multiple addresses, you can use an arrayref containing all of the addresses:

```
my $email_addrs = [
'user1@domain.com',
'user2@domain.com',
'user3@domain.com', ];

$gmail->send_message(
to => $email_addrs,
subject => 'Test Message',
msgbody => 'This is a test.'
);
```

You may also send mail using cc: and bcc:

```
$gmail->send_message(
to => $email_addrs,
cc=> $cc_email_addrs,
subject => 'Test Message',
msgbody => 'This is a test.'
);
```

Listing 10-1 shows a small script, using the Mail::Webmail::Gmail module and the Utils.pm code introduced in Chapter 7. It takes input from the keyboard, and sends the mail directly. It's exceptionally easy to understand, so no walk-through is necessary.

Listing 10-1: Sending Mail with Perl

```perl
use Utils;

$gmail = login();

# input data from keyboard
print "to:\n";
$to = <>;

print "subject:\n";
$subject = <>;

print "body:\n";
$body = <>;

$gmail->send_message( to => $to, subject => $subject, msgbody
=> $body );    # and send the message
print "message sent\n";
```

That script is, as you can see, remarkably simple. But it does provide the basis for any number of more complicated scripts. Being able to send mail from a script isn't a new thing — it's pretty easy to do without Gmail — but doing it via Gmail does give you some advantages. First, it's easier, but second, the mail is automatically archived. Using Gmail to handle outgoing mail from your applications can therefore be more resilient, certainly easier, and much more useful than doing it any other way.

In Chapter 9, you looked at downloading and reading new mail. Listing 10-2 shows a script that combines the techniques you learned there with your new-found skills at sending mail.

Listing 10-2: Reading Unread Mail and Replying

```perl
use Utils;

$gmail = login();

$messages = $gmail->get_messages();      # simply get all
messages
$id       = 1;
$num      = 0;
@nums;
```

Continued

Listing 10-2 *(continued)*

```
foreach ( @{$messages} ) {
    if ( $_->{"new"} ) {
        print $id . "\t"
            . $_->{"sender_email"} . "\t"
            . strip_bold( $_->{"subject"} )
            . "\n";
        push( @nums, $num );
        $id++;
    }
    $num++;
}

print "\n";
print "enter message number to reply to\n";
$num = <>;
print "\n";

$message = @{$messages}[ $nums[ $num - 1 ] ];
$msgid   = $message->{"id"};
if ($msgid) {     # check if message id is OK
    print "body:\n";
    $body = <>;
    $gmail->send_message(
        to      => $message->{"sender_email"},
        subject => "Re: " . strip_bold( $message->{"subject"}
),
        msgbody => $body
    );             # we are using sender and subject from the
original message
    print "message sent\n";
}
```

Running this script produces a list of the new messages and gives you the option to choose one and reply to it. You should see how this works from the code, but let's walk through it.

The start is simple enough. You're using the Utils.pm module you created in Chapter 7, and you just want to log in. Logging in creates the Gmail object used in the rest of the script:

```
use Utils;

$gmail = login();
```

You then grab all of the messages in the Inbox and set up some variables you shall use to keep track of them:

```
$messages = $gmail->get_messages();      # simply get all
messages
$id        = 1;
$num       = 0;

@nums;
```

Then you iterate through these messages, adding them to a list if they are marked as unread. You print the sender's address and the subject line of the e-mail, with a number next to it, pushing that number and the message:

```
foreach ( @{$messages} ) {
    if ( $_->{"new"} ) {
        print $id . "\t"
            . $_->{"sender_email"} . "\t"
            . strip_bold( $_->{"subject"} )
            . "\n";
        push( @nums, $num );
        $id++;
    }
    $num++;
}
```

And then you ask the user to enter the number of the message she wants to reply to:

```
print "\n";
print "enter message number to reply to\n";
$num = <>;
print "\n";
```

Finally, you retrieve the sender's e-mail and subject line from the chosen mail and request some body text from the user. Once you have that, the message is created and sent:

```
$message = @{$messages}[ $nums[ $num - 1 ] ];
$msgid   = $message->{"id"};
if ($msgid) {      # check if message id is OK
    print "body:\n";
    $body = <>;
    $gmail->send_message(
        to      => $message->{"sender_email"},
        subject => "Re: " . strip_bold( $message->{"subject"}
),
        msgbody => $body
```

```
    );             # we are using sender and subject from the
original message
    print "message sent\n";
}
```

This is, of course, an extremely simple script and well positioned to be built upon.

Sending Attachments

To attach files to a message via the WWW::Webmail::Gmail module, you only need use the send_message function as normal, but provide a file reference to the attachment. Because you're programmers, remember, you start counting from zero. So the first reference is file0, the second file1, and so on. Like so:

```
$gmail->send_message(
to => 'user@domain.com',
subject => 'Test Message',
msgbody => 'This is a test.',
file0 => ["/tmp/foo"],
file1 => ["/tmp/bar"]
);
```

And Now . . .

So, in this short chapter, you learned how to send mail. In the next chapter, you look at the much more advanced concepts of organizing your mail inside Gmail, programmatically. This will allow you to go on and use Gmail for more complicated applications.

Conquering Gmail

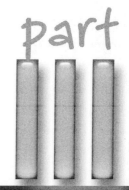

You're the man! You've learned how to use Gmail to its fullest, and now you're writing scripts that use scraped APIs to control your mail. In the rest of the book, you take your skills to the next level.

First, in Chapter 11, you look at organizing your mail—using Gmail's labeling system. Then Chapter 12 deals with e-mail addresses and the import and export of addresses to the Gmail address book.

Then, for a bit of a break, in Chapter 13 you look at the possibilities that might open up with the HTML-only version of Gmail. In the future, you might want to know about that so you can build your own API library.

After that, it's back to practicalities, when you learn how to export mail in Chapter 14, use Gmail for all sorts of interesting activities (Chapter 14), and then, in perhaps the culmination of the whole study of this fine web application, use Gmail as a mountable file system. Really. Peep Chapter 16 if you don't believe.

in this part

Chapter 11
Dealing with Labels

Chapter 12
Addressing Addresses

Chapter 13
Building an API from the HTML-Only Version of Gmail

Chapter 14
Exporting Your Mail

Chapter 15
Using Gmail to . . .

Chapter 16
Using GmailFS

Dealing with Labels

You can receive mail and you can send mail, but you have yet to play with Gmail's main feature — its immense storage capacity. You'll be using that over the next few chapters. One of the biggest draws to Gmail is the way you organize mail with labels. Labels are quite the fashionable thing on the Internet at the moment: Whether you call them labels or the commonly used idea of *tags*, it really doesn't matter. Gmail's system works in the same way as the other cult Web 2.0 sites, Flickr and del.icio.us.

In this chapter, then, you look at working with the labels programmatically, listing them, setting them, changing them, and deleting them.

in this chapter

☑ Listing existing labels

☑ Setting and editing labels

☑ Deleting old labels

Listing the Existing Labels

The simplest thing you can do with labels is list the ones you are already using. Listing 11-1 shows a script to do just that. It uses the Utils.pm module created earlier in the book, as do the rest of the scripts in this chapter.

Note You can find Utils.pm, if you don't have it already, in Listing 7-4.

The script is too simple to require any explanation, but just note that it uses Mail::Webmail::Gmail's `get_labels()` function to return an array.

Listing 11-1: Getting the Existing Labels

```
use Utils;

$gmail = login();

@labels = $gmail->get_labels();      # simply get all labels
foreach (@labels) {                  # and iterate through them
    print $_ . "\n";
}
```

Running this will simply print out a list of the labels you are using right now. That's useful, but you can extend it a little bit. Listing 11-2 does the same thing, but allows you to select a label, whereupon it prints all the messages labeled thusly. Have a look at the listing, and then you'll walk through the clever bit.

Listing 11-2: Retrieving the Messages from a Certain Label

```
use Utils;

$gmail = login();

@labels = $gmail->get_labels();      # simply get all labels
$id      = 1;
foreach (@labels) {                  # and iterate through them
    print $id . "\t" . $_ . "\n";
    $id++;
}

print "\n";
print "enter label number to retrive labeled messages:\n";
$num = <>;
print "\n";



$label = $labels[ $num - 1 ];
if ($label) {
    $messages =
      $gmail->get_messages( label => $label );
    foreach ( @{$messages} ) {
```

```
        print $_->{"sender_email"} . "\t"
        . strip_bold( $_->{"subject"} )
        . "\n";
    }
}
```

The important section to note here is the code that follows:

```
if ($label) {
    $messages =
      $gmail->get_messages( label => $label );
    foreach ( @{$messages} ) {
        print $_->{"sender_email"} . "\t"
        . strip_bold( $_->{"subject"} )
        . "\n";
    }
}
```

By this section of the script, you've printed out the labels you know about, and asked the user to choose one. So now you test to see if the number the user enters is actually a value option, and if it is, you retrieve all of the messages with the pertinent label. That's done, as ever, with the `get_messages()` function, which can be modified by passing the name of a label with it:

```
    $messages = $gmail->get_messages( label => $label );
```

And this returns messages in the same way as you dealt with in Chapter 8.

In Chapter 9, you requested new mail and gave the option to reply to it. Here, in Listing 11-3, you can do a similar thing: request mail for a certain label and give the option to reply to it.

Listing 11-3: Retrieving a Labeled Message and Replying

```
use Utils;

$gmail = login();

@labels = $gmail->get_labels();    # simply get all labels
$id     = 1;
foreach (@labels) {                # and iterate through them
    print $id . " " . $_ . "\n";
    $id++;
```

Continued

Listing 11-3 *(continued)*

```perl
}

print "\n";
print "enter label number to retrive labeled messages:\n";
$num = <>;
print "\n";

$label = $labels[ $num - 1 ];
if ($label) {
    $messages =
      $gmail->get_messages( label => $label );     # get all
labeled messages
    $id = 1;
    foreach ( @{$messages} ) {      # and iterate through them
        print $id . "\t"
            . $_->{"sender_email"} . "\t"
            . strip_bold( $_->{"subject"} )
            . "\n";                    # output message data
        $id++;
    }

    print "\n";
    print "enter message number to reply to\n";
    $num = <>;
    print "\n";

    $message = @{$messages}[ $num - 1 ];
    $msgid   = $message->{"id"};
    if ($msgid) {                    # check if message id is OK
        print "body:\n";
        $body = <>;
        $gmail->send_message(
            to      => $message->{"sender_email"},
            subject => "Re: " . strip_bold( $message-
>{"subject"} ),
            msgbody => $body
        );    # we are using sender and subject from the
original message
        print "message sent\n";
    }
}
```

This is exactly the same technique as you used in Listing 11-2, added to Chapter 10's method for sending a reply. You should now be able to see how you can build simple applications and workflows with the Gmail and the Mail::Webmail::Gmail module.

Setting New Labels

It's all very well being able to list the existing labels, but what about setting messages with them? To do that with Mail::Webmail::Gmail, use the `edit_labels` function. Listing 11-4 displays the unlabeled messages and the existing labels, and allows you to apply one to the other.

First, the listing and then how it works.

Listing 11-4: Labeling Unlabeled Messages

```
use Utils;

$gmail = login();

$messages = $gmail->get_messages();     # simply get all
messages
$id      = 1;
$num     = 0;
@nums;
foreach ( @{$messages} ) {                # and iterate through
them
    if ( $_->{"new"} ) {
        print $id . "\t"
            . $_->{"sender_email"} . "\t"
            . strip_bold( $_->{"subject"} )
            . "\n";                        # output message data
        push( @nums, $num );
        $id++;
    }
    $num++;
}

print "\n";
print "enter message number to label\n";
$num = <>;
print "\n";
```

Continued

Listing 11-4 *(continued)*

```
$message = @{$messages}[ $nums[ $num - 1 ] ];
$msgid   = $message->{"id"};

if ($msgid) {
    @labels = $gmail->get_labels();      # simply get all labels
    $id     = 1;
    foreach (@labels) {                  # and iterate through
them
        print $id . "\t" . $_ . "\n";
        $id++;
    }

    print "\n";
    print "enter label to set\n";
    $num = <>;
    print "\n";

    $label = $labels[ $num - 1 ];
    if ($label) {
        $gmail->edit_labels(
            label  => $label,
            action => "add",
            msgid  => $msgid
        );    # simply add label to message
        print "labeled message\n";
    }
}
```

The key part of the script is the edit_labels function. Here's the pertinent function call:

```
$gmail->edit_labels(
        label  => $label,
        action => "add",
        msgid  => $msgid
    );
```

You set the label attribute to the label you require, the action to "add" and the msgid to the message ID of the message you're changing. It is, as you can see, very simple to understand.

Creating a New Label

The creation of new labels is done with the same `edit_labels` function, using the `"create"` action. This code that follows creates a new label `"fish"`. Labels can have a maximum of 40 characters.

```
$gmail->edit_labels(
        label  => "fish",
        action => "create",
    );
```

When that's done, you can go back and apply that label to the messages you wish.

Removing Labels

Of course, you might go completely label crazy. In which case, one day you'll wake up with regret and want to undo all that you did before. If that's the case, use the final variation of the `edit_labels` function, like so:

```
$gmail->edit_labels(
    label  => $label,
    action => "remove",
    msgid  => $msgid
);
```

Listing 11-5 puts together the final variation of the chapter, with a script that allows you to choose a label, display the messages with that label, and choose a message to remove that label from. Complex? Not hardly!

Listing 11-5: Getting Labeled Messages and Removing Labels

```
use Utils;

$gmail = login();

@labels = $gmail->get_labels();      # simply get all labels
$id     = 1;
foreach (@labels) {                  # and iterate through them
    print $id . " " . $_ . "\n";
    $id++;
}

print "\n";
print "enter label number to retrieve labeled messages:\n";
$num = <>;
```

Continued

Listing 11-5 *(continued)*

```perl
print "\n";

$label = $labels[ $num - 1 ];
if ($label) {
    $messages =
        $gmail->get_messages( label => $label );    # get all
labeled messages

    $id  = 1;
    $num = 0;
    foreach ( @{$messages} ) {                       # and
iterate through them
        print $id . "\t"
            . $_->{"sender_email"} . "\t"
            . strip_bold( $_->{"subject"} )
            . "\n";                                  # output
message data
        $id++;
    }

    print "\n";
    print "enter message number to remove label\n";
    $num = <>;
    print "\n";

    $message = @{$messages}[ $num - 1 ];
    $msgid   = $message->{"id"};
    if ($msgid) {                                    # check if
message id is OK
        $gmail->edit_labels(
            label  => $label,
            action => "remove",
            msgid  => $msgid
        );
        print "removed label\n";
    }
}
```

And Now . . .

You should now be able to deal confidently with the mail inside Gmail. But what of your address book? In the next chapter, you look at using the Perl API to communicate with the address book and to import and export your contacts.

Addressing Addresses

Gmail's mastery of your e-mail wouldn't be of much use without an address book. Lucky for us, Gmail provides a perfectly functional one. Indeed, it was the address auto-completion, where you can start typing a known address and have it appear automatically within the To: field of a new mail, that first excited the Gmail beta testers. As an example of Ajax programming, it was, at the time, second to none.

The auto-completion system gets its addresses from, and is centered on, the Gmail Contacts list. In this chapter, you learn how to control the Contacts list from your own programs.

The Contacts List

The Contacts list is accessed from the link on the left of your Gmail screen. It looks, if you're logged into my system at least, very much like Figure 12-1.

As far as an address book goes, it's pretty simple. But combined with the auto-complete function, it provides a very useful way of dealing with your (or at least my) failing memory when it comes to e-mail addresses.

Adding and managing contacts from your browser is obvious and far below your geeky level, so let's go straight to the scripting.

Figure 12-1 The Gmail contacts list

Importing Contacts

You've got a list of contacts, and you're not going home until you've added them to your Gmail account. Hurrah, then, for Listing 12-1. This provides the basis for a script to allow you to add contacts programmatically. It uses, as ever, the Utils.pm and Mail::Webmail::Gmail modules that you've been working with since Chapter 7.

Listing 12-1: Adding a Contact

```
use Utils;

$gmail = login();

# input data from keyboard
print "name:\n";
$name = <>;
print "email:\n";
$email = <>;
print "notes:\n";
$notes = <>;
```

```
chomp($name);
chomp($email);
chomp($notes);

$gmail->add_contact( name => $name, email => $email, notes =>
$notes )
   ;    # simply add contact
print "contact added\n";
```

Running this script from the command line provides three prompts, in order, for the name, e-mail address, and notes regarding the contact. Enter those, and the script adds the contact to your Gmail account.

Tip

If you have a long list of addresses to import, sometimes it's easier to turn that list into a comma-separated values (CSV) file and use the import function that's part of the Gmail site itself.

A comma-separated values file for e-mail addresses looks like this:

```
First Name,Last Name,Email Address
Ben,Hammersley,ben.Hammersley@gmail.com
Julius,Caesar,example.account@gmail.com
```

With the first line called the *header*, defining the values separated by commas (hence the name) in the rest of the file. Most e-mail programs will export in a compatible version of CSV anyway, but if you need to make one by hand, that's how. Spreadsheets are also good programs to use to build CSV files.

So, to import large amounts of contacts, follow these steps:

1. Create a custom CSV file or export the address book from your other web-mail provider or e-mail client as a CSV file.

2. Log in to Gmail and click Contacts on the left side of the page. The Contacts list then opens in a new window.

3. Click Import Contacts.

4. Click Browse and locate the CSV file you'd like to upload.

5. Select the file and click Import Contacts. After successfully uploading the document, a dialog box displays the number of new entries that were added to your Contacts list.

Showing Your Current Contacts

Once you've got your old contacts in there and have added a load more, you might want to list those and access them programmatically. Listing 12-2 shows you how.

Listing 12-2: Getting Your Contacts

```
use Utils;

$gmail = login();

(@contacts) = @{ $gmail->get_contacts() };     # simply get all
contacts
foreach (@contacts) {                           # and iterate
though them
    print $_->{"name1"} . "\t" . $_->{"email"} . "\n";     #
output contact data
}
```

The Mail::Webmail::Gmail module provides for this with one lovely bite-sized function: get_contacts(). This returns an array hash of your contacts, in this format:

```
$contact{ 'id' }
$contact{ 'name1' }
$contact{ 'name2' }
$contact{ 'email' }
$contact{ 'note' }
```

And so, in the core of the script in Listing 12-2, you are just looping through the Arrays of Hashes and printing out the first name and e-mail address. You could, of course, change this to use the other values, too:

```
foreach (@contacts) {
    print $_->{"name1"} . $_->{"name2"} . $_->{"id"} .   "\t" .
$_->{"email"} . "\t" . $_->{"note"} . "\n";
}
```

The get_contacts() function can also be limited to the Frequently Mailed contacts with the frequent flag:

```
my $contacts = $gmail->get_contacts( frequent => 1 );
```

Exporting Contacts

Gmail is a bit greedy here. There are ample opportunities to import contacts to the system. As you've seen, you can do it with comma-separated value files or via the script in Listing 12-1. But if you want to get your contacts out again, and into a desktop address book, you're stuck.

Not quite. In Listing 12-3, there's a script to export your contacts into a large vCard file. All the modern address book or e-mail clients will be able to understand the vCard file, and re-import your addresses. It's also useful for backups, if you ever get wary of Google's ability to do that for you.

Here's the listing, and then you'll see how it works.

Listing 12-3: Exporting Contacts as vCards

```
use Utils;

$gmail = login();

open VCARDS, ">contacts.vcf";

(@contacts) = @{ $gmail->get_contacts() };     # simply get all
contacts
foreach (@contacts) {                           # and iterate
though them
    print VCARDS "BEGIN:VCARD\nVERSION:3.0\n";
    print VCARDS "FN:" . $_->{"name1"} . "\n";
    print VCARDS "EMAIL;type=INTERNET:" . $_->{"email"} .
"\n";
    print VCARDS "END:VCARD\n";
    print VCARDS "\n";
}

close VCARDS;
```

 Note A vCard is a small text file containing address data. The entire standard is complex and extensive, defined in RFC2425; you can read about it at www.imc.org/pdi/vcardoverview.html.

Here is an example of a very simple vCard file:

```
BEGIN:VCARD
VERSION:3.0
FN:Ben Hammersley
EMAIL;type=INTERNET:ben.hammersley@gmail.com
END:VCARD
```

Saving that to disk and importing it into a vCard-compatible program will result in my lovely e-mail address being embedded into your system. vCard files can contain more than one vCard within, and that's what the script in Listing 12-3 does. It's very, very simple. It opens up a filehandle to a file called contacts.vcf in the directory you're running the script in (change that line to make it go else-where, naturally), and then calls upon the Mail::Webmail::Gmail module to provide a hash of the contacts in your Contacts list. It then just iterates through them, creating vCards as it goes and printing them to the filehandle. Then it closes the filehandle and exits. Simplicity itself, really. You can then go on and import the large vCard file into your weapon of choice.

And Now . . .

In this chapter, you looked at dealing with contacts within Gmail. You should have learned how to import contacts from other applications. You should also be able to export them at will, in order to re-import them into other applications or for backup purposes. In the next chapter, you look at scraping the Gmail interface.

Building an API from the HTML-Only Version of Gmail

The problem with reverse engineering web applications — other than the complexity — is that they never stop evolving. That's the advantage of building an application on the web: It costs nothing to ship an upgrade to all of your users. Such upgrades, as mentioned previously, do, however, tend to break the third-party APIs that this book relies on.

The one thing worse than breaking an API is making it redundantly complex, and about halfway through writing this book, Gmail did just that by releasing a plain HTML version of the site. Gmail users approaching the site with an old, non-JavaScript–enabled browser are able to access a version of the application that does not rely on the JavaScript techniques discussed in previous chapters. The functionality is a little restricted, but the basic capabilities to read, write, and organize your mail are there. This chapter, therefore, looks at faking an API by scraping the HTML version — something somewhat simpler than messing with the JavaScript API.

A First Look at the HTML Version

To see the HTML version of Gmail, turn off the JavaScript in your browser, and log in as normal. (Or, you can log in and switch from standard view to basic HTML by using the choices at the bottom of the page. Either way is good.) You should see something very similar to Figure 13-1.

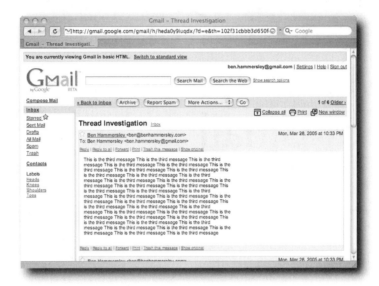

FIGURE **13-1: The HTML-only version of Gmail**

It's easy to see the differences between the JavaScript and non-JavaScript versions of the site. The non-JavaScript version has the yellow banner along the top, and — key point this — the URL of the page is both longer, and as you shall see, changes when you use the application.

The first order of business is to view the HTML source of the page. You can see that the page is all one piece — there's no iFrame nonsense here — and that it's pretty unspectacular markup. In fact, saving the HTML to disk, and running the tidy application on it produces the output in Listing 13-1.

Listing 13-1: What Happens When You Try to Tidy Gmail's HTML

```
line 7 column 26 - Warning: unescaped & or unknown entity
"&name"
line 7 column 35 - Warning: unescaped & or unknown entity "&ver"
line 12 column 30 - Warning: unescaped & or unknown entity
"&name"
line 12 column 43 - Warning: unescaped & or unknown entity
"&ver"
line 12 column 1 - Warning: <script> attribute "type" lacks
value
line 13 column 33 - Warning: unescaped & or unknown entity
"&name"
```

```
line 13 column 41 - Warning: unescaped & or unknown entity
"&ver"
line 13 column 1 - Warning: <script> attribute "type" lacks
value
line 16 column 1 - Warning: <table> attribute "summary" lacks
value
line 21 column 42 - Warning: unescaped & or unknown entity
"&answer"
line 24 column 1 - Warning: discarding unexpected </table>
line 25 column 1 - Warning: <script> attribute "type" lacks
value
line 17 column 1 - Warning: <script> isn't allowed in <tr>
elements
line 30 column 1 - Warning: <table> attribute "summary" lacks
value
line 30 column 1 - Warning: discarding unexpected <table>
line 46 column 1 - Warning: missing <td>
line 48 column 2 - Warning: discarding unexpected <td>
line 49 column 1 - Warning: <table> attribute "summary" lacks
value
line 59 column 21 - Warning: unescaped & or unknown entity "&pv"
line 62 column 1 - Error: discarding unexpected </form>
line 63 column 1 - Error: discarding unexpected </table>
line 66 column 1 - Error: discarding unexpected </table>
line 67 column 1 - Warning: <table> attribute "summary" lacks
value
line 67 column 1 - Error: discarding unexpected <table>
line 70 column 1 - Warning: <table> attribute "summary" lacks
value
line 73 column 18 - Warning: unescaped & or unknown entity "&v"
line 73 column 22 - Warning: unescaped & or unknown entity "&pv"
line 112 column 1 - Error: discarding unexpected </table>
61 warnings, 18 errors were found! Not all warnings/errors were
shown.
```

It is, in short, horrific HTML. Now, the modern-day browser is used to such things and has no problem in displaying this monstrosity on the screen. Your problems are only just beginning, however. If the page were compliant and well-formed XHTML, you would be able to use any number of XML parsing tools on the source. XPath, for example, would make your life incredibly simple. This is not to be. You're going to have to treat Gmail's HTML front page as any other horribly coded page. It's still much, much simpler than the JavaScript variety, for sure, but it's not as simple as it could be.

It is, then, time for the Old School.

Introducing Basic Scraping

Every page on the web can be *scraped*—it can be downloaded by a script and have its content mined and used as the input for a program. The complexity of this task is dependent on the way the page itself is coded: One of the key reasons why XHTML is so encouraged is that to be correct, XHTML also has to be well-formed XML. Well-formed XML can be processed with a whole raft of useful tools that make the job a simple one. Badly formed markup, like that of Gmail, is different. This "tag soup" requires a more complicated processing model. There are a few, but you're going to use the method produced by the Perl module HTML::TokeParser—Token Parsing.

HTML::TokeParser

Imagine the web page is a stream of tags. With HTML::TokeParser, you leap from tag to tag, first to last, until you reach the one you want, whereupon you can grab the content and move on. Because you start at the top of the page, and specify exactly how many times you jump, and to which tags, an HTML::TokeParser script can look a little complicated, but in reality it's pretty easy to follow. You can find the HTML::TokeParser module at `http://search.cpan.org/~gaas/HTML-Parser-3.45/lib/HTML/TokeParser.pm`.

If you flip to Appendix A, Listing A-4 shows the HTML code of the Gmail Inbox you want to walk through.

As you can see from the listing, the page is made up of lots of tables. The first displays the yellow banner advertising the JavaScript-enhanced version. The second holds the search section. The third holds the left-hand menu, the fourth the labels, and so on, and so on. It is only until you get to the table that starts with the following code that you get to the Inbox itself:

```
<table width=100% cellpadding=2 cellspacing=0 border=0 bgcolor=#e8eef7
class=th>
```

But looking at this section of the code brings you hope and joy. Listing 13-2 shows the code that displays the first and last messages in the Inbox shown in Figure 13-1.

Listing 13-2: A Single Message in the HTML-Only Inbox Source

```
<tr bgcolor=#E8EEF7>
<td width=1% nowrap>
<input type=checkbox name=t
value="1025a4065d9b40bf">
<img src="/gmail/images/cleardot.gif"
width=15 height=15 border=0 alt="">
</td>
<td width=30%>
Ben Hammersley</td>
<td width=68%>
<a href="?th=1025a4065d9b40bf&v=c">
<font size=1><font color=#006633>
</font></font>
hello me
</a></td>
<td nowrap width=1%>Feb 28


...

<td nowrap>Jan 18
<tr bgcolor=#E8EEF7>
<td>
<input type=checkbox name=t
value="101480d8ef5dc74a">
<img src="/gmail/images/star_on_2.gif"
width=15 height=15 border=0 alt=Starred>
</td>
<td >
Ben Hammersley</td>
<td >
<a href="?th=101480d8ef5dc74a&v=c">
<font size=1><font color=#006633>
Heads
</font></font>
Here's a nice message.
</a></td>


...
<tr bgcolor=#E8EEF7>
<td>
```

Continued

Listing 13-2 *(continued)*

```
<input type=checkbox name=t
value="101480d8ef5dc74a">
<img src="/gmail/images/star_on_2.gif"
width=15 height=15 border=0 alt=Starred>
</td>
<td >

Ben Hammersley</td>
<td >
<a href="?th=101480d8ef5dc74a&v=c">
<font size=1><font color=#006633>
Heads
</font></font>
Here's a nice message.
</a></td>
<td nowrap>Jan 6
```

If you look at this code, and know what you already do about the way Gmail works, it's easy to deduce the structure of the page. Each line of the Inbox is structured like this:

```
<tr bgcolor=#E8EEF7>
<td><input type=checkbox name=t value="THREAD ID">
A LINK TO A STAR IMAGE IF THE MESSAGE IS STARRED
</td>
<td >THE AUTHOR NAME</td>
<td ><a href="A RELATIVE LINK TO THE PAGE DISPLAYING THE MAIL">
<font size=1><font color=#006633>THE LABEL</font></font>
THE SUBJECT LINE
</a></td>
<td nowrap>THE DATE.
```

And so, to retrieve your Inbox, you simply retrieve this page, walk through the code until you get to the correct table, collect every instance of the preceding structure, and parse out the details. This is what you shall do now.

Parsing the Inbox

Listing 13-3 shows some Perl code that uses HTML::TokeParser to walk through the HTML-only Inbox page that you saved earlier and print out details of the messages therein. Note that it loads the page as a text file from the disk, and just prints the results out to the screen. You will need to save the Inbox source as 'gmailinboxsource.html' and save it in the same directory as this script. You'll use these results in a more meaningful way later.

Listing 13-3: Walking Through the Inbox with HTML::TokeParser

```perl
#!/usr/bin/perl

use warnings;
use strict;
use HTML::TokeParser;

open( FILEIN, "gmailinboxsource.html" );
undef $/;
my $filecontents = <FILEIN>;

my $stream = HTML::TokeParser->new( \$filecontents );

# Go to the right part of the page, skipping 8 tables (!!!)
$stream->get_tag("table");
$stream->get_tag("table");
$stream->get_tag("table");
$stream->get_tag("table");
$stream->get_tag("table");
$stream->get_tag("table");
$stream->get_tag("table");
$stream->get_tag("table");
$stream->get_tag("table");

# Now we loop through the table, getting the dates and
locations. We need to stop at the bottom of the table, so we
test for a closing /table tag.

PARSE: while ( my $tag = $stream->get_tag ) {

    my $nexttag = $stream->get_tag->[0];
    last PARSE if ( $nexttag eq 'table' );
    $stream->unget_token();

    my $input_tag = $stream->get_tag("input");
    my $threadid  = $input_tag->[1]{value};

    my $starred = $stream->get_trimmed_text() || "Not
Starred";
```

Continued

Listing 13-3 *(continued)*

```
    $stream->get_tag("td");
    my $sender = $stream->get_trimmed_text("/td");

    $stream->get_tag("td");
    $stream->get_tag("font");
    $stream->get_tag("font");
    my $label = $stream->get_trimmed_text("/font") || "No
Label";

    $stream->get_tag("/font");
    my $subject = $stream->get_trimmed_text("/td");

    $stream->get_tag("td");
    my $dateline = $stream->get_trimmed_text();
    $dateline =~ s/†/ /;

    print
"THREADID $threadid\nSTARRED $starred \nSENDER $sender\nLABEL
$label \nSUBJECT $subject\nDATE: $dateline \n\n\n";

}
```

Running this code on the saved page in Listing A-4 produces the output in
Listing 13-4.

Listing 13-4: The Result of 13-3 on A-4

```
THREADID 1025a4065d9b40bf
STARRED Not Starred
SENDER Ben Hammersley
LABEL No Label
SUBJECT hello me
DATE: Feb 28


THREADID 10237338e99e7a8c
STARRED Not Starred
SENDER Ben Hammersley
LABEL No Label
SUBJECT This is the subject line
DATE: Feb 21
```

```
THREADID 10187696869432e6
STARRED Not Starred
SENDER Ben, me (3)
LABEL No Label
SUBJECT This is the third message
DATE: Jan 18


THREADID 101865b95fc7a35a
STARRED Not Starred
SENDER Ben Hammersley
LABEL No Label
SUBJECT This is the second message
DATE: Jan 18


THREADID 101480d8ef5dc74a
STARRED Starred
SENDER Ben Hammersley
LABEL Heads
SUBJECT Here's a nice message.
```

This is a beautiful result. You can take all of the information out of the Inbox — the sender, the date, the subject line, and so on — and do something with it programmatically. You are well on the way to producing your own API.

Now, place that aside for a moment and look at the individual messages. You know that the individual message is identified by the ThreadID, and you now know how to identify that. You can also see, by looking at the HTML code — repeated here in Listing 13-5 — that the individual message is retrieved with a URL constructed like so: `http://gmail.google.com/gmail/h/CACHEBUST-INGSTRING/?th=THREADID&v=c`.

Listing 13-5: The Pertinent Bits of Listing A-4 for Finding the Individual Message

```
<base href="http://gmail.google.com/gmail/h/1m0fzst8pmgu0/">
...

<input type=checkbox name=t
value="1025a4065d9b40bf">
<img src="/gmail/images/cleardot.gif"
```

Continued

Listing 13-5 *(continued)*

```
width=15 height=15 border=0 alt="">
</td>
<td width=30%>
Ben Hammersley</td>
<td width=68%>
<a href="?th=1025a4065d9b40bf&v=c">
<font size=1><font color=#006633>
</font></font>
hello me
</a></td>
<td nowrap width=1%>Feb 28
```

So, you can now work out how to retrieve the message itself. You simply construct the correct URL, retrieve it, parse the page, and there it is.

Retrieving the Individual Page

There are two types of individual message pages, and you'll need to work out how to deal with them in a few paragraphs. In the meantime, jump to Appendix A and check out Listing A-5, which shows the code for the page depicted in Figure 13-2.

FIGURE **13-2: An individual message page, with only one message**

There is a lot going on here. You have the entire message, and all of the associated metadata — the sender, the date, the subject line, and so forth — and you have a whole collection of actions to perform on the message, with (joy of joys) a seemingly easy-to-decipher system of URLs to set them going. Later on in this chapter, you return to this listing to work on these commands.

Meanwhile, you need to get at the message contents. The technique is exactly the same as when you looked through the Inbox. Listing 13-6 shows the code that does this.

Listing 13-6: Code to Parse an Individual Message Page

```perl
#!/usr/bin/perl

use warnings;
use strict;
use HTML::TokeParser;

open( FILEIN, "Gmail - single message.html" );
undef $/;
my $filecontents = <FILEIN>;

my $stream = HTML::TokeParser->new( \$filecontents );

$stream->get_tag("table");
$stream->get_tag("table");
$stream->get_tag("table");
$stream->get_tag("table");
$stream->get_tag("table");
$stream->get_tag("table");
$stream->get_tag("table");
$stream->get_tag("table");
$stream->get_tag("table");
$stream->get_tag("table");
$stream->get_tag("table");

$stream->get_tag("b");

my $subject = $stream->get_trimmed_text("/b");

$stream->get_tag("b");
my $from_true_name = $stream->get_trimmed_text("/b");

$stream->get_tag("/font");
my $from_email_address = $stream->get_trimmed_text("/td");
```

Continued

Listing 13-6 *(continued)*

```
$stream->get_tag("td");
my $dateline = $stream->get_trimmed_text("tr");

$stream->get_tag("td");
my $to_line = $stream->get_trimmed_text("tr");

$stream->get_tag("div");
$stream->get_tag("div");
my $message_text = $stream->get_text("/div");

print
" \nSENDER $from_true_name $from_email_address \nSUBJECT
$subject\nDATE: $dateline \nTO: $to_line\nMESSAGE:
$message_text\n";
```

Running this script—again, as with Listing 13-3, it works on the page saved to disk—produces the output shown in Figure 13-3.

So this is increasingly useful: You can retrieve the Inbox, find a ThreadID, and bring down a message if the thread contains only one message. You can then take that message and grab the information out of it.

FIGURE 13-3: The result of running Listing 13-6

Dealing with Threads

Here's the problem, however: Gmail's individual message page doesn't show an individual message. Rather, it shows parts of an entire thread, and the entire message of the last one in the thread.

However, look at the top right of the individual message page. There's a link to "Expand All." Clicking this link brings you a page that shows all of the content of all of the messages within that particular ThreadID. To test this, I sent a series of messages to my Gmail account with the same subject line. Gmail naturally compiled these messages into a thread. The URL for the default view (the one displaying the latest message in full, but the previous messages' headers only) was `http://gmail.google.com/gmail/h/o1xhaxisf335/?th=102f31cbbb3d650f&v=c`.

The Expand All view's URL was `http://gmail.google.com/gmail/h/60blkj19nnjc/?d=e&th=102f31cbbb3d650f&v=c`.

The addition of the single flag `d=e` causes Gmail to return all of the information you need. You already know that the random string in the middle of the URL is a cache-busting string and can be anything, so you can say that the URL to retrieve a full message thread is `http://gmail.google.com/gmail/h/RANDOMSTRING/?d=e&th=THREADID&v=c`.

One thing remains to check. What happens if you try this URL with a ThreadID of a thread with only one message? Will it still work? The answer, which you can test yourself, is yes. It does. So now you can see how to read the mail in the Inbox. You just need to make two passes with your scraping code. The first runs through the Inbox listing, grabbing the ThreadIDs of each message. The second pass takes that ThreadID and makes it into a URL as described. You then need only to retrieve that page and scrape it to read the messages.

Dealing with Other Folders

As you may be noticing, working with the HTML-only version of Gmail is much easier than the JavaScript version — when it comes to making an API, at least. It's a very steady, almost plodding, discovery of techniques. The next thing to look for, I think, is how to read messages in the other folders: Starred, Sent Mail, All Mail, Drafts, and so on.

This is a simple matter. When I opened each of these folders, I found these URLS:

- **Inbox:** `http://gmail.google.com/gmail/h/q2fuyjw4p8mu/?`
- **Starred:** `http://gmail.google.com/gmail/h/q2fuyjw4p8mu/?s=r`
- **Sent Mail:** `http://gmail.google.com/gmail/h/q2fuyjw4p8mu/?s=s`
- **Drafts:** `http://gmail.google.com/gmail/h/q2fuyjw4p8mu/?s=d`
- **All Mail:** `http://gmail.google.com/gmail/h/q2fuyjw4p8mu/?s=a`
- **Spam:** `http://gmail.google.com/gmail/h/q2fuyjw4p8mu/?s=m`
- **Trash:** `http://gmail.google.com/gmail/h/q2fuyjw4p8mu/?s=t`

Ignoring the random seed again, you can see that the `s=` attribute sets the folder to view. Setting it to anything else but the preceding options returns an error, except, happily setting it to `s=i`, which gives you the Inbox.

So, to retrieve the mail from another folder, you simply form the URL as in the preceding list, send it to the scraping script you wrote earlier in this chapter, and proceed from there.

And Now . . .

So, you now have the basic techniques down for interacting with the HTML-only version of Gmail. You now know how to scrape the pages, and you now know how to find and, in theory, gather information from, all of the messages. In the next chapter, you learn how to export your mail, whether for re-import into another application or to back it up. As good as Gmail is, always being able to leave is sometimes a good excuse to stay.

Exporting Your Mail

The hallmark of a truly great web application is the ease with which you can remove your data should you want to leave. In the words of the poet, if you love someone set them free.

Sadly, Gmail doesn't make it easy to get your mail out of there. There's no built-in facility to do so at all, at least at the time of this writing. Of course, many would say that Gmail is so shiny that you'd be mad to stop using it. Maybe so, but in this chapter you look at how to do that anyway.

Exporting as a Massive Text File

The first way to export your mail, and the simplest, is to dump the lot to a big text file — illustrated in Listing 14-1. It's not very useful for re-importing your mail into another application, but it is good for backups of data that you'd like on paper, for example.

in this chapter

☑ Converting to a big text file

☑ Converting to Mbox

☑ Appending to IMAP

Listing 14-1: Export All Mail to a Text File

```
use Utils;

$gmail = login();

$messages = $gmail->get_messages();

open OUTPUT, ">mailarchive.txt";


foreach (@{$messages}) {

my $full_message = $gmail->get_indv_email(msg =>
$message);
....print OUTPUT "Sender:   " . $full_message-
>{$id}->{"sender_email"} . "\n";
```

Continued

Listing 14-1 *(continued)*

```
....print OUTPUT "Sent:      " . $full_message->{$id}->{"sent"}
. "\n";
....print OUTPUT "Subject: " . strip_bold($full_message-
>{$id}->{"subject"}) . "\n\n";
....print OUTPUT $full_message->{$id}->{"body"} . "\n\n----
\n";
}

close OUTPUT;
```

Running the script produces a file in the directory the script is run from called
mailarchive.txt. It will look rather like this:

```
Sender: bobette@example.com
Sent: 12:01pm
Subject: This is a mail

You are a very sexy man.
Love
Bob x


----
Sender: bobette@example.com
Sent: 11:23pm
Subject: Terrible confession

I've lost my wristwatch. Have you seen it?
Puzzled
Bob x


----
```

And so on. Very nice for printing or storing on a keychain flash drive in case of
some form of dreadful server failure at the Google farm. Of course, flippancy aside,
it is nice to have a printout of a series of mails. As you know from previous chapters how to select mails from specific labels, you can use a variation of Listing 14-1
to provide backups of mail specific to certain projects, or subjects, or whatever you
like. That is very useful, depending on your own personal work style.

Converting to Mbox

Much more useful, converting to the Mbox format allows your Gmail to be imported into most popular e-mail applications. Listing 14-2 converts your Gmail Inbox into an Mbox-compatible file. It needs two modules, in addition to the Utils.pm module you've been using for this section of the book (that, if you've forgotten, is found in Listing 7-4):

- **Mail::Internet:** Available from `http://search.cpan.org/~markov/`

- **Mail::Folder::Mbox:** Available from `http://search.cpan.org/~kjohnson`

Listing 14-2: Convert to Mbox

```
use Utils;
use Mail::Internet;
use Mail::Folder::Mbox;

$gmail = login();

$inbox = new Mail::Folder('mbox');
$inbox->create('inbox');
$inbox->open('inbox');

$messages =
  $gmail->get_messages( label =>
$Mail::Webmail::Gmail::FOLDERS{"INBOX"} )
  ;    # simply get all messages from INBOX

foreach ( @{$messages} ) {    # and iterate through them
    $message = $gmail->get_mime_email( msg => $_ );    #
retrive MIME message
    @message_lines = split( /\n/, $message );    # split
it into lines
    map { $_ .= "\n" } @message_lines;    # prevent joining of
lines in the body
    $message_inet =
      new Mail::Internet( \@message_lines )
      ;    # construct RFC822
compilant message
    $inbox->append_message($message_inet);    # and append it
into mbox
```

Continued

Listing 14-2 *(continued)*

```
}

$inbox->sync();
$inbox->close();
```

Running the script, as ever, produces an mbox file in the directory in which it is run. This one is called "inbox" and will contain the contents of your Gmail Inbox.

Note   From the previous chapters, it should be easy to see how to vary this script to deal with mail in the archive or with a specific label.

Apple Mail.app, Thunderbird, and Entorage and Eudora can all deal with importing Mbox files directly. Outlook, however, cannot. It requires an .idx file for each folder, which contains an index of the mails within. It's easy to produce one of these, however: Simply grab a copy of Eudora from `http://eudora.com/products/eudora/download/` and import into there. Then rename the folder in Eudora (and rename it back again if you like) to force it to produce an .idx file. Then you can export from Eudora, and the .idx file that Outlook needs will be there. A bit fiddly, yes, but that's what you get for using Outlook.

Appending to IMAP

The Internet Message Access Protocol, or IMAP, is by far the best protocol for accessing e-mails from a desktop client. Unlike POP3, IMAP allows you to keep your mail on a server — folders, sub-folders and all — and access it from multiple clients and devices. This means that you can, for example, have your mail synchronized between your home and work desktop machines, your laptop, and your phone. (Of course, Gmail does that too, without all the messing around, but who's quibbling at this point?)

It can be very useful to dump your Inbox into an IMAP account, and that's what Listing 14-3 does.

Listing 14-3: Appending to IMAP

```
use Utils;
use Net::IMAP;

$gmail = login();
$imap = new Net::IMAP( "IMAP SERVER ADDRESS", Debug => 1 );
$imap->login( "USERNAME", "PASSWORD" );

$messages =
  $gmail->get_messages( label =>
$Mail::Webmail::Gmail::FOLDERS{"INBOX"} )
  ;     # simply get all messages from INBOX

foreach ( @{$messages} ) {     # and iterate through them
    $message = $gmail->get_mime_email( msg => $_ );     #
retrive MIME message
    $imap->append( "INBOX", $message );     # and append it to
the IMAP INBOX
}

$imap->logout();
```

By now, as you come to the end of this book, you should be confident in dealing with mail within the archive and under different labels. I leave it to you as an exercise, therefore, to move labeled mail into the IMAP folders.

And Now . . .

For the final chapter of the book, you're going to look at the different applications that have already been written using the techniques you've learned in this section.

Using Gmail to . . .

G mail's popularity, enormous storage, search capability, and labels mean that many people have been hacking new uses for the application. This chapter, then, looks at some of the more unusual uses that people are putting the system to.

Using Gmail as a To-Do List

Around the same time as Gmail was launched, the tech world spawned a fashion for being really, really organized. To-do lists are a stylish accessory for any self-respecting geek, and, of course, Gmail can be fashioned into a fine tool for such things.

Using Filters

The first way of making to-do lists is to use plus addresses and filters. The plus address feature, as you'll remember from Chapter 3, is the one where you can add a plus sign (+) and then any string to your Gmail address without it making any difference. For example, `Ben.Hammersley+fanmail@gmail.com` is exactly the same as `Ben.Hammersley@gmail.com` or `Ben.Hammersley+hatemail@gmail.com` or `Ben.Hammersley+dinner_invitations@gmail.com` or whatever. They'll all be delivered to my address, no matter what you put after the plus sign.

However, you can set filters on the address, and push specific ones into specific labels. Figure 15-1 shows a filter set up to do just that, sending `ben.hammersley+todo@gmail.com` to the label "Todo".

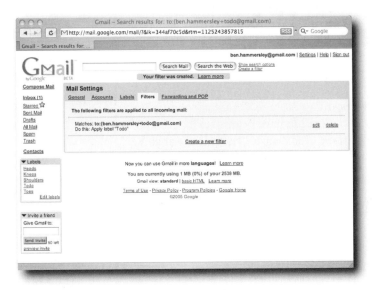

FIGURE 15-1: Setting a filter for a to-do list

What's the point of that? Well, it's easy to send e-mail, whether you're sat at your main machine or using a mobile device — and so you can send new to-do list items to your Gmail account with a few simple keystrokes. Place the to-do item itself in the subject line, and you can have a screen very much like Figure 15-2 — showing the "Todo" label index, now passing muster as a very useful to-do list in itself.

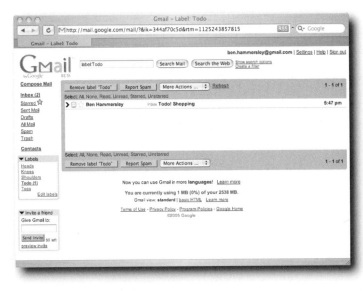

FIGURE 15-2: The Todo label listing

Using gmtodo

Gnome desktop users needn't go crazy with the preceding technique when they have a complete to-do list application to use: gmtodo, from `http://gmtodo.sourceforge.net/`.

Paul Miller's application is written in Python, and hence uses Libgmail. It also requires Pygtk, but most Linux distributions have that as standard. If you don't, you'll get an error message, and will have to download it from `www.pygtk.org`.

Once you've done that, or just gone ahead and unarchived the application, you run it from the command line with a judicious `python gmtodo.py`.

gmtodo works in exactly the same way as the plus address method, only giving it a nice GUI. The one thing you should know is that your Gmail username and password are stored in plain text in a file called .gmtodo in your home directory. If you consider that an unnecessary security risk, you've been warned.

Using Gmail to Find Information in RSS Feeds

If you're like me, you probably spend the first 37 hours or so of your working week trolling through your newsreader, in search of blog-borne snippets of wisdom and genius. Fifteen thousand blog posts about cats and new Apple rumors later, and you're none the wiser. But, still, somewhere back there, half an hour ago, there might have been something vaguely interesting. If only you could remember what it was.

Gmail, obviously, can help. By using an RSS to E-mail service, and the plus address technique discussed earlier in the chapter, you can use Gmail to store your RSS feeds, ready for the searching thereof. To do this, I like to use the free service at `www.rssfwd.com`, as shown in Figure 15-3.

By subscribing to the feeds I like to read and then setting up a plus address'n'label combo as you did in the previous section, I know that I will always have an archive of all of the old feeds I've read. I don't actually use Gmail as my newsreader — although I could, I guess — because I prefer my desktop client for that. But as a store and search system, it's perfect.

FIGURE 15-3: A screenshot of rssfwd.com

Using Gmail to Find Torrent Files

The technique used above, to filter RSS feeds into labels, can also be used to search for torrent files from your favorite Bittorrent tracker site. These sites invariably have RSS feeds of their latest offerings, but the feeds are far too fast moving, and far too full of rubbish, to be worth reading manually. Instead, forward them to Gmail in the same manner you would forward your RSS feeds, and use Gmail's search capability to find the ones you want. If you're looking for a torrent for a particular show but don't want to have to keep going back to Gmail to check, have a filter forward it to another e-mail address, as in Figure 15-4.

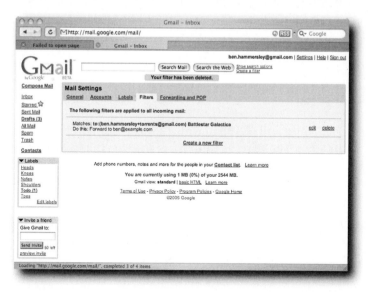

FIGURE 15-4: Not that you'll have anything to do with this naughty activity

Using Gmail as a Notepad

Jonathan Aquino, a blogger from British Columbia, called Gmail the Notepad of the web. "Today," he said at `http://jonaquino.blogspot.com/2005/03/gmail-as-notepad-of-web.html`, "I realized that Gmail's latest features make it an excellent replacement for Notepad and other basic desktop text editors. (Use its Save Draft feature so that you can edit your text whenever you want.)"

It's certainly a worthwhile insight making. Indeed, as he went on to say, Gmail has a number of advantages over Notepad or any other ordinary text editors. Gmail, he said, beats Notepad with the following:

- Filename is optional. No need to think of a unique filename to save under — just enter your content and go.
- Search all your past files at once. Try that, Notepad!
- Spell-checking on demand.

- Load/save your text files from any computer in the world.

- Cross-platform — you can access it from any make or model of machine, as long as you can get online with a web browser.

- Undo Discard. Ever wish you could retrieve your file after closing it without saving? Now you can.

This technique works pretty well — and now that Gmail has rich-text editing capabilities, it has become even more powerful. Because you might be using the Drafts folder for things other than stored notes, you might want to assign the mail a label. Figure 15-5 shows my Drafts folder with three notes within. I've labeled two.

Imaginative readers — that's all of you — will have spotted that you can easily write a script to keep your Gmail-held notes copied to your local machine. I leave that as an exercise to the newly enlightened reader.

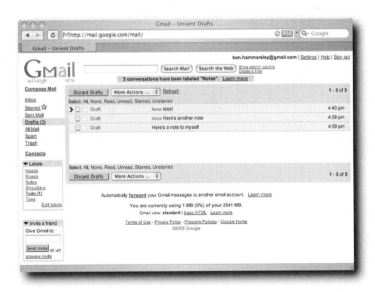

FIGURE 15-5: Using Gmail as a notepad application

Using Gmail as a Spam Filter

If there's one thing Gmail knows, it's spam. Hosting millions of e-mail addresses means millions of spam messages arrive every day—and Google must unleash their minions in the never-ending battle to stop that stuff from getting into your Inbox.

So, Gmail's spam filters are really good, and with a little bit of cunning technique, you can use the system to filter all of your mail, and not just Gmail.

You can do this because Gmail allows you to forward messages. This is a little bit complicated, so bear with me. Here's what to do:

Go to the Settings page, click the Forwarding tab, and set Gmail to forward all messages to your non-Gmail account (from now on referred to as example.com).

Once you've done that, all messages to gmail.com will go to example.com, except for the spam, which will be filtered.

Now, go to your example.com mail server and create a filter to check the headers of any incoming e-mail. Have it forward to your Gmail account if it does not find the following in the header:

```
X-Forwarded-For: user@gmail.com user@example.com
```

There are many ways to do this, and you'd be wise to ask your system administrator to advise you on it. For really advanced users, a procmail filter to do this looks like this (with your Gmail account and real mail server replacing user@gmail.com and user@example.com in the obvious places):

```
:0
* !^X-Forwarded-For: user@gmail.com user@example.com
! user@gmail.com
```

When this is set up, your server sends all the mail that Gmail hasn't seen to Gmail. Gmail filters it for spam, and then passes it back, having added in the header. The filter ignores all the messages with the X-Forwarded-For header, and so all you see in your example.com account is beautifully filtered mail.

This technique also has the advantage of saving a copy of all of your mail within Gmail, which is handy for backups. And remember, if you use Gmail as your SMTP server, too, all your outgoing mail will be saved also.

An Even Simpler Way of Doing It

There is, naturally, an even easier way to do this. Justin Blanton, this tome's noble technical editor, points out that if you can't set server-side filters but can create multiple mail accounts, you can do the following:

1. Create a new mail account (the username doesn't matter; no one will see it).

2. Forward the e-mail from your current account to Gmail.

3. Forward your Gmail e-mail to the account you just created.

4. Gmail filters your e-mail *before* forwarding it along.

5. Use your *new* mail account (you'll obviously want to set the "reply-to" and "from" fields to your current address and not the one you just created).

This is very elegant but does require multiple e-mail accounts.

Using Gmail as Storage for a Photo Gallery

As something as a transition to the final chapter, this use of Gmail is borderline naughty. Indeed, at the time of this writing, Google has taken the author's Gmail account away from him, so fiendish is his wares. Still, he fears nothing here in Chapter 14 and so will happily point to Goollery, the PHP system for using Gmail as the storage for an online photo gallery.

Figure 15-6 shows it in action on the demo site. You can download Goollery from `www.wirzm.ch/goollery/`.

The authors, Martin Wirz, Andres Villegas, and Matias Daniel Medina, have done a very nice job with Goollery. It's easy to use, requiring only PHP, curl, and ImageMagick to be installed on your server to begin with. (These are all pretty standard, and your system administrator can help you.)

Once that's done, you must create a label within your Gmail account called "pictures" and then follow the rest of the installation instructions included within the Goollery package.

Goollery uses PHP, and so libgmail, to access Gmail. In the next chapter, you see precisely how this works.

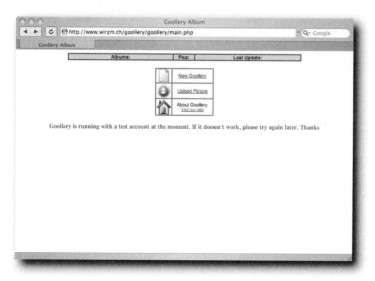

FIGURE 15-6: Goollery in action

And Now . . .

I hope that this chapter has shown you some of the interesting things you can do when you have an almost limitless amount of storage space, some cunning filters, or a bit of imagination.

To finish up the book, you're going to look at perhaps the most extreme use of Gmail—using the webmail application as a mountable file system.

Using GmailFS

Very early on in the life of the Gmail beta program, Richard Jones out-geeked everyone with the release of version 0.1 of the GmailFS — a mountable file system for Linux machines that uses Gmail as the storage mechanism. This chapter examines GmailFS and discusses how it works and how to use it.

The Underlying Idea

in this chapter

☑ Installing GmailFS

☑ Using Gmail FS

☑ How GmailFS works

The shocking thing about Gmail, apart from the cleverness of the asynchronous JavaScript and XML interface, is the amount of storage available to the user. A gigabyte is a lot of space for mail, especially when it is free. It's so much space, indeed, that the second question on a lot of people's lips (after "How do they do that" had been answered) was, "What can you do to fill it up?"

The answer, Richard Jones decided, was to use Gmail as the storage for a file system. One gigabyte is a nice size for an emergency backup, or to share files between friends. It is, after all, 200 or so good-sized MP3 files — legally downloaded, of course.

Installing GmailFS

GmailFS works on Linux machines only. For Windows machines, the equivalent program is GmailDrive.

The Correct Python

First, you need to make sure you have Python 2.3 installed. Python will probably have come pre-installed with your OS, but you need to make sure it is version 2.3 or above. There are many tests for this, depending on your system.

If you are using an RPM-based distribution — Red Hat, Mandrake, or SuSE, for example — you can get a package's version number by using `rpm`. Open a terminal window, and type the following command:

```
rpm -q python
```

This should give a result similar to the following:

```
python-2.3.0
```

If the version number is too low, you should download the update from `http://python.org/download/` and follow the instructions there.

If you're running a DEB-based distribution — Debian or Knoppix, for example — use `apt-cache` by opening a terminal and typing the following:

```
apt-cache show python
```

Again, this should give a message showing the version number. Go to `http://python.org/download/` if the number is below 2.3.

If you're not using DEB or RPM, then you need to ask for the version number from Python directly. Again, open the terminal window, and type **python**. Figure 16-1 shows the result.

FIGURE 16-1: Python showing and telling

(This screenshot, the cunning amongst you will have noticed, was done on an Apple, not a Linux box. For the sake of the Python version, this makes no difference.)

To exit Python, you have to press Ctrl+D.

Installing FUSE

The majority of the cleverness that makes up the GmailFS package comes from the FUSE library from `http://fuse.sourceforge.net/`.

Standing for File System in Userspace, FUSE is a package that allows programs to implement their own fully functional file system. Your version of Linux may have it already installed — Debian does, for example — but if not you can download it from `http://fuse.sourceforge.net/`.

The GmailFS package was developed to work with version 1.3 of FUSE, which is quite an old version. It is still available for download, however. Later versions of FUSE may well work, too; it's worth experimenting.

You also need to install the FUSE Python bindings from `http://cvs.source forge.net/viewcvs.py/fuse/`.

Once you have downloaded these packages, you just need to unpack them and follow the instructions within.

Installing Libgmail

The final tool you need before installing GmailFS is Libgmail. You've met this many times before in earlier chapters. You can get the latest version from `http://libgmail.sourceforge.net/`. Remember to download the very latest version from the CVS section of that site.

Installing GmailFS

Finally you are ready to install GmailFS. Download version 0.3 from `http://richard.jones.name/google-hacks/gmail-filesystem/gmailfs-0.3.tar.gz`, unpack it, and copy `gmailfs.py` to `/usr/local/bin`.

After doing that, copy `mount.gmailfs` to `/sbin`.

Finally, the distribution contains a configuration file called `gmailfs.conf`. It looks like Listing 16-1.

Listing 16-1: gmailfs.conf

```
[connection]
#proxy = http://user:pass@proxyhost:port
# or just
```

Continued

Listing 16-1 *(continued)*

```
#proxy = http://proxyhost:port
#retries = 3

[account]
username = gmailusername
password = gmailpassword

[filesystem]
fsname = linux_fs_3

[references]
# reference = filesystem:username:password

[logs]
# Change this to DEBUG for verbose output useful for debugging
level = INFO
```

Simply place your username and password in the obvious places, and copy the entire file to /etc.

If you are behind a proxy, you will need to enter the details into gmailfs.conf in the obvious place and also install pyOpenSSL from http://pyOpenSSL.source forge.net/, and pyOpenSSLProxy from http://richard.jones.name/ google-hacks/gmail-filesystem/pyOpenSSLProxy-0.1.tar.gz.

Once everything is installed, you are ready to use the system.

Using GmailFS

There are two ways to launch the GmailFS: You can either mount it from the command line or use fstab.

Mounting GmailFS from the Command Line

To mount from the command line, type this command, press return, and proceed to the section "Passing Commands to the File System" a bit later:

```
mount -t gmailfs /usr/local/bin/gmailfs.py /gmailfs    -o
fsname=XXXXX
```

Replace the xxxxx with a hard-to-guess string. This string, the name of the file system, must be weird and difficult to guess, because (as you will see) people can corrupt the system by sending you mail with that name in the subject line.

Mounting GmailFS from fstab

Linux machines have a file called /etc/fstab, which contains the details of all of the drives and partitions the system can see. You can add GmailFS to the fstab file to make the drive a permanent addition to your system.

To use fstab, place an entry inside /etc/fstab that looks like this:

```
/usr/local/bin/gmailfs.py /gmailfs gmailfs noauto,
fsname=XXXXX
```

Again, replace the xxxxx with the name you wish to give the file system. You will probably need root access to add things to the fstab file. Once the line has been added, reboot the machine.

Passing Commands to the File System

With the commands passed in the previous section, you now have a file system mounted at /gmailfs. So, from the command line you can use cd /gmailfs and then use any of the normal shell commands: ls, mkdir, rm, and so on. For all intents and purposes, the GmailFS is just the same as if it were a 1 gigabyte hard disk.

Copying files to and from a GmailFS directory is pretty quick, depending of course on the speed of your Internet connection, but running ls to get a directory listing takes a very long time if you have lots of mail. To understand why, take a look at how GmailFS works.

Using Multiple GmailFS Drives

Because you are giving the GmailFS system a specific, hard-to-guess name, denoted in the command line by the fsname= parameter, you are actually able to run more than one file system from the same Gmail account. You can mount as many as you like, as long as each one has a different name.

How GmailFS Works

GmailFS works with four parts: FUSE, which provides the interface to the Linux kernel that allows additional file systems to be created by programs (in what is technically known as userspace); Libgmail, which provides the interface to Gmail; Gmail, which provides the storage; and GmailFS itself, which links the three others together.

The part of the system where FUSE talks with the Linux kernel is beyond the scope of this book, and is well documented on the web. And by now you should be confident with sending and receiving mail with Libgmail. So all you need to understand is how the files are stored on Gmail.

What Makes Up a File?

To really understand the system, you need to know how a general UNIX file system identifies a file. Under an ordinary Unix file system, a file consists of three things: the content of the file itself; a file called an inode, which contains the details of the file; and a pointer to the inode inside another file that represents a directory.

This is perhaps a little confusing, so consider an example. Say you want to access a file called supersecretpasswords.txt. To display the contents of the file you would ordinarily use the command cat supersecretpasswords.txt. You can see this in Figure 16-2.

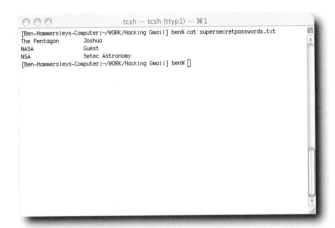

FIGURE 16-2: Displaying the contents of a file

For the `cat` command to access the file, the operating system first opens the file that represents the directory. Within that is a list of filenames, each with a corresponding name of an inode file.

The operating system then opens the inode, and it is the inode that tells the operating system where the file is on the disk and all of the rest of the data about the file. This *metadata* is quite extensive and contains the following information:

- The location of the item's contents on the disk
- What the item is (such as a file, directory, or symbolic link)
- The item's size, in bytes
- The time the file's inode was last modified — also called the ctime
- The time the file's contents were last modified — the mtime
- The time the file was last accessed — the atime
- The number of names the file has — hard links
- The file's owner — the UID
- The file's group — the GID
- The file's permissions — for example, 755

Because the file's contents, the inode, and the pointer to it from the directory are all separate, a single file can have many names. Each name is called a *hard link*. Deleting a link doesn't delete the file or the inode itself, only the link, as there may be other links pointing to the inode, and hence to the contents of the file. When a file has no hard links left, the kernel will count it as deleted and allow it to be physically overwritten on the disk itself.

So, so far you have two types of file that dictate the file system: the directory file, which matches the filename to the inode, and the inode, which matches lots of metadata to a block of data on the disk.

The third part of the file system, then, is the physical block on the disk. For most file systems, this is indeed a physical address, but as different types of storage have different ways of addressing their own bits (pun intended), this section, too, can be abstracted away into a file.

So, you have the directory pointing to the inode, the inode pointing to the datablock, and the datablock pointing to the actual data — and then, as shown in Figure 16-2, the data pointing to world domination. Excellent.

Representing All of This in E-Mail

But lest you forget, you're trying to represent all of this data in e-mail messages and not a proper storage medium. The translation between the two is the job of FUSE and GmailFS. Together, they handle the requests from the operating system for the data inside the directories, the inodes, and then the datablocks, and feed it back in the manner that the kernel expects.

To do that, GmailFS needs to store all of these different types of data within the framework that e-mail provides. Think on this: What is the framework available for data within e-mail?

It's easy, actually. You can use the subject line, the body of the message itself, and any number of attachments. That is how GmailFS works.

The Actual Data in Action

GmailFS just uses the subject line and the attachments. Nothing is held in the message body itself. There are three types of messages used.

- **Directory and file entry messages:** These hold the parent path and name of a file or a directory. The subject of these messages has a reference to the file's or directory's inode.

- **Inode messages:** The subject line of these messages holds the information found in an inode.

- **Datablock messages:** These messages hold the file's data in attachments. The subject of the messages holding these structures contains a reference to the file's inode as well as the current block number. Because Gmail has a size limit of 5MB for attachments, this message may contain more than one attachment.

So, now when you run the `cat supersecretpasswords.txt` command on a file within the GmailFS system, FUSE and the GmailFS script first use Libgmail to request the corresponding file entry message. This command points them to the inode message, which then points them to the datablock message and the data you need.

As previously mentioned in a sidebar, each of the messages' subject lines contains the file system name. This allows you to use more than one file system off the same Gmail account, and also provides some security. The security comes from the way that GmailFS adds data to itself — by sending mail to itself. Without the hard-to-guess file system name, it would be possible for an outside party to send messages to the account that added data to the file system.

And Now . . .

And so, the end is near. In this chapter, you've looked at how file systems work, and how Gmail can be used as such. Doing so allows you to host large amounts of files and applications "out there" on the Internet, with only the tiny GmailFS application needed to access it. You can, for example, carry the GmailFS application around on a so-cheap-it's-free thumbdrive and then have gigabytes of data waiting on Gmail accounts. You can even, if you're feeling very, very, very geeky, save a browser to a GmailFS drive, and check your Gmail via the browser hosting on the same account. Ah, it's all too much for me, and so, with that, we come to the end.

Long Code Listings

This book contains a lot of code. You love it really, but the designers do not. So to make the book more readable I moved all the long bits of code to this appendix. Enjoy!

Chapter 4

Listing A-1: The HTML That Displays the Inbox

```
<HTML>
  <HEAD>
    <META http-equiv="content-type"
content="text/html; charset=UTF-8"/>
    <SCRIPT>
D=(top.js&amp;&amp;top.js.init)?function(d){top.
js.P(window,d)}:function(){};if(window==top){top
.location='/gmail?search=inbox&amp;view=tl&amp;s
tart=0&amp;init=1&amp;zx=3177c401850460908955817
35&amp;fs=1';}    </SCRIPT>
    <SCRIPT>
&lt;!--
D([&quot;v&quot;,,&quot;3177c40185046090&quot;]
);
D([&quot;ud&quot;,,&quot;ben.hammersley@gmail.com
&quot;,,&quot;{\&quot;o\&quot;:\&quot;OPEN\&quot;
,\&quot;/\&quot;:\&quot;SEARCH\&quot;,\&quot;\\r
\&quot;:\&quot;OPEN\&quot;,,\&quot;k\&quot;:\&quo
t;PREV\&quot;,,\&quot;r\&quot;:\&quot;REPLY\&quot
;,\&quot;c\&quot;:\&quot;COMPOSE\&quot;,,\&quot;g
c\&quot;:\&quot;GO_CONTACTS\&quot;,,\&quot;gd\&qu
ot;:\&quot;GO_DRAFTS\&quot;,,\&quot;p\&quot;:\&qu
ot;PREVMSG\&quot;,,\&quot;gi\&quot;:\&quot;GO_INB
OX\&quot;,,\&quot;a\&quot;:\&quot;REPLYALL\&quot;
,\&quot;!\&quot;:\&quot;SPAM\&quot;,,\&quot;f\&qu
ot;:\&quot;FORWARD\&quot;,,\&quot;u\&quot;:\&quot
;BACK\&quot;
```

Continued

```
,\&quot;ga\&quot;:\&quot;GO_ALL\&quot;,,\&quot;j\&quot;:\&quot;
NEXT\&quot;,,\&quot;y\&quot;:\&quot;REMOVE\&quot;,,\&quot;n\&quo
t;:\&quot;NEXTMSG\&quot;,,\&quot;gs\&quot;:\&quot;GO_STARRED\&q
uot;,,\&quot;x\&quot;:\&quot;SELECT\&quot;,,\&quot;s\&quot;:\&qu
ot;STAR\&quot;}&quot;]
);
D([&quot;p&quot;,,[&quot;sx_em&quot;,,&quot;&quot;]
,[&quot;sx_at&quot;,,&quot;archive&quot;]
,[&quot;bx_show0&quot;,,&quot;1&quot;]
]
);
D([&quot;ppd&quot;,,0]
);
D([&quot;i&quot;,,4]
);
D([&quot;qu&quot;,,&quot;0 MB&quot;,,&quot;1000
MB&quot;,,&quot;0%&quot;,,&quot;#006633&quot;]
);
D([&quot;ft&quot;,,&quot;Use the \&lt;span
style=\&quot;color:#0000CC;text-
decoration:underline;cursor:pointer;cursor:hand;white-space:no
wrap\&quot; id=\&quot;fsb\&quot;\&gt;search\&lt;/span\&gt; box
or \&lt;span style=\&quot;color:#0000CC;text-
decoration:underline;cursor:pointer;cursor:hand;white-space:no
wrap\&quot; id=\&quot;mt_adv\&quot;\&gt;search
options\&lt;/span\&gt; to find messages quickly!&quot;]
);
D([&quot;ds&quot;,,1,0,0,0,0,0,0]
);
D([&quot;ct&quot;,,[]
]
);
D([&quot;ts&quot;,,0,50,1,0,&quot;Inbox&quot;,,&quot;100ae7248b9
&quot;,,1,[]
]
);
D([&quot;t&quot;,,[&quot;100adb8b86f18e51&quot;,,1,0,&quot;\&lt;
b\&gt;2:29pm\&lt;/b\&gt;&quot;,,&quot;\&lt;span
id=\'_user_ben@benhammersley.com\'\&gt;\&lt;b\&gt;Ben
Hammersley\&lt;/b\&gt;\&lt;/span\&gt;
(2)&quot;,,&quot;\&lt;b\&gt;&amp;raquo;\&lt;/b\&gt; &q
uot;,,&quot;\&lt;b\&gt;Skinning Gmail? That\'s so
cool!\&lt;/b\&gt;&quot;,,&quot;BEGIN PGP SIGNED MESSAGE-- Hash:
SHA1 la la la --BEGIN PGP SIGNATURE-- Version: GnuPG v1
&amp;hellip;&quot;,,[]
,&quot;&quot;,,&quot;100adb8b86f18e51&quot;,,0]
```

```
]
);
D([&quot;te&quot;]);

//--&gt;       </SCRIPT>
    <STYLE>

body {background:#fff;margin:1ex}body,td,input,textarea,select
{font-family:arial,sans-serif}input,textarea,select {font-
size:100%}form {margin:0;width:100%}select {width:20ex}.b
{font-weight:bold}.r {text-align:right}.c {text-
align:center}img {border:0}.s {font-size:80%}.xs
{font-size:70%}.sxs {font-size:87%}.lk {color:#0000CC;text-
decoration:underline;cursor:pointer;cursor:hand;white-space:no
wrap}.l {color:#0000CC;cursor:pointer;cursor:hand;white-
space:nowrap}.lc {color:#0000CC}.urlc {color:#006633}.g
{color:#444}.h {cursor:pointer;cursor:hand}.ilc {text-
decoration:underline;cursor:pointer;cursor:hand;white-space:no
wrap;font-weight:bold}.nfc {color:#AA0000;font-weight:bold}.gr
{color:#006633}.ab {font-size:85%;vertical-
align:middle;padding:0 10 0 10}.ct
{color:#006633;font-size:80%}.mh {font-size:80%}.mh div
{padding-bottom:4}.asl {font-weight:bold;text-
align:right;vertical-align:top;padding-top:4px;width:1%}.asbu
{font-size:80%}.nt table {background:#FAD163;font-
size:80%;font-weight:bold;white-space:nowrap}.nm {padding:0 15
1}.phd {padding:6 0 10}.phd table {background:#FAD163;font-
weight:bold;margin:auto;font-size:80%}.ph {padding:7 12}.nl
{font-size:80%;white-space:nowrap;padding:2 0 2 8}.cv {font-
size:80%;width:100%}.nb
{width:100%;background:white;table-layout:fixed}.nb div
{white-space:nowrap;overflow:hidden;text-overflow:ellipsis}.cs
{color:#063}.rv {color:#00c}.cs, .rv {font-size:70%;padding:0
2 2;width:100%;text-overflow:ellipsis}.th td {font-
size:80%;}.tlc
{table-layout:fixed;cursor:pointer;cursor:hand}.tlc col {font-
size:80%}.tlc td {border-bottom:1px #bbb
solid;font-size:80%;empty-cells:show}.cti {padding:20;}.ctn
{margin:10;font-size:110%;font-weight:bold}#cbs, #cts {text-
align:left;padding-left:20px;white-space:nowrap}#cit
{width:1%;font-size:80%;white-space:nowrap}.ctlf {padding-
left:3em;width:1%;text-align:right;vertical-align:top;white-sp
ace:nowrap}.ctrf {white-space:nowrap}.cted {font-
size:80%;padding:1em 0 0}.clc td {padding-right:1ex}.tlc td
{width:100%;white-space:nowrap;overflow:hidden;text-
overflow:ellipsis}.tlc img {width:15;height:15}.rr
{background:#E8EEF7}.rr b {font-weight:normal}.sr
{background:#FFFFCC}.p {color:#777}.p b {font-weight:bold}.lb
```

Continued

```
{color:#080}#tt {padding:3 0}.msg {display:inline-block}#mm
{width:100%}#mm td {font-size:80%;white-space:nowrap}.rc
{width:100%;table-layout:fixed}.rc div {white-
space:nowrap;overflow:hidden;text-overflow:ellipsis}.au
{font-weight:bold}.mb {font-size:80%;padding:6 0 0 10}.ma
{}.att td {font-size:80%}.mc {font-size:70%;padding:4 0 0
10;background:#eee}.q {color:#505}.e {display:none}.ea {font-
size:80%;color:#5c6efc;padding:5;cursor:pointer;cursor:hand}.s
g, .sg *, .ad, .ad * {color:#888888}.st0
{background:#ffff88}#ap {font-size:80%;padding-
bottom:1.5ex}.al {padding-bottom:1ex}.ai
{vertical-align:middle}.cg {background:#eee}.cf
{background:#c3d9ff}.cb2 #cft, .cb2 #cfb {display:none}#cft td
{background-color:inherit}.ci {background:#e0ecff;vertical-
align:top}.cf td, .cg td {font-size:80%}.cn, .cto, .cn table,
.cto table {height:100%}.cn .tl {background-image:none}.cd
{padding:4 5 2 10;}.cd button {text-align:center;font-
size:80%}.tb {padding:5;width:100%}.sp
{display:none;background:#e8f1ff;padding:7px;border:1px black
solid;cursor:default;overflow:auto;height:100%}.ms {text-
decoration:underline;cursor:pointer;cursor:hand;font-weight:bo
ld}.un {color:red}.cr {color:green}.mr {text-
decoration:none}.sm {position:absolute;display:none;margin:2px
0px;font-family:arial,sans-serif;background-
color:#c3d9ff;border:2px solid;border-color:#e8f1ff #9daecd
#9daecd #e8f1ff;z-index:1}.si {font-family:arial,sans-
serif;display:block;padding:3px
1em;white-space:nowrap;font-size:83%;cursor:default}.ih
{background-color:#66c;color:white}.sy {font-size:90%;font-
weight:bold}.hm {background-color:#ffff00}.tbo
{background:#c3d9ff;padding:2;-moz-user-select:none}.tbr
{cursor:default;width:100%;padding-left:0;vertical-
align:middle;-moz-user-select:none}.tbb {border:solid #c3d9ff
1px;padding:0 2 0 2;-moz-user-select:none}.tbm {font-
size:80%;-moz-user-select:none}.db {border:1px
solid;border-color:#9daecd #e8f1ff #e8f1ff #9daecd}.ob
{background:#e8f1ff;border:1px solid;border-color:#9daecd
#e8f1ff #e8f1ff #9daecd}.hb {border:1px solid;border-
color:#e8f1ff #9daecd #9daecd #e8f1ff}.sv
{margin-left:12px}.pt
{display:none;position:absolute;background:#bbb;padding:2px}.p
t table {background:#bbb}.pt table td
{width:15px;height:15px;padding:0px;margin:0px;border:1px
solid #bbb}.ef {width:100%}.nw {white-space:nowrap}.hd
{display:none}.iv
```

```
{position:absolute;left:0;right:0;width:0;height:0;padding:0;m
argin:0;border:0}#hm { position:absolute;z-index:3;border:1px
#000 outset;background:#eee;padding:2}.ac span {text-
decoration:none;color:#00c;display:block;cursor:default;paddin
g:0 10 0 10;font-size:80%;white-space:nowrap}.ac span.sel
{background:#c4e4ff}.chc {background:#FAD163;padding:2 4 0
9}.chc, .chc td {font-size:80%;white-space:nowrap}#ctf {font-
size:80%}#ctm {padding:9 8 5 0;white-space:nowrap}.ctum
{padding:5 8;font-weight:bold}.ctsm {padding:5
8;background:#FFFFF8;font-weight:bold}.y
{background:#FFFFF8}.z {background:#FFFFCC}.pr
{background:#FAD163}#pt {font-weight:bold;padding-
left:4;padding-top:3}#pm {padding:6 0 3;font-size:80%}#pm span
{font-weight:bold}#pp {background:#FFF7D7;padding:8}.pum
{padding:3 8}.psm {padding:3 8;background:#FFF7D7}table.pe
{font-size:80%}.pl {color:#063;font-weight:bold}.tl
{background:url(/gmail/images/corner_tl.gif) top left}.bl
{background:url(/gmail/images/corner_bl.gif) bottom left}.tr
{background:url(/gmail/images/corner_tr.gif) top right}.br
{background:url(/gmail/images/corner_br.gif) bottom right}.tl,
.bl, .tr, .br {background-repeat:no-repeat;padding-
left:4;width:4}.ctop
{background:url(/gmail/images/card_top.gif) top repeat-
x;padding:1;width:100%}.ctl
{background:url(/gmail/images/card_tl.gif) top left}.ctr
{background:url(/gmail/images/card_tr.gif) top right}.stl
{background:url(/gmail/images/card_stl.gif) top left}.cbot
{background-image:url(/gmail/images/card_bot.gif);background-
position:bottom;background-repeat:repeat-x;padding:1;width:100
%}.cbl {background-
image:url(/gmail/images/card_bl.gif);background-position:botto
m left}.cbr {background-
image:url(/gmail/images/card_br.gif);background-position:botto
m right}.cb {background-
image:url(/gmail/images/card_left.gif);background-position:lef
t;background-repeat:repeat-y;border-right:1px #e8e8e8
solid;}.cb2 {background-
image:url(/gmail/images/card_left2.gif);background-position:le
ft;background-repeat:repeat-y;border-right:1px #e8e8e8
solid;}.ctl, .ctr, .stl, .cbl, .cbr {background-repeat:no-
repeat}.ctl, .cbl, .stl {padding:0 10 0 0}.ctr, .cbr
{padding:0 9 0 0}#rh {background:white}.metatable {margin-
bottom:10} .metatable td {font-size:70%;padding:2 2 8 2}.rhh
{color:#333;text-align:center}    </STYLE>
  </HEAD>

  <BODY>
    <TABLE width="100%" cellspacing="0" cellpadding="0">
```

Continued

Listing A-1 *(continued)*

```
    <TBODY>
      <TR>
        <TD width="149" valign="top" rowspan="2">
          <DIV id="ds_inbox" style="padding-top: 1ex;"
class="h">
            <IMG width="143" height="59"
src="/gmail/help/images/logo.gif"/>
          </DIV>
        </TD>
        <TD valign="top" align="right">
          <DIV class="s" style="padding-bottom: 2px; text-
align: right;">
            <B>
ben.hammersley@gmail.com                </B>
|               <SPAN id="prf_g" class="lk">
Settings            </SPAN>
|               <A target="_blank" href="/support/"
class="lc" id="help">
Help          </A>
|               <A target="_top"
                onclick="return
top.js._Main_OnLink(window,this,event)" class="lk"
href="?logout">
Sign out            </A>
          </DIV>
        </TD>
      </TR>
      <TR>
        <TD valign="bottom">
          <DIV class="s" id="mt1">
            <TABLE cellspacing="0" cellpadding="0">
              <TBODY>
                <TR>
                  <TD valign="bottom">
                    <FORM onsubmit="return
top.js._MH_OnSearch(window,0)"
                          style="padding-bottom: 5px; white-
space: nowrap;" class="s" id="s">
                      <INPUT value="" name="q"
maxlength="2048" size="28"/>
                       <INPUT type="submit"
value="Search Mail"/>
                       <INPUT type="submit"
                        onclick="return
top.js._MH_OnSearch(window,1)" value="Search the Web"/>
```

```
                               </FORM>
                            </TD>
                            <TD>
                                <TABLE cellspacing="0" cellpadding="0"
style="vertical-align: top; padding-bottom: 4px;">
                                <TBODY>
                                    <TR>
                                    <TD>
                                        <SPAN id="mt_adv" style="font-
size: 65%;" class="lk">
Show search options
</SPAN>
                                        </TD>
                                    </TR>
                                    <TR>
                                    <TD>
                                        <SPAN id="mt_cf1"
                                            style="font-size: 65%;
vertical-align: top;" class="lk">
Create a filter                              </SPAN>
                                    </TD>
                                    </TR>
                                </TBODY>
                                </TABLE>
                            </TD>
                        </TR>
                    </TBODY>
                </TABLE>
            </DIV>
            <DIV
                    style="height: 2.1ex; padding-right: 149px;
visibility: hidden;" class="nt" id="nt1"/>
            </TD>
        </TR>
    </TBODY>
    </TABLE>
    <DIV style="padding-bottom: 1px;" id="mt2"/>
    <DIV class="nt" id="nt2" style="display: none;"/>
    <DIV id="nav" style="position: absolute; left: 1ex; width:
14ex;">
        <DIV class="nl">
            <SPAN id="comp" class="lk">
                <B>
Compose Mail            </B>
            </SPAN>
        </DIV>
        <DIV style="padding-top: 9px;">
            <TABLE cellspacing="0" cellpadding="0" border="0"
```

Continued

Listing A-1 *(continued)*

```
                style="background: rgb(195, 217, 255) none
repeat scroll 0%; -moz-background-clip: initial; -moz-
background-origin: initial; -moz-background-inline-policy:
initial;" class="cv">
        <TBODY>
          <TR height="2">
            <TD width="8" class="tl"/>
          </TR>
          <TR>
            <TD/>
            <TD>
              <SPAN id="ds_inbox" class="lk b">
                <B>
Inbox (1)                    </B>
              </SPAN>
            </TD>
          </TR>
          <TR height="2">
            <TD class="bl"/>
          </TR>
        </TBODY>
      </TABLE>
      <DIV class="nl">
        <SPAN id="ds_starred" class="lk">
Starred            <IMG width="13" height="13"
src="/gmail/images/star_on_sm_2.gif" id="_ss"/>
        </SPAN>
      </DIV>
      <DIV class="nl">
        <SPAN id="ds_sent" class="lk">
Sent Mail        </SPAN>
      </DIV>
      <DIV class="nl">
        <SPAN id="ds_drafts" class="lk">
Drafts        </SPAN>
      </DIV>
      <DIV class="nl">
        <SPAN id="ds_all" class="lk">
All Mail         </SPAN>
      </DIV>
      <DIV class="nl">
        <SPAN id="ds_spam" class="lk">
Spam          </SPAN>
      </DIV>
      <DIV class="nl">
```

```
            <SPAN id="ds_trash" class="lk">
Trash            </SPAN>
        </DIV>
      </DIV>
      <DIV style="padding-top: 8px;">
        <DIV class="nl">
          <SPAN id="cont" class="lk">
            <B>
Contacts           </B>
          </SPAN>
        </DIV>
      </DIV>
      <DIV id="nb_0" style="padding-top: 8px;">
        <DIV style="width: 95%;">
          <TABLE width="100%" cellspacing="0" cellpadding="0"
bgcolor="#b5edbc">
            <TBODY>
              <TR height="2">
                <TD class="tl"/>
                <TD class="tr"/>
              </TR>
            </TBODY>
          </TABLE>
          <DIV style="padding: 0pt 3px 1px; background:
rgb(181, 237, 188) none repeat scroll 0%; -moz-background-
clip: initial; -moz-background-origin: initial;
-moz-background-inline-policy: initial;">
            <DIV id="nt_0" class="s h">
              <IMG width="11" height="11"
src="/gmail/images/opentriangle.gif"/>
 Labels            </DIV>
            <TABLE cellspacing="2" class="nb">
              <TBODY>
                <TR>
                  <TD>
                    <DIV align="right" id="prf_l" class="lk
cs">
Edit labels                    </DIV>
                  </TD>
                </TR>
              </TBODY>
            </TABLE>
          </DIV>
          <TABLE width="100%" cellspacing="0" cellpadding="0"
bgcolor="#b5edbc">
            <TBODY>
              <TR height="2">
                <TD class="bl"/>
```

Continued

Listing A-1 *(continued)*

```
              <TD class="br"/>
            </TR>
          </TBODY>
        </TABLE>
      </DIV>
    </DIV>
    <DIV id="nb_2" style="padding-top: 7px;"/>
    <DIV style="padding-top: 7px;" class="s">
      <SPAN style="color: rgb(170, 0, 0);" class="ilc"
id="il">
Invite 4 friends              <BR/>
to Gmail          </SPAN>
            </DIV>
    </DIV>
    <DIV style="margin-left: 14ex;" id="co">
      <DIV id="tc_top">
        <TABLE width="100%" cellspacing="0" cellpadding="0"
bgcolor="#c3d9ff">
          <TBODY>
            <TR height="2">
              <TD class="tl"/>
              <TD class="tr"/>
            </TR>
          </TBODY>
        </TABLE>
        <TABLE width="100%" cellspacing="0" cellpadding="0"
              style="background: rgb(195, 217, 255) none
repeat scroll 0%; -moz-background-clip: initial; -moz-
background-origin: initial; -moz-background-inline-policy:
initial;" class="th">
          <TBODY>
            <TR>
              <TD width="8"/>
              <TD>
                <BUTTON style="font-weight: bold;"
id="ac_rc_^i" class="ab" type="button">
Archive                 </BUTTON>
                  <BUTTON style="width: 8em; text-
align: center;" id="ac_sp"
                        class="ab" type="button">
Report Spam              </BUTTON>
                  <SELECT id="tamu"

onchange="top.js._TL_OnActionMenuChange(window,this)"
                        onfocus="return
top.js._TL_MaybeUpdateActionMenus(window,this)"
```

```
                                onmouseover="return
top.js._TL_MaybeUpdateActionMenus(window,this)"
style="vertical-align: middle;">
                <OPTION style="color: rgb(119, 119, 119);"
id="mac">
More Actions ...                        </OPTION>
                <OPTION style="color: rgb(119, 119, 119);"
disabled="" id="nil">
--------                        </OPTION>
                <OPTION style="color: rgb(119, 119, 119);"
disabled="" id="al">
Apply label:                    </OPTION>
                <OPTION value="new">
   New label...                  </OPTION>
            </SELECT>
                      <SPAN id="refresh" class="lk">
Refresh             </SPAN>
            </TD>
            <TD align="right">
                   <SPAN style="white-space: nowrap;">
                <B>
1                </B>
 -                 <B>
1                </B>
 of                <B>
1                </B>
            </SPAN>
          </TD>
          <TD width="4"/>
        </TR>
        <TR>
          <TD/>
          <TD valign="bottom" style="padding-top: 3px;"
colspan="2">
Select:                 <SPAN id="sl_a" class="l">
All            </SPAN>
,               <SPAN id="sl_r" class="l">
Read             </SPAN>
,               <SPAN id="sl_u" class="l">
Unread              </SPAN>
,               <SPAN id="sl_s" class="l">
Starred              </SPAN>
,               <SPAN id="sl_t" class="l">
Unstarred               </SPAN>
,               <SPAN id="sl_n" class="l">
None              </SPAN>
          </TD>
        </TR>
```

Continued

Listing A-1 *(continued)*

```
            <TR height="3">
              <TD/>
            </TR>
          </TBODY>
        </TABLE>
      </DIV>
      <DIV style="border-left: 9px solid rgb(195, 217, 255);">
        <DIV id="tbd">
          <FORM target="hist" method="post" name="af"
action="/gmail?search=inbox&amp;view=tl&amp;start=0">
            <INPUT type="hidden" name="act"/>
            <INPUT type="hidden" name="at"/>
            <INPUT type="hidden" name="vp"/>
            <TABLE width="100%" cellspacing="0"
cellpadding="1" id="tb" class="tlc">
              <COL style="width: 31px; text-align: right;"/>
              <COL style="width: 20px;"/>
              <COL style="width: 24ex;"/>
              <COL style="width: 2ex;"/>
              <COL/>
              <COL style="width: 17px;"/>
              <COL style="width: 8ex;"/>
              <TBODY>
                <TR id="w_0" class="ur">
                  <TD align="right">
                    <INPUT type="checkbox"/>
                  </TD>
                  <TD>
                    <IMG src="/gmail/images/star_off_2.gif"/>
                  </TD>
                  <TD>
                    <SPAN id="_user_ben@benhammersley.com">
                      <B>
Ben Hammersley                        </B>
                    </SPAN>
  (2)                  </TD>
                  <TD>
                 </TD>
                  <TD>
                    <B>
Skinning Gmail? That's so cool!                  </B>
                    <SPAN class="p">
 - BEGIN PGP SIGNED MESSAGE-- Hash: SHA1 la la la --BEGIN PGP
SIGNATURE-- Version: GnuPG v1 &hellip;
</SPAN>
                  </TD>
```

```
                        <TD>
                               </TD>
                        <TD>
                          <B>
2:29pm                                  </B>
                        </TD>
                      </TR>
                    </TBODY>
                  </TABLE>
                </FORM>
                <DIV style="padding: 0pt 20px;" class="s c">
                  <BR/>
                  <BR/>
                  <BR/>
                  <BR/>
                  <BR/>
                  <BR/>
                  <BR/>
                  <BR/>
                </DIV>
              </DIV>
            </DIV>
            <IMG width="9" height="11"
src="/gmail/images/chevron.gif"
                style="position: absolute; display: none;"
id="ar"/>
            <DIV id="tc_bot">
              <TABLE width="100%" cellspacing="0" cellpadding="0"
                     style="background: rgb(195, 217, 255) none
repeat scroll 0%; -moz-background-clip: initial; -moz-
background-origin: initial; -moz-background-inline-policy:
initial;" class="th">
                <TBODY>
                  <TR height="2">
                    <TD/>
                  </TR>
                  <TR>
                    <TD width="8"/>
                    <TD>
Select:                     <SPAN id="sl_a" class="l">
All                   </SPAN>
,                     <SPAN id="sl_r" class="l">
Read                    </SPAN>
,                     <SPAN id="sl_u" class="l">
Unread                     </SPAN>
,                     <SPAN id="sl_s" class="l">
Starred                     </SPAN>
,                     <SPAN id="sl_t" class="l">
```

Continued

Listing A-1 *(continued)*

```
Unstarred                      </SPAN>
,                   <SPAN id="sl_n" class="l">
None                  </SPAN>
               </TD>
          </TR>
          <TR height="4">
             <TD/>
          </TR>
          <TR>
             <TD/>
             <TD>
                <BUTTON style="font-weight: bold;"
id="ac_rc_^i" class="ab" type="button">
Archive                </BUTTON>
                  <BUTTON style="width: 8em; text-
align: center;" id="ac_sp"
class="ab" type="button">
Report Spam             </BUTTON>
                  <SELECT id="bamu"

onchange="top.js._TL_OnActionMenuChange(window,this)"
                  onfocus="return
top.js._TL_MaybeUpdateActionMenus(window,this)"
                  onmouseover="return
top.js._TL_MaybeUpdateActionMenus(window,this)"
style="vertical-align: middle;">
               <OPTION style="color: rgb(119, 119, 119);"
id="mac">
More Actions ...                </OPTION>
               <OPTION style="color: rgb(119, 119, 119);"
disabled="" id="nil">
--------              </OPTION>
               <OPTION style="color: rgb(119, 119, 119);"
disabled="" id="al">
Apply label:              </OPTION>
               <OPTION value="new">
   New label...                </OPTION>
               </SELECT>
             </TD>
             <TD align="right">
                <SPAN style="white-space: nowrap;">
                <B>
1                </B>
 -                <B>
1                </B>
 of                <B>
```

```
1                    </B>
                   </SPAN>
                  </TD>
                <TD width="4"/>
              </TR>
            </TBODY>
          </TABLE>
          <TABLE width="100%" cellspacing="0" cellpadding="0"
bgcolor="#c3d9ff">
            <TBODY>
              <TR height="2">
                <TD class="bl"/>
                <TD class="br"/>
              </TR>
            </TBODY>
          </TABLE>
        </DIV>
      </DIV>
      <DIV style="padding: 0ex 14ex;" id="ft">
        <DIV style="margin-top: 20px;" class="c s">
Use the          <SPAN id="fsb" style="color: rgb(0, 0, 204);
text-decoration: underline; cursor: pointer; white-space:
nowrap;">
search          </SPAN>
 box or          <SPAN id="mt_adv" style="color: rgb(0, 0,
204); text-decoration: underline; cursor: pointer; white-
space: nowrap;">
search options          </SPAN>
 to find messages quickly!      </DIV>
        <DIV style="margin-top: 12px; color: rgb(0, 102, 51);"
class="c s b">
You are currently using 0 MB (0%) of your 1000 MB.      </DIV>
        <DIV style="margin-top: 4px;" class="c xs">
          <DIV>
            <A href="/gmail/help/terms_of_use.html"
target="_blank" class="lc">
Terms of Use          </A>
 -          <A href="/gmail/help/privacy.html"
target="_blank" class="lc">
Privacy Policy          </A>
 -          <A href="/gmail/help/program_policies.html"
target="_blank" class="lc">
Program Policies          </A>
 -          <A href="http://www.google.com/" target="_blank"
class="lc" id="googh">
Google Home          </A>
        </DIV>
        <DIV style="color: rgb(68, 68, 68); margin-top: 4px;">
```

Continued

Listing A-1 *(continued)*

```
&copy;2004 Google          </DIV>
        </DIV>
    </DIV>
    <SCRIPT>
var fp='9cf0974955f546da';     </SCRIPT>
    <SCRIPT>
var loaded=true;D(['e']);      </SCRIPT>
    <SCRIPT>
try{top.js.L(window,45,'f4ba224ac4');}catch(e){}    </SCRIPT>
    <DIV id="tip" style="border-style: outset; border-width:
1px; padding: 2px; background: rgb(255, 255, 221) none repeat
scroll 0%; position: absolute; -moz-background-clip: initial;
-moz-background-origin: initial; -moz-background-inline-
policy: initial; left: 309px; top: 125px; display: none;">
        <CENTER>
          <SMALL>
ben@benhammersley.com          </SMALL>
        </CENTER>
    </DIV>
  </BODY>
</HTML>
```

Listing A-2: The Complete CSS Listing

```css
body#gmail-google-com {
    background-color: #ffffff !important;
}

body#gmail-google-com img{
   display: none !important;
}

/* regular links */
body#gmail-google-com span.lk,
body#gmail-google-com a.lc,
body#gmail-google-com a.lk
{
    text-decoration: none !important;
    color: #191b4c !important;
}


/* The Search Form */
```

```css
body#gmail-google-com  div#mt1 form{
display: none !important;
}

body#gmail-google-com  div#mt1 table{
display: none !important;
}

/*------------------------------------------------------------
*/
/*The Navigation Menu */


body#gmail-google-com span#comp {
font-family: cursive;
}


/* sidebar links */
body#gmail-google-com div#nav table.cv,
body#gmail-google-com div#nav table.cv td {
    background: #ffffff !important;
}

body#gmail-google-com table.cv td.tl,
body#gmail-google-com table.cv td.bl {
    height: 0 !important;
}

/* both current and other */
body#gmail-google-com table.cv td span.lk,
body#gmail-google-com div.nl span.lk{
    display: block !important;
    background: #ffffff !important;
    color: #191b4c;
    border: none !important;
    padding: 2px !important;
    margin-right: 5px !important;
}

/* Override the background color for the unselected options*/
body#gmail-google-com div.nl span.lk {
    background: #ffffff !important;
    border: none !important;
}


/* For the mouse-over color change */
```

Continued

Listing A-2 *(continued)*

```css
body#gmail-google-com div.nl span.lk:hover {
    background: #d3cbb8 !important;
    border-color: #fef759 !important;
}

/* hide "New!" super-script */
body#gmail-google-com div#nav sup {
    display: none !important;
}


/* remove the colored left border of the inbox */
body#gmail-google-com div#co div {
    border: 0 !important;
}

/*-------------------------------------------------------*/

/* labels */
body#gmail-google-com div#nb_0 {
display: none !important;
}


/* The Invitation Link */
body#gmail-google-com #il {
    display: none !important;
}


/* The footer */
body#gmail-google-com div#ft {
    display: none !important;
}


/*-------------------------------------------------------
*/
/* THE APPLICATION AREA */

/* top bar */
body#gmail-google-com div#tc_top table,
body#gmail-google-com div#tc_top table td.tl,
body#gmail-google-com div#tc_top table td.tr,
```

```
body#gmail-google-com div#tc_top table.th,{
    background: #ffffff !important;
    border: none !important;
    padding: 2px !important;
    margin: 5px 0 5px 0 !important;
}


/* bottom bar*/
body#gmail-google-com div#tc_bot table,
body#gmail-google-com div#tc_bot table td.bl,
body#gmail-google-com div#tc_bot table td.br,
body#gmail-google-com div#tc_bot table.th{
    display: none !important;
}

/* selection links in bar */
body#gmail-google-com div#co div#tc_top span.l{
    color: #191b4c !important;
}


/* mailbox contents */
body#gmail-google-com div#co div#tbd {
    background: #ffffff !important;
    border: none !important;
    padding: 4px 0 4px 0 !important;
}


/* unread mail row inside the inbox */
body#gmail-google-com table.tlc tr.ur {
    background-color: #d7d7d7 !important;
    height: 30px;
}

/*read mail row inside the inbox */
body#gmail-google-com table.tlc tr.rr {
    background-color: #ffffff !important;
}

body#gmail-google-com table.tlc tr.ur td,
body#gmail-google-com table.tlc tr.rr td{
    border: 0 !important;
}
```

Continued

Listing A-2 *(continued)*

```css
/* message hovering snippet expansion */
body#gmail-google-com table.tlc tr.ur:hover,
body#gmail-google-com table.tlc tr.rr:hover{
    background-color: #ffffff !important;
}

body#gmail-google-com table.tlc tr.ur:hover td,
body#gmail-google-com table.tlc tr.rr:hover td{
    border: none !important;
    vertical-align: top !important;
}

body#gmail-google-com table.tlc tr.ur:hover .sn,
body#gmail-google-com table.tlc tr.rr:hover .sn{
    display: block !important;
    white-space: normal !important;
}

/* and email address display */
body#gmail-google-com table.tlc tr.ur:hover td span,
body#gmail-google-com table.tlc tr.rr:hover td span {
    display: block; !important;
    color: #ff0000;
}

/* labels should still be inline */
body#gmail-google-com table.tlc tr.ur:hover td span.ct,
body#gmail-google-com table.tlc tr.rr:hover td span.ct{
    display: inline;
}

body#gmail-google-com table.tlc tr.ur:hover td span[id]:after,
body#gmail-google-com table.tlc tr.rr:hover td span[id]:after{
  content: attr(id);
  display: block;
  margin-left: -38px; /* hack to hide "user_" id prefix */
  color: #b6af9e;
}

/*--------------------------------------------------------
*/
```

Chapter 5

Listing A-3: The Edited Boot Sequence

```
192.168.016.053.64142-216.239.057.106.00080: GET / HTTP/1.1

Host: gmail.google.com


216.239.057.106.00080-192.168.016.053.64142: HTTP/1.1 302
Moved Temporarily

Location:
https://gmail.google.com/?dest=http%3A%2F%2Fgmail.google.com%2
Fgmail

Cache-control: private
Content-Length: 0
Content-Type: text/html
Server: GFE/1.3
Date: Sun, 16 Jan 2005 17:11:18 GMT



192.168.016.053.64143-216.239.057.106.00443
LOTS OF ENCRYPTED TRAFFIC CLIPPED OUT FROM THIS SECTION


192.168.016.053.64147-066.102.007.104.00080: GET / HTTP/1.1
Host: www.google.com
Cookie: GMAIL_RTT2=290




066.102.007.104.00080-192.168.016.053.64147: HTTP/1.1 302
Found
Location:
http://www.google.it/cxfer?c=PREF%3D:TM%3D1105895484:S%3Dy1QWQ
vOGa-clmjwi&prev=/
Set-Cookie:
PREF=ID=1ded507398eab78d:CR=1:TM=1105895484:LM=1105895484:S=fq
J6wL_U141gaHs1; expires=Sun, 17-Jan-2038 19:14:07 GMT; path=/;
domain=.google.com
```

Continued

Listing A-3 *(continued)*

```
Content-Type: text/html
Server: GWS/2.1
Content-Length: 214
Date: Sun, 16 Jan 2005 17:11:24 GMT
<HTML><HEAD><TITLE>302 Moved</TITLE></HEAD><BODY>
<H1>302 Moved</H1>
The document has moved
<A
HREF="http://www.google.it/cxfer?c=PREF%3D:TM%3D1105895484:S%3
Dy1QWQvOGa-clmjwi&amp;prev=/">here</A>.
</BODY></HTML>


192.168.016.053.64148-216.239.063.104.00080: GET
/cxfer?c=PREF%3D:TM%3D1105895484:S%3Dy1QWQvOGa-clmjwi&prev=/
HTTP/1.1
Host: www.google.it



216.239.063.104.00080-192.168.016.053.64148: HTTP/1.1 302
Found
Location: http://www.google.it/
Set-Cookie:
PREF=ID=5f2f91cd13521ebf:LD=it:TM=1105895484:LM=1105895485:S=J
4G_HJAk1i5fY0Ip; expires=Sun, 17-Jan-2038 19:14:07 GMT;
path=/; domain=.google.it
Content-Type: text/html
Server: GWS/2.1
Content-Length: 151
Date: Sun, 16 Jan 2005 17:11:25 GMT
<HTML><HEAD><TITLE>302 Moved</TITLE></HEAD><BODY>
<H1>302 Moved</H1>
The document has moved
<A HREF="http://www.google.it/">here</A>.
</BODY></HTML>


192.168.016.053.64148-216.239.063.104.00080: GET / HTTP/1.1
Host: www.google.it
Cookie:PREF=ID=5f2f91cd13521ebf:LD=it:TM=1105895484:LM=1105895
485:S=J4G_HJAk1i5fY0Ip

216.239.063.104.00080-192.168.016.053.64148: HTTP/1.1 200 OK
Cache-Control: private
```

```
Content-Type: text/html
Server: GWS/2.1
Transfer-Encoding: chunked
Date: Sun, 16 Jan 2005 17:11:25 GMT
a98

<html><head><meta http-equiv="content-type"
content="text/html; charset=UTF-
8"><title>Google</title><style><!--
body,td,a,p,.h{font-family:arial,sans-serif;}
.h{font-size: 20px;}
.q{color:#0000cc;}
//-->
</style>
<script>
<!--
function sf(){document.f.q.focus();}
// -->
</script>
</head><body bgcolor=#ffffff text=#000000 link=#0000cc
vlink=#551a8b alink=#ff0000 onLoad=sf()><center><img
src="/intl/it_it/images/logo.gif" width=276 height=110
alt="Google"><br><br>
<form action=/search name=f><script><!--
function qs(el) {if (window.RegExp &&
window.encodeURIComponent) {var
qe=encodeURIComponent(document.f.q.value);if
(el.href.indexOf("q=")!=-1) {el.href=el.href.replace(new
RegExp("q=[^&$]*"),"q="+qe);} else {el.href+="&q="+qe;}}return
1;}
// -->
</script><table border=0 cellspacing=0 cellpadding=4><tr><td
nowrap><font size=-1><b>Web</b>    <a
id=1a class=q href="/imghp?hl=it&tab=wi" onClick="return
qs(this);">Immagini</a>    <a id=2a
class=q href="/grphp?hl=it&tab=wg" onClick="return
qs(this);">Gruppi</a>    <a id=3a class=q
href="/dirhp?hl=it&tab=wd" onClick="return
qs(this);">Directory</a>    <a id=4a
class=q href="/nwshp?hl=it&tab=wn" onClick="return qs(this)
216.239.063.104.00080-192.168.016.053.64148:
;">News</a>    </font></td></tr></table><t
able cellspacing=0 cellpadding=0><tr><td
width=25%> </td><td align=center><input type=hidden
name=hl value=it><input maxLength=256 size=55 name=q
value=""><br><input type=submit value="Cerca con Google"
name=btnG><input type=submit value="Mi sento fortunato"
name=btnI></td><td valign=top nowrap width=25%><font size=-
2>  <a href=/advanced_search?hl=it>Ricerca
```

Continued

Listing A-3 *(continued)*

```
avanzata</a><br>  <a
href=/preferences?hl=it>Preferenze</a><br>  <a
href=/language_tools?hl=it>Strumenti per le
lingue</a></font></td></tr><tr><td colspan=3
align=center><font size=-1>Cerca: <input id=all type=radio
name=meta value="" checked><label for=all> il
Web</label><input id=lgr type=radio name=meta
value="lr=lang_it" ><label for=lgr> pagine in
Italiano</label><input id=cty type=radio name=meta
value="cr=countryIT" ><label for=cty>pagine provenienti da:
Italia</label></font></td></tr></table></form><br><font size=-
1><a href="http://www.google.it/tsunami_relief.html">Come
aiutare le popolazioni colpite dal
maremoto</a></font><br><br><br><font size=-1><a
href=/intl/it/ads/>Pubblicit..</a> - <a
href=/intl/it/about.html>Tutto su Google</a> - <a
href=http://www.google.it/jobs/>Stiamo Assumendo</a> - <a
href=http://www.google.com/ncr>Google.com in
English</a></font><p><font size=-2>&copy;2005 Google - Ricerca
effettuata su 8.058.044.651 pa
216.239.063.104.00080-192.168.016.053.64148: gine
Web.</font></p></center></body></html>

0




192.168.016.053.64149-066.102.007.104.00443:
MORE ENCRYPTED TRAFFIC REMOVED FROM HERE




192.168.016.053.64150-216.239.057.106.00080: GET
/gmail?_sgh=9f1fe07d6a3a70c03b32d8a3ebc7577e HTTP/1.1

Host: gmail.google.com
Cookie: GMAIL_RTT2=290;
PREF=ID=1ded507398eab78d:CR=1:TM=1105895484:LM=1105895484:S=fq
J6wL_U141gaHs1;
GMAIL_LOGIN2=T1105895481223/1105895481223/1105895499818;
SID=DQAAAGsAAADNYMqIE3HRTYLVLhM-
DesqryUuzAxHlGKckFg7QgImGX4Y7tBrplUvz8Z8NHOJCuVrRKX64rmEMzaSoS
```

TdAy3QWJ4WE2GSEN46IOOMzBr14uI0wGOX_3Fnd-WUQIFpDxFrpuMP5-
J5OPEVdaxV2Y59

216.239.057.106.00080-192.168.016.053.64150: HTTP/1.1 200 OK

Set-Cookie: GV=101017c822e49-b58a8eed922f7d0f8c9e1901388b8beb;
Domain=gmail.google.com; Path=/gmail
Set-Cookie: GMAIL_AT=58c7bf063b77e796-1017c822e4c; Path=/
Set-Cookie: GMAIL_RTT=; Expires=Sat, 15-Jan-05 17:11:41 GMT;
Path=/
Set-Cookie: GMAIL_RTT2=; Domain=google.com; Expires=Sat, 15-
Jan-05 17:11:41 GMT; Path=/
Set-Cookie: S=gmail=ZnUe1o8mp44:gmproxy=kROzNYRS5DA;
Domain=.google.com; Path=/
Cache-control: private
Content-Type: text/html; charset=utf-8
Expires: Sat, 05 Feb 2005 17:11:41 GMT
ETag: "79be7effb0cf7b45"
Transfer-Encoding: chunked
Server: GFE/1.3
Date: Sun, 16 Jan 2005 17:11:41 GMT

487

```
<title>Gmail</title><link rel="alternate"
type="application/atom+xml" title="Gmail Atom Feed"
href="https://gmail.google.com/gmail/feed/atom"
/><noscript>Javascript is disabled in your browser. Gmail
requires Javascript to be enabled in order to operate.<p>To
use Gmail, enable Javascript by changing your browser
preferences.<p>After enabling Javascript, <a href=/gmail>try
again</a>.</noscript><script>var fs_time=(new
Date()).getTime();var testcookie =
'jscookietest=valid';document.cookie = testcookie;if
(document.cookie.indexOf(testcookie) == -1) {top.location =
'/gmail/html/nocookies.html';}document.cookie = testcookie +
';expires=' + new Date(0).toGMTString();var agt =
navigator.userAgent.toLowerCase();if (agt.indexOf('msie')!= -1
&& document.all) {var control = (a
216.239.057.106.00080-192.168.016.053.64150: gt.indexOf('msie
5') != -1) ? 'Microsoft.XMLHTTP' : 'Msxml2.XMLHTTP';try {new
ActiveXObject(control);} catch (e) {top.location =
'/gmail/html/noactivex.html';}}</script><frameset
rows='100%,*' border=0><frame name=main
src=/gmail/html/loading.html frameborder=0 noresize
```

Continued

Listing A-3 *(continued)*

```
scrolling=no><frame name=js
src=/gmail?view=page&name=js&ver=84b4499b9788ada frameborder=0
noresize></frameset>

0

192.168.016.053.64150-216.239.057.106.00080: GET
/gmail/html/loading.html HTTP/1.1
Host: gmail.google.com
Referer:
http://gmail.google.com/gmail?_sgh=9f1fe07d6a3a70c03b32d8a3ebc
7577e
Cookie: GV=101017c822e49-b58a8eed922f7d0f8c9e1901388b8beb;
PREF=ID=1ded507398eab78d:CR=1:TM=1105895484:LM=1105895484:S=fq
J6wL_U141gaHs1;
GMAIL_LOGIN2=T1105895481223/1105895481223/1105895499818;
SID=DQAAAGsAAADNYMqIE3HRTYLVLhM-
DesqryUuzAxHlGKckFg7QgImGX4Y7tBrplUvz8Z8NHOJCuVrRKX64rmEMzaSoS
TdAy3QWJ4WE2GSEN46IOOMzBr14uI0wGOX_3Fnd-WUQIFpDxFrpuMP5-
J5OPEVdaxV2Y59; GMAIL_AT=58c7bf063b77e796-1017c822e4c;
S=gmail=ZnUe1o8mp44:gmproxy=kROzNYRS5DA

216.239.057.106.00080-192.168.016.053.64150: HTTP/1.1 200 OK
Last-Modified: Sun, 09 Jan 2005 20:54:50 GMT
Cache-control: public
Expires: Mon, 16 Jan 2006 17:11:41 GMT
Content-Type: text/html
Server: GFE/1.3
Transfer-Encoding: chunked
Date: Sun, 16 Jan 2005 17:11:41 GMT
<font size=+1>Loading...</font>

192.168.016.053.64150-216.239.057.106.00080: GET
/gmail?view=page&name=js&ver=84b4499b9788ada HTTP/1.1
Host: gmail.google.com
```

```
Referer:
http://gmail.google.com/gmail?_sgh=9f1fe07d6a3a70c03b32d8a3ebc
7577e
Cookie: GV=101017c822e49-b58a8eed922f7d0f8c9e1901388b8beb;
PREF=ID=1ded507398eab78d:CR=1:TM=1105895484:LM=1105895484:S=fq
J6wL_U141gaHs1;
GMAIL_LOGIN2=T1105895481223/1105895481223/1105895499818;
SID=DQAAAGsAAADNYMqIE3HRTYLVLhM-
DesqryUuzAxHlGKckFg7QgImGX4Y7tBrplUvz8Z8NHOJCuVrRKX64rmEMzaSoS
TdAy3QWJ4WE2GSEN46IOOMzBr14uI0wGOX_3Fnd-WUQIFpDxFrpuMP5-
J5OPEVdaxV2Y59; GMAIL_AT=58c7bf063b77e796-1017c822e4c;
S=gmail=ZnUe1o8mp44:gmproxy=kROzNYRS5DA



216.239.057.106.00080-192.168.016.053.64150: HTTP/1.1 200 OK
Cache-control: public
Content-Type: text/html; charset=utf-8
Expires: Sat, 05 Feb 2005 17:11:42 GMT
ETag: "84b4499b9788ada"
Last-Modified: Fri, 05 Sep 2003 02:11:15 GMT
Transfer-Encoding: chunked
Server: GFE/1.3
Date: Sun, 16 Jan 2005 17:11:42 GMT
f3ce
<script><!--
var js_load_time=(new Date()).getTime();var product_name =
'Gmail';var js_version='84b4499b9788ada';var
js_url='/gmail?view=page&name=js&ver=84b4499b9788ada';
try {

THE REST OF THE JAVASCRIPT GOES HERE.

--></script>

0




192.168.016.053.64150-216.239.057.106.00080: GET /favicon.ico
HTTP/1.1
216.239.057.106.00080-192.168.016.053.64150: HTTP/1.1 200 OK


192.168.016.053.64150-216.239.057.106.00080: GET
/gmail/html/hist1.html HTTP/1.1
```

Continued

Listing A-3 *(continued)*

```
Host: gmail.google.com
Referer:
http://gmail.google.com/gmail?view=page&name=js&ver=84b4499b97
88ada

Cookie: GV=101017c822e49-b58a8eed922f7d0f8c9e1901388b8beb;
PREF=ID=1ded507398eab78d:CR=1:TM=1105895484:LM=1105895484:S=fq
J6wL_U141gaHs1;
GMAIL_LOGIN2=T1105895481223/1105895481223/1105895499818;
SID=DQAAAGsAAADNYMqIE3HRTYLVLhM-
DesqryUuzAxHlGKckFg7QgImGX4Y7tBrplUvz8Z8NHOJCuVrRKX64rmEMzaSoS
TdAy3QWJ4WE2GSEN46IOOMzBr14uI0wGOX_3Fnd-WUQIFpDxFrpuMP5-
J5OPEVdaxV2Y59; GMAIL_AT=58c7bf063b77e796-1017c822e4c;
S=gmail=ZnUe1o8mp44:gmproxy=kROzNYRS5DA; TZ=-60



216.239.057.106.00080-192.168.016.053.64150: HTTP/1.1 200 OK
Last-Modified: Sun, 09 Jan 2005 20:54:50 GMT
Cache-control: public
Expires: Mon, 16 Jan 2006 17:11:48 GMT
Content-Type: text/html
Server: GFE/1.3
Transfer-Encoding: chunked
Date: Sun, 16 Jan 2005 17:11:48 GMT
<body onload="OnLoad()">
<script>
function OnLoad() {
  try {
    if (top.js.init) {
      top.js.HI_OnNavigateHistory();
    }
  } catch(e) {
  }
}
var loaded = true;
</script>
</body>


0

192.168.016.053.64150-216.239.057.106.00080: GET
/gmail/html/hist2.html HTTP/1.1
```

```
Host: gmail.google.com
Referer:
http://gmail.google.com/gmail?view=page&name=js&ver=84b4499b97
88ada
Cookie: GV=101017c822e49-b58a8eed922f7d0f8c9e1901388b8beb;
PREF=ID=1ded507398eab78d:CR=1:TM=1105895484:LM=1105895484:S=fq
J6wL_U141gaHs1;
GMAIL_LOGIN2=T1105895481223/1105895481223/1105895499818;
SID=DQAAAGsAAADNYMqIE3HRTYLVLhM-
DesqryUuzAxHlGKckFg7QgImGX4Y7tBrplUvz8Z8NHOJCuVrRKX64rmEMzaSoS
TdAy3QWJ4WE2GSEN46IOOMzBr14uI0wGOX_3Fnd-WUQIFpDxFrpuMP5-
J5OPEVdaxV2Y59; GMAIL_AT=58c7bf063b77e796-1017c822e4c;
S=gmail=ZnUe1o8mp44:gmproxy=kROzNYRS5DA; TZ=-60


216.239.057.106.00080-192.168.016.053.64150: HTTP/1.1 200 OK
Last-Modified: Sun, 09 Jan 2005 20:54:50 GMT
Cache-control: public
Expires: Mon, 16 Jan 2006 17:11:49 GMT
Content-Type: text/html
Server: GFE/1.3
Transfer-Encoding: chunked
Date: Sun, 16 Jan 2005 17:11:49 GMT
<body onload="OnLoad()">
<script>
function OnLoad() {
  try {
    if (top.js.init) {
      top.js.HI_OnNavigateHistory();
    }
  } catch(e) {
  }
}
var loaded = true;
</script>
</body>


192.168.016.053.64150-216.239.057.106.00080: GET
/gmail?ik=&search=inbox&view=tl&start=0&init=1&zx=z6te3fe41hms
jo HTTP/1.1
Host: gmail.google.com
Referer: http://gmail.google.com/gmail/html/hist2.html
```

Continued

```
Cookie: GV=101017c822e49-b58a8eed922f7d0f8c9e1901388b8beb;
PREF=ID=1ded507398eab78d:CR=1:TM=1105895484:LM=1105895484:S=fq
J6wL_U141gaHs1;
GMAIL_LOGIN2=T1105895481223/1105895481223/1105895499818;
SID=DQAAAGsAAADNYMqIE3HRTYLVLhM-
DesqryUuzAxHlGKckFg7QgImGX4Y7tBrplUvz8Z8NHOJCuVrRKX64rmEMzaSoS
TdAy3QWJ4WE2GSEN46IOOMzBr14uI0wGOX_3Fnd-WUQIFpDxFrpuMP5-
J5OPEVdaxV2Y59; GMAIL_AT=58c7bf063b77e796-1017c822e4c;
S=gmail=ZnUe1o8mp44:gmproxy=kROzNYRS5DA; TZ=-60
```

```
216.239.057.106.00080-192.168.016.053.64150: HTTP/1.1 200 OK
Set-Cookie: SID=DQAAAGsAAADNYMqIE3HRTYLVLhM-
DesqryUuzAxHlGKckFg7QgImGX4Y7tBrplUvz8Z8NHOJCuVrRKX64rmEMzaSoS
TdAy3QWJ4WE2GSEN46IOOMzBr14uI0wGOX_3Fnd-WUQIFpDxFrpuMP5-
J5OPEVdaxV2Y59;Domain=.google.com;Path=/
Cache-control: no-cache
Pragma: no-cache
Content-Type: text/html; charset=utf-8
Transfer-Encoding: chunked
Server: GFE/1.3
Date: Sun, 16 Jan 2005 17:11:49 GMT
<html><head><meta content="text/html; charset=UTF-8" http-
equiv="content-type"></head><script>D=(top.js&&top.js.init)?fu
nction(d){top.js.P(window,d)}:function(){};if(window==top){top
.location="/gmail?ik=&search=inbox&view=tl&start=0&init=1&zx=z
6te3fe41hmsjo&fs=1";}</script><script><!--
D(["v","84b4499b9788ada","33fc762357568758"]
);
D(["ud","ben.hammersley@gmail.com","{\"o\":\"OPEN\",\"/\":\"SE
ARCH\",\"\\r\":\"OPEN\",\"k\":\"PREV\",\"r\":\"REPLY\",\"c\":\
"COMPOSE\",\"gc\":\"GO_CONTACTS\",\"gd\":\"GO_DRAFTS\",\"p\":\
"PREVMSG\",\"gi\":\"GO_INBOX\",\"m\":\"IGNORE\",\"a\":\"REPLYA
LL\",\"!\":\"SPAM\",\"f\":\"FORWARD\",\"u\":\"BACK\",\"ga\":\"
GO_ALL\",\"j\":\"NEXT\",\"y\":\"REMOVE\",\"n\":\"NEXTMSG\",\"g
s\":\"GO_STARRED\",\"x\":\"SELECT\",\"s\":\"STAR\"}","344af70c
5d","/gmail?view=page&name=contacts&ver=50c1485d48db7207"]
);
D(["su","33fc762357568758",["l","/gmail/help/images/logo.gif",
"i","Invite a friend to Gmail","j","Invite PH_NUM friends to
Gmail"]
```

```
]
);
D(["p",["bx_hs","1"]
,["bx_show0","1"]
,["bx_sc","0"
216.239.057.106.00080-192.168.016.053.64150: ]
,["bx_pe","1"]
,["bx_ns","1"]
]
);
D(["ppd",0]
);
D(["i",6]
);
D(["qu","1 MB","1000 MB","0%","#006633"]
);
D(["ft","Compose a message in a new window by pressing
\"Shift\" while clicking Compose Mail or Reply."]
);
D(["ds",0,0,0,0,0,20,0]
);
D(["ct",[]
]
);
D(["ts",0,50,1,0,"Inbox","1017c824dee",1,]
);
D(["t",["101480d8ef5dc74a",0,0,"Jan 6","<span
id=\'_user_ben@benhammersley.com\'>Ben
Hammersley</span>","<b>&raquo;</b> ","Here\'s a nice
message.",,[]
,"","101480d8ef5dc74a",0,"Thu Jan 6 2005_4:44AM"]
]
);
D(["te"]);

//--></script><script>var
fp='9055a1297cd86ff2';</script><script>var
loaded=true;D(['e']);</script><script>try{top.js.L(window,43,'
204c380d43');}catch(e){}</script>



192.168.016.053.64150-216.239.057.106.00080: GET
/gmail/help/images/logo.gif
216.239.057.106.00080-192.168.016.053.64150: HTTP/1.1 200 OK
```

Continued

Listing A-3 *(continued)*

```
192.168.016.053.64150-216.239.057.106.00080: GET
/gmail/images/corner_tl.gif
216.239.057.106.00080-192.168.016.053.64150: HTTP/1.1 200 OK


192.168.016.053.64150-216.239.057.106.00080: GET
/gmail/images/corner_bl.gif
216.239.057.106.00080-192.168.016.053.64150: HTTP/1.1 200 OK


192.168.016.053.64150-216.239.057.106.00080: GET
/gmail/images/star_on_sm_2.gif
216.239.057.106.00080-192.168.016.053.64150: HTTP/1.1 200 OK


192.168.016.053.64150-216.239.057.106.00080: GET
/gmail/images/corner_tr.gif
216.239.057.106.00080-192.168.016.053.64150: HTTP/1.1 200 OK


192.168.016.053.64150-216.239.057.106.00080: GET
/gmail/images/opentriangle.gif
216.239.057.106.00080-192.168.016.053.64150: HTTP/1.1 200 OK

192.168.016.053.64150-216.239.057.106.00080: GET
/gmail/images/corner_br.gif
216.239.057.106.00080-192.168.016.053.64150: HTTP/1.1 200 OK


192.168.016.053.64150-216.239.057.106.00080: GET
/gmail/images/star_off_2.gif
216.239.057.106.00080-192.168.016.053.64150: HTTP/1.1 200 OK


192.168.016.053.64150-216.239.057.106.00080: GET
/gmail/images/chevron.gif
216.239.057.106.00080-192.168.016.053.64150: HTTP/1.1 200 OK



192.168.016.053.64150-216.239.057.106.00080: GET
/gmail?view=page&name=contacts&ver=50c1485d48db7207 HTTP/1.1
Host: gmail.google.com
Cookie: GV=101017c822e49-b58a8eed922f7d0f8c9e1901388b8beb;
PREF=ID=1ded507398eab78d:CR=1:TM=1105895484:LM=1105895484:S=fq
```

```
J6wL_U141gaHs1;
GMAIL_LOGIN2=T1105895481223/1105895481223/1105895499818;
SID=DQAAAGsAAADNYMqIE3HRTYLVLhM-
DesqryUuzAxHlGKckFg7QgImGX4Y7tBrplUvz8Z8NHOJCuVrRKX64rmEMzaSoS
TdAy3QWJ4WE2GSEN46IOOMzBr14uI0wGOX_3Fnd-WUQIFpDxFrpuMP5-
J5OPEVdaxV2Y59; GMAIL_AT=58c7bf063b77e796-1017c822e4c;
S=gmail=ZnUe1o8mp44:gmproxy=kROzNYRS5DA; TZ=-60; GMAIL_SU=1
Pragma: no-cache
Cache-Control: no-cache



216.239.057.106.00080-192.168.016.053.64150: HTTP/1.1 200 OK
Cache-control: private
Content-Type: text/html; charset=utf-8
Expires: Sat, 05 Feb 2005 17:11:53 GMT
ETag: "50c1485d48db7207"
Last-Modified: Fri, 05 Sep 2003 02:11:15 GMT
Transfer-Encoding: chunked
Server: GFE/1.3
Date: Sun, 16 Jan 2005 17:11:53 GMT
56

[["ben@benhammersley.com","Hacking Gmail"]
,["BHerrmann@wiley.com","Brian Herrmann"]
]



192.168.016.053.64150-216.239.057.106.00080: GET
/gmail?view=page&name=blank_modal&ver=6ae1910f12c398eb
HTTP/1.1
Host: gmail.google.com
Referer:
http://gmail.google.com/gmail?view=page&name=js&ver=84b4499b97
88ada
Cookie: GV=101017c822e49-b58a8eed922f7d0f8c9e1901388b8beb;
PREF=ID=1ded507398eab78d:CR=1:TM=1105895484:LM=1105895484:S=fq
J6wL_U141gaHs1;
GMAIL_LOGIN2=T1105895481223/1105895481223/1105895499818;
SID=DQAAAGsAAADNYMqIE3HRTYLVLhM-
DesqryUuzAxHlGKckFg7QgImGX4Y7tBrplUvz8Z8NHOJCuVrRKX64rmEMzaSoS
TdAy3QWJ4WE2GSEN46IOOMzBr14uI0wGOX_3Fnd-WUQIFpDxFrpuMP5-
J5OPEVdaxV2Y59; GMAIL_AT=58c7bf063b77e796-1017c822e4c;
S=gmail=ZnUe1o8mp44:gmproxy=kROzNYRS5DA; TZ=-60; GMAIL_SU=1
```

Continued

Listing A-3 *(continued)*

```
216.239.057.106.00080-192.168.016.053.64150: HTTP/1.1 200 OK
Cache-control: private
Content-Type: text/html; charset=utf-8
Expires: Sat, 05 Feb 2005 17:11:53 GMT
ETag: "6ae1910f12c398eb"
Last-Modified: Fri, 05 Sep 2003 02:11:15 GMT
Transfer-Encoding: chunked
Server: GFE/1.3
Date: Sun, 16 Jan 2005 17:11:53 GMT
<html><head><style>body{margin:0;background:#FFF}
body,td,button{font-family:sans-serif;font-size:85%}
.tl {
background-image: url(/gmail/images/corner_tl.gif);
background-position:top left;
background-repeat:no-repeat;
}
.tr {
background-image: url(/gmail/images/corner_tr.gif);
background-position:top right;
background-repeat:no-repeat;
}
.bl {
background-image: url(/gmail/images/corner_bl.gif);
background-position:bottom left;
background-repeat:no-repeat;
}
.br {
background-image: url(/gmail/images/corner_br.gif);
background-position:bottom right;
background-repeat:no-repeat;
}
.bubble {
background-color:#C3D9FF;
}
.button {vertical-align:middle;padding:0 10;margin:0 5}
#title   {font-weight:bold;padding:2 10}
#message {font-size:95%;padding:10 0 0 10}
#buttons {text-align:center;margin-top:15}
#main {border:2px #c3D9FF solid;padding:10 10 10 0}
</style></head><body>
<table id=main width=100% height=100% cellpadding=0
cellspacing=0>
<tr><td>
```

```
</table>
</body>
</html>
```

```
192.168.016.053.64151-066.102.007.104.00080: GET /setgmail
HTTP/1.1
Host: www.google.com
User-Agent: Mozilla/5.0 (Macintosh; U; PPC Mac OS X Mach-O;
en-GB; rv:1.7.5) Gecko/20041110 Firefox/1.0
Accept: image/png,*/*;q=0.5
Accept-Language: en-gb,en;q=0.5
Accept-Charset: ISO-8859-1,utf-8;q=0.7,*;q=0.7
Keep-Alive: 300
Connection: keep-alive
Referer:
http://gmail.google.com/gmail?ik=&search=inbox&view=tl&start=0
&init=1&zx=z6te3fe41hmsjo
Cookie:
PREF=ID=1ded507398eab78d:CR=1:TM=1105895484:LM=1105895484:S=fq
J6wL_U141gaHs1;
GMAIL_LOGIN2=1105895481223/1105895481223/1105895499818/1105895
502118/1105895508496/1105895509753/1105895510624/false/false;
SID=DQAAAGsAAADNYMqIE3HRTYLVLhM-
DesqryUuzAxHlGKckFg7QgImGX4Y7tBrplUvz8Z8NHOJCuVrRKX64rmEMzaSoS
TdAy3QWJ4WE2GSEN46IOOMzBr14uI0wGOX_3Fnd-WUQIFpDxFrpuMP5-
J5OPEVdaxV2Y59; S=gmail=ZnUe1o8mp44:gmproxy=kROzNYRS5DA
```

```
066.102.007.104.00080-192.168.016.053.64151: HTTP/1.1 204 No
Content
Set-Cookie:
PREF=ID=1ded507398eab78d:CR=1:TM=1105895484:LM=1105895514:GM=1
:S=7pA3w_PCISy_m6mm; expires=Sun, 17-Jan-2038 19:14:07 GMT;
path=/; domain=.google.com
Content-Type: text/html
Server: GWS/2.1
Content-Length: 0
Date: Sun, 16 Jan 2005 17:11:54 GMT
```

Chapter 13

Listing A-4: The HTML-Only Gmail Inbox Source

```html
<html>
<head>
<title>Gmail - Inbox</title>
<meta http-equiv=Content-Type content="text/html; charset=UTF-
8">
<link rel="stylesheet" type="text/css"
href="/gmail/h/?view=page&name=css&ver=4e9d6884374d2804">
<style type="text/css">
@import
url("/gmail/h/?view=page&name=css2&ver=e5dcae215b68fea6");
</style>
<base href="http://gmail.google.com/gmail/h/1m0fzst8pmgu0/">
<script
src="/gmail?view=page&name=browser&ver=b8da0131e81235c4"></scr
ipt>
<script
src="/gmail/h/?view=page&name=js&ver=198b37c9e12e6f72"></scrip
t>
</head>
<body bgcolor=#ffffff>
<table width=100% cellpadding=4 cellspacing=0 border=0
class=bn>

<tr>
<td id=bm bgcolor=#FAE5B0>
<b>For a better Gmail experience, use a
fully supported browser.  
<a href="/support/bin/answer.py?ctx=gmail&answer=15046"
target=_blank
>Learn more</a></b>
</td>
</table>
<script>
<!--
sbm()
//-->
</script>
<table width=100% cellpadding=0 cellspacing=0 border=0>
<tr>
<td width=143 rowspan=3>
<a href="?">
<img src="/gmail/help/images/logo.gif"
```

```
width=143 height=59 border=0
alt="Gmail by Google">
</a>
</td>

<td width=1 rowspan=3> </td>
<td height=25 colspan=2 align=right valign=top>
<b>ben.hammersley@gmail.com</b> |
<a href="?v=pr">Settings</a> |
<a href="/support/?ctx=gmail" target=_blank>Help</a> |
<a href="?logout">Sign out</a>
<tr>
<form action=? name=sf method=GET>
<input type=hidden name=s value=q>
<td>

<table width=100% cellpadding=0 cellspacing=0 border=0>
<tr>
<td width=1% height=25 nowrap>
<input size=28 maxlength=2048
name=q value=""
> <input type=submit name=site value="Search Mail"
> <input type=submit name=site value="Search the Web">
</td>
<td>
<font size=1>
 <a href="?v=as&pv=tl"
>Show search options</a>
</font>
</form>
</table>
<tr>
<td height=25 colspan=2>
</table>

<table width=100% cellpadding=0 cellspacing=0 border=0>
<tr>
<td width=120 valign=top>
<table width=100% cellpadding=2 cellspacing=0 border=0
class=m>
<tr>
<td>
<b><a href="?ct=n&v=b&pv=tl"
>Compose Mail</a></b>
<tr>
<td height=5>
<tr>
<td bgcolor=#C3D9FF>
```

Continued

```
<b><a href="?"
>Inbox</a></b>
<tr>
<td>

<a href="?s=r"
>Starred <img src="/gmail/images/star_on_sm_2.gif"
width=13 height=13 border=0 alt="star"></a>
<tr>
<td>
<a href="?s=s"
>Sent Mail</a>
<tr>
<td>
<a href="?s=d"
>Drafts</a>
<tr>
<td>
<a href="?s=a"
>All Mail</a>
<tr>
<td>
<b><a href="?s=m"
>Spam (1)</a></b>

<tr>
<td>
<a href="?s=t"
>Trash</a>
<tr>
<td height=8>
<tr>
<td>
<b><a href="?v=cl">Contacts</a></b>
<tr>
<td height=8>
</table>
<table width=100% cellpadding=2 cellspacing=0 border=0
class=l>
<tr>
<td class=lb>
<font color=#000000>Labels</font><br>

<a href="?l=Heads&s=l"><font color=#006633
    >Heads</font></a>
<br>
```

```
<a href="?l=Knees&s=l"><font color=#006633
    >Knees</font></a>
<br>
<a href="?l=Shoulders&s=l"><font color=#006633
    >Shoulders</font></a>
<br>
<a href="?l=Toes&s=l"><font color=#006633
    >Toes</font></a>
<br>
</td>
</table>
</td>
<td valign=top>
<table width=100% cellpadding=0 cellspacing=0 border=0>

<tr>
<td width=5 bgcolor=#C3D9FF> </td>
<td>
<form action="?at=946adde382e122c-102ca495e7d" name=f
method=POST>
<input type=hidden name=redir
value="?">
<table width=100% cellpadding=2 cellspacing=0 border=0
bgcolor=#C3D9FF>
<tr>
<td>
<input type=submit name=a value="Archive">  <input
type=submit name=a value="Report Spam">  
<select name=tact>
<option value="">More Actions...</option>
<option value=rd>Mark as read</option>
<option value=ur>Mark as unread</option>
<option value=st>Add star</option>

<option value=xst>Remove star</option>
<option value=tr>Move to Trash</option>
<option value="" disabled>--------</option>
<option value="" disabled>Apply label:</option>
<option value="ac_Heads"
>Heads
</option>
<option value="ac_Knees"
>Knees
</option>
<option value="ac_Shoulders"
>Shoulders
</option>
<option value="ac_Toes"
```

Continued

```
>Toes
</option>
<option value="" disabled>--------</option>

<option value="" disabled>Remove label:</option>
<option value="rc_Heads"
>Heads
</option>
<option value="rc_Knees"
>Knees
</option>
<option value="rc_Shoulders"
>Shoulders
</option>
<option value="rc_Toes"
>Toes
</option>
</select> <input type=submit name=tbu value=Go> 
<a href="?">Refresh</a>
</td>
<td align=right>
<b>1 - 5</b> of <b>5</b>

</table>
<table width=100% cellpadding=2 cellspacing=0 border=0
bgcolor=#e8eef7 class=th>
<tr bgcolor=#E8EEF7>
<td width=1% nowrap>
<input type=checkbox name=t
value="1025a4065d9b40bf">
<img src="/gmail/images/cleardot.gif"
width=15 height=15 border=0 alt="">
</td>
<td width=30%>
Ben Hammersley</td>
<td width=68%>
<a href="?th=1025a4065d9b40bf&v=c">
<font size=1><font color=#006633>
</font></font>
hello me
</a></td>
<td nowrap width=1%>Feb 28

<tr bgcolor=#E8EEF7>
<td>
<input type=checkbox name=t
```

```
value="10237338e99e7a8c">
</td>
<td >
Ben Hammersley</td>
<td >
<a href="?th=10237338e99e7a8c&v=c">
<font size=1><font color=#006633>
</font></font>
This is the subject line
</a></td>
<td nowrap>Feb 21
<tr bgcolor=#E8EEF7>
<td>

<input type=checkbox name=t
value="10187696869432e6">
</td>
<td >
Ben, me (3)</td>
<td >
<a href="?th=10187696869432e6&v=c">
<font size=1><font color=#006633>
</font></font>
This is the third message
</a></td>
<td nowrap>Jan 18
<tr bgcolor=#E8EEF7>
<td>
<input type=checkbox name=t
value="101865b95fc7a35a">
</td>

<td >
Ben Hammersley</td>
<td >
<a href="?th=101865b95fc7a35a&v=c">
<font size=1><font color=#006633>
</font></font>
This is the second message
</a></td>
<td nowrap>Jan 18
<tr bgcolor=#E8EEF7>
<td>
<input type=checkbox name=t
value="101480d8ef5dc74a">
<img src="/gmail/images/star_on_2.gif"
width=15 height=15 border=0 alt=Starred>
</td>
```

Continued

```
<td >

Ben Hammersley</td>
<td >
<a href="?th=101480d8ef5dc74a&v=c">
<font size=1><font color=#006633>
Heads
</font></font>
Here's a nice message.
</a></td>
<td nowrap>Jan 6
</table>
<table width=100% cellpadding=2 cellspacing=0 border=0
bgcolor=#C3D9FF>
<tr>
<td>
<input type=submit name=a value="Archive">  <input
type=submit name=a value="Report Spam">  
<select name=bact>

<option value="">More Actions...</option>
<option value=rd>Mark as read</option>
<option value=ur>Mark as unread</option>
<option value=st>Add star</option>
<option value=xst>Remove star</option>
<option value=tr>Move to Trash</option>
<option value="" disabled>--------</option>
<option value="" disabled>Apply label:</option>
<option value="ac_Heads"
>Heads

</option>
<option value="ac_Knees"
>Knees
</option>
<option value="ac_Shoulders"
>Shoulders
</option>
<option value="ac_Toes"
>Toes
</option>
<option value="" disabled>--------</option>
<option value="" disabled>Remove label:</option>
<option value="rc_Heads"
>Heads
</option>
```

```
<option value="rc_Knees"
>Knees
</option>
<option value="rc_Shoulders"
>Shoulders
</option>

<option value="rc_Toes"
>Toes
</option>
</select> <input type=submit name=bbu value=Go> 
<a href="?">Refresh</a>
</td>
<td align=right>
<b>1 - 5</b> of <b>5</b>
</table>
</tr>
</form>

</table>
<table cellpadding=2 cellspacing=0 border=0 align=center
class=ft>
<tr>
<td align=center>
Search accurately with <a style=color:#0000CC target=_blank
href="/support/bin/answer.py?ctx=gmail&answer=7190">operators<
/a> including <b>from:</b>  <b>to:</b>
 <b>subject:</b>.
<tr>
<td align=center>
<font color="#006633">

<b>You are currently using 1 MB
(0%)
of your 1000 MB.</b>
</font>
<script>
<!--
wsl();
//-->
</script>
<tr>
<td align=center>
<font size=1>
<a href="/gmail/help/terms_of_use.html"
target=_blank>Terms of Use</a> -
<a href="/gmail/help/privacy.html"
target=_blank>Privacy Policy</a> -
```

Continued

Listing A-4 *(continued)*

```
<a href="/gmail/help/program_policies.html"
target=_blank>Program Policies</a> -

<a href="http://www.google.com" target=_blank>Google Home</a>
</font>
<tr>
<td align=center>
<font size=1>&copy;2005 Google</font>
</table>
</table>
</body>
</html>
```

Listing A-5: Code That Produces Figure 13-2

```
<html>
<head>
<title>Gmail - hello me</title>
<meta http-equiv=Content-Type content="text/html; charset=UTF-
8">
<link rel="stylesheet" type="text/css"
href="/gmail/h/?view=page&name=css&ver=4e9d6884374d2804">
<style type="text/css">
@import
url("/gmail/h/?view=page&name=css2&ver=e5dcae215b68fea6");
</style>
<base href="http://gmail.google.com/gmail/h/gmqifu8n7ale/">
<script
src="/gmail?view=page&name=browser&ver=b8da0131e81235c4"></scr
ipt>
<script
src="/gmail/h/?view=page&name=js&ver=198b37c9e12e6f72"></scrip
t>
</head>
<body bgcolor=#ffffff>
<table width=100% cellpadding=4 cellspacing=0 border=0
class=bn>
<tr>
<td id=bm bgcolor=#FAE5B0>
<b>For a better Gmail experience, use a
fully supported browser.  
```

```
<a href="/support/bin/answer.py?ctx=gmail&answer=15046"
target=_blank
>Learn more</a></b>
</td>
</table>
<script>
<!--
sbm()
//-->
</script>
<table width=100% cellpadding=0 cellspacing=0 border=0>
<tr>
<td width=143 rowspan=3>
<a href="?">
<img src="/gmail/help/images/logo.gif"
width=143 height=59 border=0
alt="Gmail by Google">
</a>
</td>
<td width=1 rowspan=3> </td>
<td height=25 colspan=2 align=right valign=top>
<b>ben.hammersley@gmail.com</b> |
<a href="?v=pr">Settings</a> |
<a href="/support/?ctx=gmail" target=_blank>Help</a> |
<a href="?logout">Sign out</a>
<tr>
<form action=? name=sf method=GET>
<input type=hidden name=s value=q>
<td>
<table width=100% cellpadding=0 cellspacing=0 border=0>
<tr>
<td width=1% height=25 nowrap>
<input size=28 maxlength=2048
name=q value=""
> <input type=submit name=site value="Search Mail"
> <input type=submit name=site value="Search the Web">
</td>
<td>
<font size=1>
 <a href="?th=1025a4065d9b40bf&v=as&pv=cv"
>Show search options</a>
</font>
</form>
</table>
<tr>
<td height=25 colspan=2>
</table>
```

Continued

Listing A-5 *(continued)*

```html
<table width=100% cellpadding=0 cellspacing=0 border=0>
<tr>
<td width=120 valign=top>
<table width=100% cellpadding=2 cellspacing=0 border=0
class=m>
<tr>
<td>
<b><a href="?th=1025a4065d9b40bf&ct=n&v=b&pv=cv"
>Compose Mail</a></b>
<tr>
<td height=5>
<tr>
<td bgcolor=#C3D9FF>
<b><a href="?"
>Inbox</a></b>
<tr>
<td>
<a href="?s=r"
>Starred <img src="/gmail/images/star_on_sm_2.gif"
width=13 height=13 border=0 alt="star"></a>
<tr>
<td>
<a href="?s=s"
>Sent Mail</a>
<tr>
<td>
<a href="?s=d"
>Drafts</a>
<tr>
<td>
<a href="?s=a"
>All Mail</a>
<tr>
<td>
<b><a href="?s=m"
>Spam (1)</a></b>
<tr>
<td>
<a href="?s=t"
>Trash</a>
<tr>
<td height=8>
<tr>
<td>
<b><a href="?v=cl">Contacts</a></b>
<tr>
```

```
<td height=8>
</table>
<table width=100% cellpadding=2 cellspacing=0 border=0
class=l>
<tr>
<td class=lb>
<font color=#000000>Labels</font><br>
<a href="?l=Heads&s=l"><font color=#006633
    >Heads</font></a>
<br>
<a href="?l=Knees&s=l"><font color=#006633
    >Knees</font></a>
<br>
<a href="?l=Shoulders&s=l"><font color=#006633
    >Shoulders</font></a>
<br>
<a href="?l=Toes&s=l"><font color=#006633
    >Toes</font></a>
<br>
</td>
</table>
<td valign=top>
<table width=100% cellpadding=0 cellspacing=0 border=0>
<tr>
<td width=5 bgcolor=#C3D9FF> </td>
<td>
<table width=100% cellpadding=2 cellspacing=0 border=0
bgcolor=#C3D9FF>
<form
action="?t=1025a4065d9b40bf&at=b2e38396b0a9faf8-102e93a7156"
name=f method=POST>
<tr>
<td>
<input type=hidden name=redir
value="?">
<b><a href="?"
>&laquo; Back to Inbox</a></b>  
<input type=submit name=a value="Archive">  <input
type=submit name=a value="Report Spam">
  <select name=tact>
<option value="">More Actions...</option>
<option value=rd>Mark as read</option>
<option value=ur>Mark as unread</option>
<option value=st>Add star</option>
<option value=xst>Remove star</option>
<option value=tr>Move to Trash</option>
<option value="" disabled>--------</option>
<option value="" disabled>Apply label:</option>
```

Continued

Listing A-5 *(continued)*

```
<option value="ac_Heads"
>Heads
</option>
<option value="ac_Knees"
>Knees
</option>
<option value="ac_Shoulders"
>Shoulders
</option>
<option value="ac_Toes"
>Toes
</option>
</select> <input type=submit name=tbu value=Go>
</td>
<td align=right>
<b>1</b> of <b>5</b>
<a
href="?next=1&th=1025a4065d9b40bf&v=c"><b>Older &#8250;</
b></a>
</tr>
</form>
</table>
<table width=100% cellpadding=2 cellspacing=0 border=0
bgcolor=#E0ECFF>
<tr>
<td align=right>
<table cellpadding=0 cellspacing=0 border=0 class=ac>
<tr>
<td>
<a href="?th=1025a4065d9b40bf&v=pt" class=nu target=_blank
><img src="/gmail/images/print_icon.gif"
width=16 height=16 border=0 alt="Print conversation"
> <span class=u>Print</span></a>   
</td>
<td>
<a href="?th=1025a4065d9b40bf&v=c" class=nu target=_blank
><img src="/gmail/images/tearoff_icon.gif"
width=16 height=16 border=0 alt="Open conversation in new
window"
> <span class=u>New window</span></a> 
</td>
</table>
</table>
<table width=98% cellpadding=0 cellspacing=0 border=0
align=center class=h>
<tr>
```

```
<td>
<font size=+1><b>hello me</b></font>  
<a href="?"
><font size=1 color=#006633>Inbox</font></a> 
</table>
<table width=98% cellpadding=1 cellspacing=0 border=0
bgcolor=#cccccc
align=center>
<tr>
<td>
<a name=m_1025a4065d9b40bf></a>
<table width=100% cellpadding=1 cellspacing=0 border=0
bgcolor=#efefef>
<tr>
<td>
<a
href="?m=1025a4065d9b40bf&a=st&th=1025a4065d9b40bf&at=b2e38396
b0a9faf8-102e93a7156&v=c#m_1025a4065d9b40bf">
<img src="/gmail/images/star_off_sm_2.gif"
width=13 height=13 border=0 alt="Add star"></a> 
<font color=#00681C>
<b>Ben Hammersley</b>
</font>
&lt;ben@benhammersley.com&gt;
</td>
<td align=right valign=top>
Mon, Feb 28, 2005 at 10:35AM
<tr>
<td colspan=2>
To: Ben Hammersley &lt;ben.hammersley@gmail.com&gt;
<tr>
<td colspan=2>
<div class=r>
<font size=1>
<a
href="?rm=1025a4065d9b40bf&th=1025a4065d9b40bf&ct=rn&v=b&pv=cv
">Reply</a> |
<a
href="?rm=1025a4065d9b40bf&th=1025a4065d9b40bf&ct=ran&v=b&pv=c
v">Reply to all</a> |
<a
href="?rm=1025a4065d9b40bf&th=1025a4065d9b40bf&ct=fn&v=b&pv=cv
">Forward</a> |
<a href="?msgs=1025a4065d9b40bf&th=1025a4065d9b40bf&v=pt"
target=_blank>Print</a> |
<a
href="?m=1025a4065d9b40bf&a=dm&at=b2e38396b0a9faf8-102e93a7156
">Trash this message</a> |
```

Continued

Listing A-5 *(continued)*

```
<a href="?th=1025a4065d9b40bf&v=om" target=_blank>Show
original</a>
</font>
</div>
<tr bgcolor=#ffffff>
<td colspan=2>
<div class=msg>
hello!<br><br>
</div>
</table>
<a name=m_></a>
<table width=100% cellpadding=1 cellspacing=0 border=0
bgcolor=#e0ecff
class=qr>
<tr>
<td bgcolor=#c3d9ff>
<b>Quick Reply</b>
<tr>
<td>
<table width=1% cellpadding=0 cellspacing=0 border=0
bgcolor=#e0ecff>
<form
action="?rm=1025a4065d9b40bf&fv=cv&th=1025a4065d9b40bf&at=b2e3
8396b0a9faf8-102e93a7156&ct=qfnq&v=b&pv=cv&qrt=n"
name=qrf method=POST>
<input type=hidden name=redir
value="?v=c">
<tr>
<td colspan=2>
<table width=100% cellpadding=1 cellspacing=0 border=0>
<tr>
<td width=99%>
<b>To:</b>
<input type=hidden name=qrr value=o>
Ben Hammersley &lt;ben@benhammersley.com&gt;
</td>
<td width=1% valign=bottom>
<input type=submit name=bu value="More Reply Options">
</td>
</table>
<tr>
<td>
<textarea name=body rows=10 cols=50 wrap=virtual>
</textarea>
<tr>
<td>
```

```
<input type=submit name=bu value=Send> 
<input type=submit name=bu value="Save Draft"> 
<input type=checkbox id=diqt name=diqt value=1 checked>
<label for=diqt>Include quoted text with reply</label>
</tr>
</form>
</table>
</table>
</td>
</tr>
</table>
<br>
<table width=100% cellpadding=2 cellspacing=0 border=0
bgcolor=#C3D9FF>
<form
action="?t=1025a4065d9b40bf&at=b2e38396b0a9faf8-102e93a7156"
name=f method=POST>
<tr>
<td>
<input type=hidden name=redir
value="?">
<b><a href="?"
>&laquo; Back to Inbox</a></b>  
<input type=submit name=a value="Archive">  <input
type=submit name=a value="Report Spam">
  <select name=bact>
<option value="">More Actions...</option>
<option value=rd>Mark as read</option>
<option value=ur>Mark as unread</option>
<option value=st>Add star</option>
<option value=xst>Remove star</option>
<option value=tr>Move to Trash</option>
<option value="" disabled>--------</option>
<option value="" disabled>Apply label:</option>
<option value="ac_Heads"
>Heads
</option>
<option value="ac_Knees"
>Knees
</option>
<option value="ac_Shoulders"
>Shoulders
</option>
<option value="ac_Toes"
>Toes
</option>
</select> <input type=submit name=bbu value=Go>
</td>
```

Continued

Listing A-5 *(continued)*

```
<td align=right>
<b>1</b> of <b>5</b>
<a
href="?next=1&th=1025a4065d9b40bf&v=c"><b>Older &#8250;</
b></a>
</tr>
</form>
</table>
</table>
<table cellpadding=2 cellspacing=0 border=0 align=center
class=ft>
<tr>
<td align=center>
Search accurately with <a style=color:#0000CC target=_blank
href="/support/bin/answer.py?ctx=gmail&answer=7190">operators<
/a> including <b>from:</b>  <b>to:</b>
 <b>subject:</b>.
<tr>
<td align=center>
<font color="#006633">
<b>You are currently using 1 MB
(0%)
of your 1000 MB.</b>
</font>
<script>
<!--
wsl();
//-->
</script>
<tr>
<td align=center>
<font size=1>
<a href="/gmail/help/terms_of_use.html"
target=_blank>Terms of Use</a> -
<a href="/gmail/help/privacy.html"
target=_blank>Privacy Policy</a> -
<a href="/gmail/help/program_policies.html"
target=_blank>Program Policies</a> -
<a href="http://www.google.com" target=_blank>Google Home</a>
</font>
<tr>
<td align=center>
<font size=1>&copy;2005 Google</font>
</table>
</table>
</body>
</html>
```

Index

SYMBOLS

backslash (/) keyboard shortcut, 18
exclamation (!) keyboard shortcut, 19
hyphen (–) operator, 24
parentheses ( ) operator, 25
quotes (" ") operator, 25

A

a keyboard shortcut, 19
abort( ) method, 59
addresses
    contacts
        adding contacts, 178–179
        Contacts list, 177
        current contacts, showing, 180
        exporting contacts, 181–182
        importing contacts, 178–179
    header, 179
    overview, 177
    vCards, 181–182
advertising, removing Google, 51–52
after: operator, 25
All Mail folder, 196
AOL Instant Messenger, new mail count to, 144–149
Aquino, Jonathan (notepad use of Gmail), 207
Araujo, Robson Braga (random signatures), 115
array getAttachmentsOf( ) method, 120
array getStandardBox( ) method, 120
attachments
    executables sent as, 23–24
    overview, 155
    sending, 166

B

backslash (/) keyboard shortcut, 18
bcc: operator, 25
before: operator, 25
Blanton, Justin (spam filters), 210
Bloglines, displaying, 92–100
bool connect( ) method, 119
bool connectNoCookie( ) method, 119
bool fetch( ) method, 119
bool fetchBox( ) method, 119
bool fetchContact( ) method, 119
bool getAttachment( ) method, 120
bool isconnected( ) method, 119
bool performAction( ) method, 120

bool send( ) method, 120
boot sequence
    labels, 80
    log for, cleaning up, 68
    login procedure, 75
    long code listings for edited, 243–257
    steps for
        cookie, setting code for, 71–74
        inbox, loading, 74–80
        logging in, 69–71
        multiple messages in inbox, 76–78
        one message in inbox, 78–79
        reading an individual mail, 81–89
    storage space, 80
    watching, preparing for, 67–68
bottom section of screen
    HTML code for, 43–44
    overview, 42–43
box_name property, 123
box_pos property, 123
box_total property, 123
Brown, Jed (WebMailCompose), 7

C

c keyboard shortcut, 18
cc: operator, 25
central activity area of screen
    HTML code for, 39–42
    overview, 38
certain label, retrieving messages from, 170–171
checking for mail
    in Perl
        AOL Instant Messenger, new mail count to, 144–149
        overview, 137–139
        RSS, new mail count in, 137–139
    in PHP, 139–140
    in Python, 140–141
    RSS, new mail count in, 142–144
    using Libgmail, 139–140
    using Mail::Webmail::Gmail
        AOL Instant Messenger, new mail count to, 144–149
        overview, 137–139
        RSS, new mail count in, 142–144
combo-keys shortcuts, 19
command line, mounting GmailFS from, 216–217

comma-separated values (CSV) file, 179

constants, 122–123

contacts

    adding contacts, 178–179

    Contacts list, 177

    current contacts, showing, 180

    exporting contacts, 181–182

    importing contacts, 178–179

Contacts list, 177

`contacts_all` property, 125

`contacts_freq` property, 125

`conv_id` property, 124

`conv_labels` property, 124

`conv_starred` property, 124

`conv_title` property, 124

`conv_total` property, 124

cookie, setting code for, 71–74

Copy as XML function, 53

Couvreur, Julien (MailtoComposeInGmail), 111

CSS listing, long code listings for complete, 238–242

CSV (comma-separated values) file, 179

current contacts, showing, 180

customization

    advertising, removing Google, 51–52

    Gmail Lite, 45

    new style, applying, 44

    style sheets, 45–51

D

data

    accessing all data of a message, 152

    e-mail used to represent all, 220

datablock messages, 220

Delete button, adding, 101–108

`delete_message( )` function, 131

desktop integration

    `mailto:` link redirection

        in Mac OS X, 8

        for Mozilla, 7–8

        for multiplatform, 7–8

        overview, 6

        in Windows, 7

    new mail notification

        in Linux, 5–6

        in Mac OS X, 5

        overview, 3

        in Windows, 3–4

direct use of Gmail SMTP, 162

directory file, 219

directory messages, 220

DOM inspector

    Copy as XML function, 53

    interface with, 30–33

downloading

    Gmailer, 118

    Libgmail, 131

    Mail::Webmail::Gmail, 127

Drafts folder, 196, 208

drives, using multiple, 217

E

`edit_archive( )` function, 129

`edit_labels( )` function, 128–129

`edit_star( )` function, 129

Elson, Jeremy (Tcpflow), 62

`Enter` keyboard shortcut, 18

`esc` keyboard shortcut, 19

exclamation (`!`) keyboard shortcut, 19

existing labels

    certain label, retrieving messages from, 170–171

    listing, 169–173

    retrieving a labeled message and replying, 171–173

exporting contacts, 181–182

exporting mail

    to IMAP account, 200–201

    Mail::Folder::Mbox module, 199

    Mail::Internet module, 199

    Mbox format conversion, 199–200

    as text file, 197–198

F

`f` keyboard shortcut, 19

file entry messages, 220

file, identifying a, 218–219

File System in Userspace (FUSE), 215

file system, passing commands to, 217

`filename:` operator, 25

filters

    overview, 21

    and to-do lists, 203–204

Firefox, 44

first message in inbox, reading

    Gmailer, 126

    Libgmail, 134–135

folders

    and HTML::TokeParser, 195–196

    Inbox folder, 196

    Sent Mail folder, 196

    Spam folder, 196

    Starred folder, 196

    Trash folder, 196

`from:` operator, 24

fstab, mounting GmailFS from, 217
functions, 128–131
FUSE (File System in Userspace), 215

G

g then a keyboard shortcut, 19
g then c keyboard shortcut, 19
g then d keyboard shortcut, 19
g then i keyboard shortcut, 19
g then s keyboard shortcut, 19
Gan, Yin Hung (Gmailer), 118
gCount (Spindel), 5
getAllResponseHeaders( ) method, 59
get_contacts( ) function, 130
get_indv_email( ) function, 130
get_labels( ) function, 128
getMessagesByFolder method, 133
getMessagesByLabel method, 133
getMessagesByQuery method, 133
get_mime_email( ) function, 130
getQuotaInfo method, 134
getResponseHeader( ) method, 60
getUnreadMsgCount method, 134
GM_ACT_APPLYLABEL constant, 122
GM_ACT_ARCHIVE constant, 122
GM_ACT_DELFOREVER constant, 123
GM_ACT_INBOX constant, 122
GM_ACT_READ constant, 122
GM_ACT_REMOVELABEL constant, 122
GM_ACT_SPAM constant, 122
GM_ACT_STAR constant, 122
GM_ACT_TRASH constant, 123
GM_ACT_UNREAD constant, 122
GM_ACT_UNSPAM constant, 122
GM_ACT_UNSTAR constant, 122
GM_ACT_UNTRASH constant, 123
Gmail Lite, 45
Gmail Loader (Lyon), 11–12
Gmail SMTP
    attachments, sending, 166
    direct use of Gmail SMTP, 162
    Mail::Webmail::Gmail and, 162–166
    overview, 161–162
    Perl and, 162–166
    unread mail, reading and replying to, 163–166
Gmailer
    array getAttachmentsOf( ) method, 120
    array getStandardBox( ) method, 120
    bool connect( ) method, 119
    bool connectNoCookie( ) method, 119
    bool fetch( ) method, 119
    bool fetchBox( ) method, 119
    bool fetchContact( ) method, 119
    bool getAttachment( ) method, 120
    bool isconnected( ) method, 119
    bool performAction( ) method, 120
    bool send( ) method, 120
    box_name property, 123
    box_pos property, 123
    box_total property, 123
    constants, 122–123
    contacts_all property, 125
    contacts_freq property, 125
    conv_id property, 124
    conv_labels property, 124
    conv_starred property, 124
    conv_title property, 124
    conv_total property, 124
    downloading, 118
    first message in inbox, reading, 126
    GM_ACT_APPLYLABEL constant, 122
    GM_ACT_ARCHIVE constant, 122
    GM_ACT_DELFOREVER constant, 123
    GM_ACT_INBOX constant, 122
    GM_ACT_READ constant, 122
    GM_ACT_REMOVELABEL constant, 122
    GM_ACT_SPAM constant, 122
    GM_ACT_STAR constant, 122
    GM_ACT_TRASH constant, 123
    GM_ACT_UNREAD constant, 122
    GM_ACT_UNSPAM constant, 122
    GM_ACT_UNSTAR constant, 122
    GM_ACT_UNTRASH constant, 123
    GMailSnapshot get Snapshot( ) method, 120
    gmail_ver property, 123
    GM_CONTACT constant, 122
    GM_CONVERSATION constant, 122
    GM_LABEL constant, 122
    GM_QUERY constant, 122
    GM_STANDARD constant, 122
    GM_USE_COOKIE constant, 123
    GM_USE_PHPSESSION constant, 123
    have_invit property, 123
    inbox, retrieval of, 121–122
    installation of, 118
    label_list property, 123
    label_new property, 123
    logging in with, 120–121
    methods for, 119–120
    overview, 118
    quota_mb property, 123
    quota_per property, 123
    Snapshots, 123–124
    std_box_new property, 123

Continued

Gmailer *(continued)*
    `string dump( )` method, 120
    using, 119–126
    `void disconnect( )` method, 120
    `void setLoginInfo` method, 119
    `void setProxy` method, 119
    `void setSessionMethod` method, 119
GmailerXP, 8
GmailFS
    command line, mounting GmailFS from, 216–217
    datablock messages, 220
    directory messages, 220
    drives, using multiple, 217
    e-mail used to represent all data, 220
    file entry messages, 220
    file, identifying a, 218–219
    file system, passing commands to, 217
    `fstab`, mounting GmailFS from, 217
    FUSE, installing, 215
    how it works, 218
    inode messages, 220
    installation of, 213–215
    Libgmail, installing, 215
    overview, 213, 218
    Python 2.3 needed for, 213–214
    use of, 216–217
GmailFS (Jones), 213
GmailSecure, 108–110
`GMailSnapshot get Snapshot( )` method, 120
GmailStatus, 8
GmailStatus (Guenther), 5
Gmailto, 8
`gmail_ver` property, 123
`GM_CONTACT` constant, 122
`GM_CONVERSATION` constant, 122
`GM_LABEL` constant, 122
`GM_QUERY` constant, 122
`GM_STANDARD` constant, 122
gmtodo (Miller), 205
`GM_USE_COOKIE` constant, 123
`GM_USE_PHPSESSION` constant, 123
Goollery, 210
Greasemonkey
    installation of, 91
    overview, 91–92
    userscripts
        Bloglines, displaying, 92–100
        Delete button, adding, 101–108
        GmailSecure, 108–110
        hide invites, 115
        how it works, 100–101
        HTTPS, forcing Gmail to use, 108–110

        installation of, 92
        MailtoComposeInGmail, 110–114
        mark read button, 114–115
        multiple signatures, 115
        random signatures, 115
Guenther, Carsten (GmailStatus), 5
Gzip encoding, 64

H

hard link, 219
`has:attachment` operator, 24
`have_invit` property, 123
header, 179
heartbeat, Gmail's unencoded, 65–66
hiding invites, userscript for, 115
Holman, Allen (Mail::Webmail::Gmail), 127
HTML code. *See also* HTML version of Gmail
    for bottom section of screen, 43–44
    for central activity area, 39–42
    long code listings
        boot sequence, edited, 243–257
        CSS listing, complete, 238–242
        HTML-only Gmail inbox source, 258–266
        inbox, displaying, 223–238
        individual message page with only one message,
            266–274
    for navigation menu, 36–38
    for top section of screen, 34–35
    `XMLHttpRequest`, 56–59
HTML version of Gmail
    All Mail folder, 196
    Drafts folder, 196
    HTML::TokeParser
        folders and, 195–196
        inbox, parsing, 188–192
        individual page, retrieving, 192–194
        overview, 186–188
        threads and, 195
    Inbox folder, 196
    overview, 183
    scraping
        HTML::TokeParser, 186–194
        overview, 186
    Sent Mail folder, 196
    Spam folder, 196
    Starred folder, 196
    Trash folder, 196
    viewing, 183–185
HTML::TokeParser
    folders and, 195–196
    inbox, parsing, 188–192
    individual page, retrieving, 192–194

overview, 186–188
    threads and, 195
HTTPS, forcing Gmail to use, 108–110
hyphen (–) operator, 24

I

IMAP (Internet Message Access Protocol)
    exporting mail to, 200–201
    integration into your existing mail accounts, 14
importing contacts, 178–179
importing your mail into Gmail
    with Gmail Loader, 11–12
    overview, 11
in:anywhere operator, 25
inbox
    loading, 74–80
    long code listings for, 223–238
    parsing, 188–192
    retrieval of, 121–122
Inbox folder, 196
individual message page with only one message, long code
        listings for, 266–274
individual page, retrieving, 192–194
in:inbox operator, 25
inode, 219
inode messages, 220
in:spam operator, 25
installation
    of FUSE, 215
    of Gmailer, 118
    of Greasemonkey, 91
    of Libgmail, 132, 215
    of Mail::Webmail::Gmail, 127
integration into your existing mail accounts
    IMAP and, 14
    importing your mail into Gmail
        with Gmail Loader, 11–12
        overview, 11
    Pop mail access, setting up, 12–14
interface
    bottom section of screen
        HTML code for, 43–44
        overview, 42–43
    central activity area
        HTML code for, 39–42
        overview, 38
    Delete button, adding, 101–108
    with DOM inspector, 29–33
    HTML code for
        bottom section, 43–44
        central activity area, 39–42
        navigation menu, 36–38
        top section, 34–35

navigation menu
    HTML code for, 36–38
    overview, 35–36
    overview, 29–33
    preloading, 54
    top section of screen
        HTML code for, 34–35
        overview, 33–34
Internet Message Access Protocol (IMAP)
    exporting mail to, 200–201
    integration into your existing mail accounts, 14
in:trash operator, 25
is:read operator, 25
is:starred operator, 25
is:unread operator, 25

J

j keyboard shortcut, 18
Jones, Richard (GmailFS), 213

K

keyboard shortcuts
    a key, 19
    / (backslash) key, 18
    c key, 18
    combo-keys shortcuts, 19
    Enter key, 18
    esc key, 19
    ! (exclamation) key, 19
    f key, 19
    g then a keys, 19
    g then c keys, 19
    g then d keys, 19
    g then i keys, 19
    g then s keys, 19
    j key, 18
    k key, 18
    n key, 18
    overview, 15–17
    p key, 18
    r key, 19
    s key, 19
    spam filters and, 17
    tab then enter keys, 19
    u key, 18
    x key, 19
    y key, 18
    y then o keys, 19

L

label: operator, 24
label_list property, 123
label_new property, 123

labels
    existing labels
        certain label, retrieving messages from, 170–171
        listing, 169–173
        retrieving a labeled message and replying, 171–173
    new labels
        creating, 175
        unlabeled messages, labeling, 173–174
    overview, 80, 169
    removing labels, 175–176
Lawton, Jim (mark read button), 115
Lefort, Jean-Yves (Mail Notification), 6
Libgmail
    checking for mail, 139–140
    downloading, 131
    first message in inbox, reading, 134–135
    getMessagesByFolder method, 133
    getMessagesByLabel method, 133
    getMessagesByQuery method, 133
    getQuotaInfo method, 134
    getUnreadMsgCount method, 134
    gmtodo, 205
    installation of, 132, 215
    login method, 132
    overview, 131
    using, 132–135
libraries
    Gmailer
        array getAttachmentsOf( ) method, 120
        array getStandardBox( ) method, 120
        bool connect( ) method, 119
        bool connectNoCookie( ) method, 119
        bool fetch( ) method, 119
        bool fetchBox( ) method, 119
        bool fetchContact( ) method, 119
        bool getAttachment( ) method, 120
        bool isconnected( ) method, 119
        bool performAction( ) method, 120
        bool send( ) method, 120
        box_name property, 123
        box_pos property, 123
        box_total property, 123
        constants, 122–123
        contacts_all property, 125
        contacts_freq property, 125
        conv_id property, 124
        conv_labels property, 124
        conv_starred property, 124
        conv_title property, 124
        conv_total property, 124
        downloading, 118
        first message in inbox, reading, 126
        GM_ACT_APPLYLABEL constant, 122

GM_ACT_ARCHIVE constant, 122
GM_ACT_DELFOREVER constant, 123
GM_ACT_INBOX constant, 122
GM_ACT_READ constant, 122
GM_ACT_REMOVELABEL constant, 122
GM_ACT_SPAM constant, 122
GM_ACT_STAR constant, 122
GM_ACT_TRASH constant, 123
GM_ACT_UNREAD constant, 122
GM_ACT_UNSPAM constant, 122
GM_ACT_UNSTAR constant, 122
GM_ACT_UNTRASH constant, 123
GMailSnapshot get Snapshot( )
    method, 120
gmail_ver property, 123
GM_CONTACT constant, 122
GM_CONVERSATION constant, 122
GM_LABEL constant, 122
GM_QUERY constant, 122
GM_STANDARD constant, 122
GM_USE_COOKIE constant, 123
GM_USE_PHPSESSION constant, 123
have_invit property, 123
inbox, retrieval of, 121–122
installation of, 118
label_list property, 123
label_new property, 123
logging in with, 120–121
methods for, 119–120
overview, 118
quota_mb property, 123
quota_per property, 123
Snapshots, 123–124
std_box_new property, 123
string dump( ) method, 120
using, 119–126
void disconnect( ) method, 120
void setLoginInfo method, 119
void setProxy method, 119
void setSessionMethod method, 119
Libgmail
    downloading, 131
    first message in inbox, reading, 134–135
    getMessagesByFolder method, 133
    getMessagesByLabel method, 133
    getMessagesByQuery method, 133
    getQuotaInfo method, 134
    getUnreadMsgCount method, 134
    installation of, 132
    login method, 132
    overview, 131
    using, 132–135

Mail::Webmail::Gmail
    delete_message( ) function, 131
    downloading, 127
    edit_archive( ) function, 129
    edit_labels( ) function, 128–129
    edit_star( ) function, 129
    functions, 128–131
    get_contacts( ) function, 130
    get_indv_email( ) function, 130
    get_labels( ) function, 128
    get_mime_email( ) function, 130
    installation of, 127
    logging in, 128
    overview, 127
    send_message( ) function, 131
    size_usage( ) function, 130
    update_prefs( ) function, 129
    using, 128–131
overview, 117
Perl
    libwww-perl module, 136
    MailFolder module, 136
    MD5 module, 136
    MIME-Base64 module, 136
    MIME-tools module, 136
    Utils.pm module, 135
    for PHP coders, 118–126
libwww-perl module, 136
Lieuallen, Anthony (Delete button, adding), 101
listing existing labels, 169–173
listing mail and displaying chosen message, 153–155
Liyanage, Marc (OS X package), 62
login method, 132
login procedure
    boot sequence and, 69–71, 75
    with Gmailer, 120–121
    Mail::Webmail::Gmail, 128
long code listings
    boot sequence, edited, 243–257
    CSS listing, complete, 238–242
    HTML-only Gmail inbox source, 258–266
    inbox, displaying, 223–238
    individual message page with only one message,
        266–274
Lyon, Mark (Gmail Loader), 11–12

M

Mac OS X
    gCount, 5
    GmailStatus, 5
    mailto: link redirection, 8
    new mail notification, 5

Mail Notification (Lefort), 6
MailFolder module, 136
Mail::Folder::Mbox module, 199
Mail::Internet module, 199
mailto: link redirection
    in Mac OS X, 8
    for Mozilla, 7–8
    for multiplatform, 7–8
    overview, 6
    in Windows, 7
MailtoComposeInGmail, 110–114
MailtoComposeInGmail (Couvreur), 111
Mail::Webmail::Gmail
    all data of a message, accessing, 152
    AOL Instant Messenger, new mail count to, 144–149
    attachments, 155
    delete_message( ) function, 131
    downloading, 127
    edit_archive( ) function, 129
    edit_labels( ) function, 128–129
    edit_star( ) function, 129
    functions, 128–131
    get_contacts( ) function, 130
    get_indv_email( ) function, 130
    get_labels( ) function, 128
    get_mime_email( ) function, 130
    installation of, 127
    listing mail and displaying chosen message, 153–155
    logging in, 128
    overview, 127
    reading mail, 151–152
    RSS feed of inbox, creating, 155–159
    RSS, new mail count in, 142–144
    sending mail and, 162–166
    send_message( ) function, 131
    size_usage( ) function, 130
    update_prefs( ) function, 129
    using, 128–131
mark read button, userscript for, 114–115
marking a group of e-mails, 23
Mbox format conversion, 199–200
MD5 module, 136
Medina, Matias Daniel (Goollery), 210
metadata, 219
methods for Gmailer, 119–120
Miller, Paul (gmtodo), 205
MIME-Base64 module, 136
MIME-tools module, 136
Mozilla, 7–8
multiplatforms, 7–8
multiple messages in inbox, 76–78
multiple signatures, userscript for, 115

N

n keyboard shortcut, 18
navigation menu
    HTML code for, 36–38
    overview, 35–36
Neale, Chris (URIid extension), 44
network traffic
    boot sequence
        log for, cleaning up, 68
        steps for, 68–89
        watching, preparing for, 67–68
    overview, 62
    Tcpflow
        Gzip encoding, 64
        heartbeat, Gmail's unencoded, 65–66
        new mail, checking for, 63–65
        overview, 62
new labels
    creating, 175
    unlabeled messages, labeling, 173–174
new mail, checking for, 63–65
new mail notification
    in Linux
        Mail Notification, 6
        overview, 5
        Wmgmail, 6
    in Mac OS X, 5
    in Windows
        Gmail Notifier, 4
        Mozilla Gmail Notifier, 4
        overview, 3
new style, applying, 44
newsreaders
    overview, 205
    torrent files, finding, 206
notepad application, using Gmail as, 207–208

O

object methods
    abort( ) method, 59
    getAllResponseHeaders( ) method, 59
    getResponseHeader( ) method, 60
    open( ) method, 60
    send( ) method, 60
    setRequestHeader( ) method, 60
object properties
    onreadystatechange property, 60
    readyState property, 60
    responseText property, 60
    responseXML property, 60
    status property, 60
    statusText property, 60

one message in inbox, 78–79
onreadystatechange property, 60
open( ) method, 60
OR operator, 24
OS X package (Liyanage), 62

P

p keyboard shortcut, 18
parentheses ( ) operator, 25
Parparita, Mihai (style sheet), 51
password needed for sending mail, 161
Pederick, Chris (Web Developer Extension), 29
Perl
    all data of a message, accessing, 152
    AOL Instant Messenger, new mail count to, 144–149
    attachments, 155
    libwww-perl module, 136
    listing mail and displaying chosen message, 153–155
    MailFolder module, 136
    MD5 module, 136
    MIME-Base64 module, 136
    MIME-tools module, 136
    reading mail, 151–152
    RSS feed of inbox, creating, 155–159
    RSS, new mail count in, 137–139
    sending mail and, 162–166
    Utils.pm module, 135
photo gallery, using Gmail as storage for a, 210
PHP
    checking for mail, 139–140
    Goollery, 210
    libraries for coders, 118–126
Pilgrim, Mark (GmailSecure), 108
plus addressing, 20–23
Pop mail access, setting up, 12–14
power tips
    attachments, sending executables as, 23–24
    filtering, 21
    keyboard shortcuts
        a key, 19
        / (backslash) key, 18
        c key, 18
        combo-keys shortcuts, 19
        Enter key, 18
        esc key, 19
        ! (exclamation) key, 19
        f key, 19
        g then a keys, 19
        g then c keys, 19
        g then d keys, 19
        g then i keys, 19
        g then s keys, 19

j key, 18
k key, 18
n key, 18
overview, 15–17
p key, 18
r key, 19
s key, 19
spam filters and, 17
tab then enter keys, 19
u key, 18
x key, 19
y key, 18
y then o keys, 19
marking a group of e-mails, 23
plus addressing, 20–23
searching, advanced, 24–26
preloading interface, 54
Pygtk, 205
Python
checking for mail, 140–141
gmtodo, 205
Python 2.3, 213–214

Q

quota_mb property, 123
quota_per property, 123
quotes (" ") operator, 25

R

r keyboard shortcut, 19
random signatures, userscript for, 115
reading mail
individual mail, 81–89
with Perl
all data of a message, accessing, 152
attachments, 155
listing mail and displaying chosen message,
153–155
overview, 151–152
RSS feed of inbox, creating, 155–159
Utils.pm module used for, 153–155
readyState property, 60
removing labels, 175–176
responseText property, 60
responseXML property, 60
retrieving a labeled message and replying, 171–173
RSS feeds
of inbox, creating, 155–159
new mail count in, 142–144
overview, 205
torrent files, finding, 206

S

s keyboard shortcut, 19
Savolainen, Pasi (Wmgmail), 6
scraping HTML::TokeParser, 186–194
search operators
after: operator, 25
bcc: operator, 25
before: operator, 25
cc: operator, 25
filename: operator, 25
from: operator, 24
has:attachment operator, 24
- (hyphen) operator, 24
in:anywhere operator, 25
in:inbox operator, 25
in:read operator, 25
in:spam operator, 25
in:starred operator, 25
in:trash operator, 25
in:unread operator, 25
label: operator, 24
OR operator, 24
overview, 26
( ) (parentheses) operator, 25
" " (quotes) operator, 25
subject: operator, 24
to: operator, 24
overview, 186
searching, advanced, 24–26
send( ) method, 60
sending mail
with Gmail SMTP
attachments, sending, 166
direct use of, 162
Mail::Webmail::Gmail and, 162–166
overview, 161–162
Perl and, 162–166
unread mail, reading and replying to, 163–166
password needed for, 161
send_message( ) function, 131
Sent Mail folder, 196
setRequestHeader( ) method, 60
size_usage( ) function, 130
Snapshots, 123–124
spam filters, 17, 209–210
Spam folder, 196
Spindel, Nathan (gCount), 5
Starred folder, 196
status property, 60
statusText property, 60
std_box_new property, 123
storage space, 80

`string dump( )` method, 120
style sheets, 45–51
style sheets (Parparita), 51
`subject:` operator, 24

T

`tab then enter` keyboard shortcut, 19
Tcpflow
    Gzip encoding, 64
    heartbeat, Gmail's unencoded, 65–66
    new mail, checking for, 63–65
    overview, 62
    thread, retrieving a, 83–88
    trace from reading a message, 81–83
Tcpflow (Elson), 62
text-editing, 208
text file, exporting mail as, 197–198
threads
    and HTML::TokeParser, 195
    retrieving, 83–88
`to:` operator, 24
to-do lists
    filters and, 203–204
    gmtodo, using, 205
    overview, 203
top section of screen
    HTML code for, 34–35
    overview, 33–34
torrent files, finding, 206
trace from reading a message, 81–83
Trash folder, 196

U

`u` keyboard shortcut, 18
unlabeled messages, labeling, 173–174
unread mail, reading and replying to, 163–166
`update_prefs( )` function, 129
URIid extension (Neale), 44
userscripts
    Bloglines, displaying, 92–100
    Delete button, adding, 101–108
    GmailSecure, 108–110
    hide invites, 115

    how it works, 100–101
    HTTPS, forcing Gmail to use, 108–110
    installation of, 92
    MailtoComposeInGmail, 110–114
    mark read button, 114–115
    multiple signatures, 115
    random signatures, 115
Utils.pm module, 135, 153–155

V

vCards, 181–182
viewing HTML version of Gmail, 183–185
Villegas, Andres (Goollery), 210
`void disconnect( )` method, 120
`void setLoginInfo` method, 119
`void setProxy` method, 119
`void setSessionMethod` method, 119

W

Web Developer Extension (Pederick), 29
WebMailCompose (Brown), 7
Windows
    Gmail Notifier, 4
    `mailto:` link redirection, 7
    Mozilla Gmail Notifier, 4
    new mail notification, 3–4
    overview, 3
Wirz, Martin (Goollery), 210
Wmgmail (Savolainen), 6

X

`x` keyboard shortcut, 19
`XMLHttpRequest`
    within Gmail code, 61
    HTML code for, 56–59
    object methods, 59–60
    object properties, 60
    overview, 55
    using yourself, 55–60

Y

`y` keyboard shortcut, 18
`y then o` keyboard shortcut, 19

How to take it to the Extreme.

If you enjoyed this book, there are many others like it for you. From *Podcasting* to *Hacking Firefox*, ExtremeTech books can fulfill your urge to hack, tweak and modify, providing the tech tips and tricks readers need to get the most out of their hi-tech lives.

EXTREMETECH™   Available wherever books are sold.